The Perils of Passion

Christopher David

authorHOUSE®

AuthorHouse™ UK Ltd.
500 Avebury Boulevard
Central Milton Keynes, MK9 2BE
www.authorhouse.co.uk
Phone: 08001974150

First published by AuthorHouse   9/2/2010

ISBN: 978-1-4520-6577-9 (sc)

This book is printed on acid-free paper.

The Perils of Passion

In gratitude
To my family
Many friends
Angela Charles
And especially
My wife Gill

We shall not cease from exploration
And the end of all our exploring
Will be to arrive where we started
And know the place for the first time

TS Eliot (Little Gidding)

Contents

Illustrations

Introduction

If there is one thread that holds this story of my life together it is a yearning for a spiritual purpose; a God who is Love. Otherwise it is muddled, describing perhaps one of the most zigzag paths that anyone could take in life. It soars high and plunges deep and finds itself best described in Francis Thompson's epic poem, The Hound of Heaven;

> *'I fled Him down the nights and down the days, I fled Him down the arches of the years, I fled Him down the labyrinthine ways of my own mind, and in the midst of tears I hid from Him and under running laughter.'*

For the most part I have written about a series of events that are also reflections on the Church, as it was and as it is, not in its essential nature which has to be spiritual to make any sense, but on the way it has evolved and on its management today. It is not written in chronological order but it is all absolutely true.

It is easy to see corruption at every level of society but not easy to see it in oneself. When G.K.Chesterton was asked what 'is wrong with the world?' He answered 'I am.' Yet to stop there would indeed be gloom. There are two sides to everyone and to every institution, to blow the dying flame into more life, whether in that of an individual or an institution, is better than blowing it out. The institution of the Church is indeed far from dying but, as in every other age, deserves to be criticised for the way it presents itself to the world, and appears at times to disguise the Treasure it holds.

It is the year in which Cardinal Henry Newman is likely to be beatified and there has been fierce argument in the Church about the meaning of his remark to the Duke of Norfolk, 'I will drink to the Pope but to conscience first.' It is claimed that Newman did not mean everyone should follow their private conscience rather than obey the teaching of the Church. There is a fine line to follow indeed for all who believe that Christ gave Authority to the Church, but that Authority is not always wisely exercised which is where the limits to obedience and belief become evident.

Everyone relates to life differently and builds up their own value system which need not harmonise that well with that of other people. I hope only that some of the insights and experiences I have had and recorded here may have a value and be of interest to you, the Reader. I believe that everything we have and enjoy in life is pure gift and should be shared, but whatever ambitions we have, Hilaire Belloc's verse gives us (in my view) the bottom line:

> *From quiet home and first beginning*
> *Out to the undiscovered ends There*
> *is nothing worth the wear of winning*
> *Than laughter and the love of*
> *friends.*

Part 1
Living as a Priest in Holywell

Chapter 1
A Less than Quiet Beginning

I travelled from Hereford to Chester by train and went on to Holywell by bus. I was more fearful than I had ever been. The Church was huge and the Presbytery next door forbidding but a small woman opened the door and immediately made me welcome.

"Your tea is ready," she said, "and Monsignor will see you later."

She chattered on and showed me my room up a steep stairway. It was large, with two gothic, church-like windows and a small gas fire. I found myself living at the end of a large rambling house that was very old, part of it three or four centuries old. It was half way up a very steep street called Well Street, and at the bottom of the street was a spring or well, but no ordinary well. I would come to know it and write about it and almost live there at times. The house was connected with the huge church through a long passage, but it was a house infested with mice. I could not get over the strangeness of it. Bridget, for that was her name, was rambling on about the mice. She seemed to think that was the problem I had come to sort out. There was a strict house rule, no poison, only traps. Bridget needed me more than the parish did, she was close to despair, and I began setting traps at her bidding. It was September 1955. I had been ordained a priest in April and returned from Rome two months before. I was 28.

We caught mice every night, sometimes two at a time, and it became my task to remove the bodies. Bridget was grateful and calmed down, Monsignor, unaware of any problem, was living on another plane and I could not even suggest that what he really needed was a cat, not a curate. He assigned me various duties but otherwise expected me to discover the needs of the parish on my own. He himself lived on the other side of the house, the posh side. He seldom came into the servants' quarters, the kitchen and rooms above, where I now lived. He was the Vicar General of the diocese, concerned with important matters, spending most of his days in the offices of the bishop in Wrexham. He was not, therefore, much concerned with mice but he did disapprove of them dying under his nose, so to speak; hence the 'no poison' rule. The parish was Holywell in Flintshire, North Wales, and the diocese at the time was Menevia.

The tension rose when I failed one morning to remove a dead mouse from a trap. It was the first event of the day, remove corpse, reset trap. This particular trap was under the kitchen table but I had been distracted and forgot to remove the large and very dead contents. It was not there the next day, the mouse and trap had gone. This was highly mysterious and rather worrying. Bridget swore she had not touched it. The idea that Monsignor might have come in and removed mouse and trap was unthinkable. Bridget and I were still conjecturing as to what might have happened, when suddenly an enormous rat crossed the floor, immediately in front of us. Bridget screamed. The rat lumbered away faster and climbed over quite a high step, the bottom one of the staircase to my room. It disappeared through a doorway on the other side. It had a hole behind a bookcase and the bookcase backed on to the bathroom wall. I followed its path and eventually discovered another hole inside the bathroom cupboard which went through the wall and clearly linked up with the back of the bookcase. The trap was lying on the floor of the cupboard. It was blood stained but empty. The mouse had clearly been eaten whole, head, tail, the lot. Nothing was left but a few hairs. I realised with some misgiving that the enormous creature must be hiding behind the bookcase at that moment. I had no desire to find out. It was also obvious that it had come back into the kitchen looking for another dead mouse. I did not mention that little fact to Bridget but was astonished that the rat had managed to haul mouse and trap across the kitchen floor, up and over a high step, drag it behind the bookshelves, get it through the hole in the wall, and only then settle down to have its supper.

Bridget was panic stricken. She was sitting white-faced on a chair, her hair in disarray, fear in her eyes. She was small, a bundle of energy, carelessly dressed, never any sign of make-up, but now she was paralysed and having hysterics. There was poison available. I didn't think we could cope with the rat without poison.

"We are not supposed to put down poison, Bridget."

"I can't stand it. I can't stand it any longer."

"OK, we'll put down poison. But what happens if I'm fired?"

Bridget managed a laugh.

"You don't know Monsignor. He won't do anything abut it."

"So we put down poison. *I* put down poison."

What was I doing disobeying the rules and poisoning a rat? I went out, bought the stuff and put it on a saucer in the cupboard. We did not see the rat again. It preferred to move around at night but it obviously enjoyed its meal. It ate the lot. The next night I put down the same quantity. Only half was eaten this time. All was quiet. I was sure the rat was now dead and I felt a bit like Hamlet after he had killed Polonius. "Where is Polonius?" asked the king, to which Hamlet replied, "If you find him not this month you will nose him as you go up the stairs to the lobby." I hoped the rat would be sensible and go out of the house to die, but of course it was not at all sensible. The consequences were unfortunate. My career, such as it was, was in jeopardy after only a month in the place.

Obviously, I should have had the courage to consult Monsignor about the rat. I should have waited until he returned from Wrexham. He seemed to be always in Wrexham or locked up in his study. In any case, I am sure he would have suggested a larger trap and, neither Bridget nor I, were prepared to bait such a trap or deal with the consequences. The rat had decided to stay in the house, which was warm and comfortable, and the result of its negligence became evident within a few weeks. An unpleasant smell seeped into the corridor connecting the house with the church. The smell was strongest as you past Monsignor's room. Indeed the whole of Monsignor's side of the house began to smell. He became irritable. He had the cellars, which were under his room, lime washed. No relief. Soon he found it impossible to work in his study and would bring his papers into the dining room. He was portly and serious and not in the best of humour. It was rather tiresome having him in the dining room which impeded our freedom of movement. The weeks passed slowly. Bridget and I would skirt round Monsignor's chair and his mountain of papers, hurry past his study to the front door, the waiting room or the church, and pretend we had no idea what the cause of the problem was. Bridget was poker faced. We both waited anxiously.

"Where do you think the rat is, Bridget?" She found the situation very funny. She had a sort of giggle which was infectious.

"It's not funny, Bridget."

"It's probably in Monsignor's room, but there is nothing we can do about it now." She had stopped going into his room to clean. He had stopped going in at all.

When the stench had become quite unbearable and was seeping through the ceiling of the study into his bedroom, Monsignor became grim and purposeful. He could not, after all, actually *live* in Wrexham. He had his furniture taken out, his precious furniture and carpets now cluttered up the hall. He had the floor boards taken up. It was a huge operation involving several men. They found the enormous decomposed carcass of the rat immediately under his desk.

It was the end of our suspense and worth celebrating. Bridget brought me a Guinness that night and we drank to Monsignor's health, but I was expecting fireworks. I could hardly believe Bridget's confidence that if you did something he did not like, he would not mind. After all he did not like as much as a tiny mouse dying under his nose. The next morning I approached the breakfast table with some trepidation but there were no recriminations, not even an enquiry. Monsignor said not a word. I realised then that it was not altogether surprising. He did not know where the rat had come from. He did not know that Bridget and I had actually met the rat. These were matters I had not troubled him with. Bridget was surprisingly sanguine about it all, apparently unmoved by the discomfort we had caused the great man. He certainly paid her little attention.

Monsignor wielded power but he was a recluse as well. During the nine years I was with him I never discovered where he lived. His wing of the house, from the stairs upwards, was out of bounds. Downstairs he hid away in his study which had a second, baize-covered door fitted, to shut out noise. It was unnerving opening both doors to approach the great man and the conversation was always brief. He did not like initiatives, nor could one discuss with him the plight of this family or that. He simply did not know what was going on in the parish and was not in that sense a parish priest. But he liked conventions. He always appeared at meal times wearing his cassock and purple stock, aware of his ecclesiastical importance and always approached the altar wearing his biretta. He liked his biretta, the oddest kind of clerical gear you can imagine. He was probably disappointed that he could not wear it all the time.

The episode of the rat and its demise in such a place, immediately under the great man's desk, became in retrospect prophetic. Despite all the wonderful people within the Church the structure was creaking badly. Within ten years there would be an upheaval. They would literally dig up the floor and look at the foundations. Michael Novak would write in his book, The Open Church, 'the non-historical Church of the last few generations has produced its saints, but it has also presented a withered, wrinkled face to the world.' It had become a religion of rules and was beset by guilt. The Gospel message of good news had become obscured. An Argentinian bishop, Monsignor Iriarte, was quoted as saying:

> *"We have to proclaim the Christian message from the height of our marble altars and Episcopal palaces, in the incomprehensible baroque of our pontifical Masses and in the even stranger definitions of our ecclesiastical language, while we appear before our people clad in purple and our people call us 'Your Grace' and genuflect to kiss our ring."*

Inside the Church this was accepted but outside the institution it could not only be an obstacle to entering in but also an object of ridicule. But the words of Bishop Iriarte would only be uttered aloud when John 23rd became Pope and called the Second Vatican Council. Thus, the rat became an excuse for reflecting on the state of the Church. The strange thing is that no more mice appeared in the house and I do not remember setting a single trap in the next nine years. The rat had been a sign of things to come and life became a good deal more serious.

Chapter 2
Failures of an Ill-equipped Marriage Counsellor

I could have had a career in the army, indeed I was commissioned in the Rifle Brigade, the 95th, a Scout regiment, which meant marching twice as fast as anyone else. The recruiting officer, who came to Ampleforth College where I ended my erratic education, did not mention that little fact in his enthusiastic peroration. I was 17 and signed on, seven years with the colours and five with the reserve. It was October 1943.

We had been pretending to be soldiers in the College, wearing puttees and high collars like soldiers in the Crimean war. We crawled around the meadows with ancient rifles, and drilled on the square in front of the school. On one memorable day the head of school, who was pompous and played the role of RSM, forgot there was a large tank of water behind him and, wishing to project his voice to more effect, stepped backwards and disappeared from view. There was a loud splash. The whole parade was in hysterics and all further drill was cancelled. No such happy events occurred in the York barracks. We paraded and marched and drilled in all weathers and that November, through to January, it was freezing cold most of the time. Pay was 3 shillings a day. On Fridays we paraded and when called to the officer's desk, saluted, shouted your number and received 20 shillings. One shilling was taken off for 'breakages.' Nobody knew what this meant but you never got it back. With the rest, a princely sum in those days, you could go into town on a Saturday.

We were issued with khaki gloves, mine disappeared. Our corporal found me another pair. They disappeared too. I bought a really good pair and marked the backs with CD in indelible ink, it spoilt the gloves but they disappeared all the same, and one day on the firing range, in freezing weather, I found a boy wearing them. At that moment an officer called me, so I gave the boy wearing *my* gloves *my* rifle too, a useless ploy. When I returned, my rifle was missing as well. I was learning about life from the cockney conscript point of view.

There were three of us considered officer material. We were the ones who wore pyjamas in bed and the vest and pants brigade found that very funny. The kindly corporal gave everybody a lecture on pyjamas but I wished he would give everyone a lecture on bad language, though I soon discovered that it was his language as well. Even so, it was boring being reminded of sex all the time. Of course they went further than that. They huddled over nude pictures, people making love.

"Get rid of them," I said from my pedestal.

"Why? It's perfectly natural."

Indeed the army seemed to think it perfectly natural. The medical officer simply lectured everybody on taking precautions, and some of the boys, stimulated by the subject, drew lewd pictures on their desks while he was speaking.

One hut in the camp was a library with some comfortable chairs. I took refuge there but a group of young lads, not at all interested in books, were swapping dirty stories. That made reading impossible. I went out and slammed the door and to my surprise all the lights went out. I walked off but I could hear their cries for help from some distance away and decided I was not going back. They would fall over the tables and chairs and find the door eventually and the darkness they were in seemed altogether appropriate. The other hut I retreated to sometimes was the RC chapel. Our sergeant found religion quaint. He paraded us on Sundays and bawled out

"Anglicans and Roman Catholics, one step forward. All other fictitious religions fall out." Most fell out.

Religion is burdensome and I envied those who did not have strict rules to keep, especially those concerning sex, but I was already in some strange way committed, the only one who actively supported the Padre. I went round the barracks, self- conscious and fearful, announcing Mass times, and served the Sunday Mass. I did not know, at that time, if I would ever be doing anything more. But it happened, and I discovered the actual work of the priest was not at all what I had expected. I had no idea I would become a social worker and marriage counsellor and would be ill equipped for either. The memories shame me still. First shock, a pretty young secretary drives over from Liverpool in a flashy red sports car, an impressive vehicle. She sat opposite me across the table in the waiting-room. Few ever advanced beyond the waiting-room. There was another big door to open before you actually entered the Presbytery, unknown and mysterious to almost everyone. I was mesmerised by her. She was highly attractive and I listened to her story with difficulty but with ever increasing sympathy. Sadly, I failed to understand what was really on her mind. I could have guessed that it was not just a long-standing relationship with her boss. That would not have brought her all the way from Liverpool. I found myself making weak comments about finding another job. She could not be responsible for breaking up a marriage and so on. We talked for quite a time but only later, long after she had left, did I realise she was pregnant. That was the agonising thing she wanted to tell somebody and could not tell me, too obviously young and inexperienced.

Shortly afterwards a recently married woman from the parish called to complain that her husband behaved like an animal. Oh dear, what was I supposed to do about that?

"You mean he makes love to you in a way you don't like?"

Her head nodded, eyes down.

"Can't you help him, discuss it with him?"

She had a phobia about such things and it was possible at that time to remain completely ignorant and discover what marriage was about only after the event. The nuns were not that good at preparing their protégés, having had little experience themselves. These days a priest faced with a problem like that would no doubt send people with marriage problems to a Counsellor but such people did not exist, as far as I was aware, 50 years ago

"To put oneself at the disposal of another is to love that person," I said, hopefully. Then I tried to tell her St Paul's ideas about marriage. 'The husband must give his wife what she has the right to expect, and so too the wife to her husband. The wife has no rights over her own body; it is the husband who has them. In the same way the husband has no rights over his body; his wife has them. Do not refuse each other except by mutual consent.' But she was not listening and I was not helping her. Within another year she had left him. The army, on the other hand, had no problems with sex. They just thought it great fun. I once called on a couple in the afternoon in Holywell when they were indeed having great fun. Shift work made such things likely and, aware, half way up the pathway, I retreated hastily but I remember being glad that not all ex-convent girls in the parish were that inhibited.

Holywell seemed to specialise in marriage break-ups, and though I tried, I could not view them dispassionately. All the secretaries in the parish seemed to be at risk. This particular one worked for a lawyer, her husband worked shifts at Courtaulds, most of the able-bodied population in Holywell worked at Courtaulds or the Shotton steel works in those days. This lady had taken up dancing once a week while her husband went to a pub, not too unusual. Then, suddenly, with no warning at all, she left him.

I went to the house. Their son opened the door and I entered a darkened room and could only just make out a shape, slumped in a chair. I was told the husband had gone blind but could that be true?

"Pull the curtains, son," he said

"I can't see," he told me. The doctor doesn't understand why but I do."

"You do?"

"I've been stabbed in the 'eart, Father. Left me she did with no warning, not even a note."

His blindness proved indeed to be psychosomatic and after some weeks his sight returned but he was completely devastated and his son, who was only 16, was looking after him. He asked me to go and see his wife and told me where he thought she might be. It was not a place easy to find and I was reluctant even to try, but eventually I found her in a terraced house with her new boy friend. It was somewhere in the hills near Pentre Halkyn. The boy friend was, fortunately, not at home. She received me coldly but at least she did not leave me standing at the door. It was a cold day.

"Your husband went blind," I began

"He was blind already."

"Are you so heartless?"

"He just wanted me around, wanted his meals cooked, did not care for me."

"But you made promises for life. Marriage is not something you can walk away from when it gets difficult."

"Not just difficult, it was impossible."

"Impossible, because you fell in love with someone else?"

"What's the point of asking me questions? I've made my decision."

"And quite likely risking your soul."

"What do you mean by that?"

"Just that. Don't you believe that hell exists?"

"Damn you, get out of here."

Her voice had risen to a high pitch and, of course, I had no choice. Outside the terraced house the cold was uncomfortable enough and the splendid view, down towards the Dee Estuary and across to the Wirral, was no consolation, other heads had appeared at doors along the terrace, curious to know who the intruder was which increased my embarrassment. I was not among friends, but it was a lesson too. I had shown no interest in the woman. I did not begin gently, ask how she was or make a serious attempt to listen to her or understand her.

Since then the fires of hell have tended to burn rather low, if not go out altogether, and the fiery Friar Aloysius Webb OFM Cap., destined for promotion, would have to modify his vivid illustrations. They were mission sermons kindly meant to discourage wayward behaviour but the wayward themselves did not bother to come and listen.

This little episode was not the only time I discovered that too much zeal could be counter productive, looking for the wayward ones and suggesting unfortunate consequences if they did not return to the fold seemed to be in line with Christ's parable of leaving the 99 in the desert and going out to find the one sheep that had got itself lost, but I know now I had completely missed the point of the story. He did not use a big stick and drive the lost sheep home; he carried it back on his shoulders.

I got it wrong again when I had the temerity to pray aloud in somebody's house without the poor man's permission. He needed prayer but he did not need it imposed upon him in his sitting-room. He saw me as a kind of evangelical policeman after that, and would not open the door at all, indeed if he saw me in the street he would scuttle home and batten down the hatches.

It was only a year or so later the unhappy husband, still cared for by their only son, got cancer. I visited him several times and was with him the night before he died. She did not come to the funeral. It was winter time and a huddle of about twenty people gathered at the snow covered graveside. I was able to tell them he had died in peace and that the day before when I brought him Communion he had said, 'It is enough, I need nothing more.'

I was instructing a woman who called at the presbytery and asked if she could become a Catholic, as she was a shift worker we had to vary the timetable. Instruction of a convert usually took place once a week and lasted six months. She seemed very sincere and was always at Mass but she had not told her husband.

"Your husband ought to know that you are coming here once a week."

"I don't think he will understand, not yet anyway."

"Would he ever understand?"

"I hope so."

We had been talking about the Passover, the extraordinary escape of the Israelites from Egypt, the Paschal meal, the blood of the lamb on the doorposts of the houses.

"I have to wonder if you are escaping from something. You are not going to leave your husband are you?"

"Oh no, I love him. It is just that things have changed a bit. We have his mother living with us now. He was adopted as a child."

"How do you get on with her?"

"Not well. She has taken over the house."

"You must talk to your husband openly. It is no good becoming a Catholic because you are unhappy at home."

"Will you talk to him?"

It was the last thing I wanted to do, but I did go round to his house. A large woman came to the door with an unfriendly face.

"I have come to see your son."

"Why?"

"It's about his wife."

"What's wrong with her then?"

"Nothing, but I need to speak to her husband."

She let me in, but I realised there was indeed something wrong. Never before or since have I faced such a hostile atmosphere; it seemed to me positively evil. The husband sat in an armchair. The woman sat down too. They did not suggest I sit down.

"Your wife wants to become a Catholic," I said. The woman laughed. The man said:

"Why couldn't she tell me that herself? Do you have to come and tell me? Not that I care. She can do what she likes. And now if you've said what you want to say you can go away."

He had a twelve bore shot gun leaning against the door. I was stupid enough to say:

"I like your gun."

"If you come round again I'll have it ready for you."

I didn't know what to do now. I knew exactly what Monsignor would say. It would be negative. 'Don't get involved with those kinds of people. You are wasting your time.'

The woman came again for her next lesson.

"Well," I said, cautiously, "How did your husband take the news?"

"He was angry, but he said he did not care. I am so happy now. Thank you for going there. Make me a Catholic as quickly as you can."

So we plodded on, concentrating on Christ's message, on Christ's love. I would have liked to have cut down these talks. Then suddenly she appeared at the door in floods of tears. It was her afternoon shift and she should have been at work. I had to wait quite a time before she could bring herself to tell me what was wrong.

"My husband...I had a headache and was given permission to leave work. When I got home I found.... I found my husband in bed with his mother."

She stopped crying and just looked wildly at me.

"So that explains it," I said. "I knew there was something wrong. You must have guessed there was something wrong?"

"Yes, I wasn't happy."

"You have not got much choice now. You have to tell your husband he has to choose between you and his mother."

She went home, calm at last, and did just that. The mother-in-law left. It was not the end of the story. It was a painful business remaking her relationship with her husband and I was surprised she was brave enough and able to forgive him.

Chapter 3
Privileged Life Style

Society changed dramatically after the war, it was less authoritarian and more liberal. Tiresome theologians were digging under the foundations of the Church as well, and were viewed by the Authorities with alarm. The post-war euphoria, the welfare society, the brave new world of greater equality and openness was exciting, but all the while the old world lingered on and poverty seemed to be everywhere.

Lluesty hospital, on the edge of Holywell, was no longer a workhouse but still served as a refuge for 'men of the road' who would also make the presbytery a port of call. Bridget would make tea and cut sandwiches but it was unofficial, something that happened quietly at the back door. Monsignor turned a blind eye to it, but I felt pretty sure he would not have turned a blind eye to the liberty I took which was much more serious. A young man came to the door one day, dirty and unshaven. He looked as though he had been sleeping rough for several days. Could he please use our bathroom for a wash and shave? He said he had a chance of a job. Monsignor was in his study that day; it was only on such days that he ever came into my side of the house. It was easier for him to use my bathroom when he needed to, rather than climb the stairs to his own. But looking at the poor man standing at the door it was obvious that he had no chance of a job with anyone in his present state. So I took him into my bathroom, lent him all that he needed for a wash and shave, and stood guard outside. It was such a pity I could not consult Monsignor, warn him not to use the bathroom for at least 20 minutes. It was an anxious interminable wait and even Bridget did not approve. Yet it was no big deal, I just could not face Monsignor saying his inevitable, 'No'. There was not a thought in those days that the Church should have, by definition, 'an option for the poor.' It seems so obvious now and for many in the Church it was always obvious, but human organisations tend to have other priorities, particularly the one of self-preservation, and the Church does not escape that temptation. It could have had a stronger voice against Nazi tyranny if it had worried less about its own survival. To faithfully follow Christ is not easy, it was not easy working in a Church, the barque of St Peter, encrusted with barnacles, conservation, preservation, safety first, all obstacles to preaching the Gospel. The privilege of the priesthood has nothing to do with a privileged lifestyle. I wrote this verse at the time but not for anyone to see.

> We talk so much of love,
> Find ourselves properly concerned
> 'Keep yourselves warm we say, and eat.'
> We put some money in a box
> Glibly talk and ponder human need,
> Find war an agony and hold our peace
> We will be catholic and love, without a limit, every one
> And then we book our central heated room
> And say our grace.
> So prudence insulates our lives from overwork and sharper pain
> Ensures the ease of comfortable prayer
> While others hate and drift along
> The road despair.

That Sunday I was aware of Monsignor's presence in the Sacristy. He often listened to me when I was preaching and occasionally he would make comments. The text was 'Give and it will be given to you in full measure, pressed down and running over.' The church was packed as usual for the 11am Mass and though there was no microphone it was not difficult to make oneself heard. This is the essence of what I tried to say.

"We can exist and survive but only when we *give* do we really live. The reason is simple. We are ourselves a gift, our life is a gift, not one that was made once only and then forgotten. It is a continuous gift from the One whose very life is giving. In order to share this life we too have to be givers, and the more we become givers the more we live. What is happening is that we are learning, slowly perhaps, to give ourselves back to God. We have to peel off the protective layers that limit our capacity to give.

We are commanded to love our neighbour as ourselves. Our strongest impulse is to care first for ourselves and only afterwards for our neighbour. To reverse that order and care first for our neighbour is to take a risk but only then will the promise come true; 'Give and it will be given to you, full measure, pressed down and running over.'"

"You must keep your sermons simple," Monsignor commented. "The people won't understand a word of that."

But I thought he was wrong. With regard to relieving poverty I thought Confucius was right. Five hundred years before Christ he wrote: 'Relieving people's poverty ought to be handled as though one were rescuing them from fire or saving them from drowning. One dare not hesitate.' But how many would have listened to him then and how many deaf ears would greet such a message today.

It was a painful time, so many came knocking at the door. There was need in the parish itself. 'The road despair' was a real enough image.

Next door to the Hospice there was a big hall which acted as a social club and youth club alternately. Upstairs there was a room used for 'Enquiry classes' for anyone wanting to enquire about the Church, and Sodality meetings, the Children of Mary or the Knights of St. Columba. Up another flight of stairs was the scout room. The whole place was heated by a large boiler in the basement. One evening I could see from my window a light on in the boiler room and went down to investigate. The caretaker was there. He had filled a sack with coal.

"I have to let the boiler go out," he said lamely.

There was no obvious connection between that statement and the fact that he had filled a sack with coal.

"You have to let the boiler go out," I repeated and then to myself, 'I wish I could let the boiler man go out.'

Where did my responsibility lie? I was not the parish priest. We both stood there awkwardly. I knew him well. He had a quarrelsome wife and was living in a damp house further down the valley. At last I said sadly, pointing at the sack.

"I think you had better tip it out again. I won't say anything to anybody."

Now, Bridget was complaining again, not about coal. We had an oil-fired boiler in the cellar. Such is the difference between the standard of living of the clergy and that of the poor, but Bridget was not bothered about coal. She was concerned about something relatively trivial, the disappearance of votive candles from the Lady Chapel. No money was going into the offertory box, she said, in alarm. I watched one day from the organ loft and saw a man in a shabby overcoat come in and fill his pockets with candles. I said, in a sepulchral voice,

"There is one above who see-eth all."

The poor man nearly jumped out of his skin and scuttled out. Bridget was not amused.

"That must have been so-and-so who lives in a garden shed."

I was suitably humbled and went round with a paraffin lamp for him but he was not there. I put it down outside the shed. It was a hard time for so many, but I learnt not to lend money. That was a sure way to break a relationship. Any help had to be a gift. I learnt too not to trust the antics of some, the request for a train ticket to London when only the price of one was needed, or the swoon from hunger faked so well. Yet there was desperate need, the dark side of post-war Britain.

Chapter 4
The Past and the Present

Our experiences in life do have an effect on the kind of people we become. I had been anxious about the army. I certainly never wanted to shoot anybody but I believed we had to defend ourselves and had to fight and it was not fair to let other people do that and stand aside.

After surviving York barracks I was called to take part in a week-end course in a large house that belonged to the Duke of Westminster, near Chester. It had been converted into a War Office Selection Board, or WOSB, and was full of boisterous young men from public schools. The first task was making a raft. Eight would-be officers had to find a way of putting together a jumble of wood and rope in order to get across the river. You can imagine the altercation and arguments. I just stood aside and watched them, they did not need me. The officer in charge took notes and would have noticed my reluctance to take part. The assault course too was beastly, especially the six foot high wall, apparently we had to be athletic as well as potential leaders. The agility or ingenuity test was deciding how to get from 'a' to 'b' in a complicated structure of rope ladders, walkways, jumps, swings and slides. You studied a model and made your decision alone with an officer. When I got to the bottom of the first ladder I was due to climb, another cadet came charging up, I let him go up first.

"Why?" asked the officer.

"Because he was in such a hurry," I answered lamely.

I was clearly wimpish and my hopes of becoming an officer were fading fast. That night we had a debate. I excelled in the debate because it was about communism and I knew the world should really worry about that. One of the would-be generals came to me afterwards and said: "That probably saved you."

Whether it did or not I went with the group to Bushfield Camp near Winchester, first rung on the ladder. Our pay increased to five shillings a day, 35 splendid shillings a week!

I was not getting any pay now as a priest. The only pocket money we had was in the form of Mass stipends. Usually the stipend was 5 shillings, so, curiously, my income was much the same as that of a cadet in the army, though less secure.

There were lots of nuns in the parish. They ran two schools and prepared children for their First Confession and First Communion. I remember two little girls arguing about what to say at their First Confession.

"I'm going to tell the priest I told my Guardian Angel to go to hell."

"He won't like that,' said the other. "Just tell him you're a nasty little girl, always telling lies." That started a fight.

Confession was considered essential before receiving Communion. The big Sodalities, Children of Mary and Knights of St. Columba, had their monthly Holy Communion days and besieged the confessionals the night before. My name was on the door of one, Monsignor's on the other.

St Winefride's Well had made Holywell not only into a parish but into a pilgrimage centre as well. The Hospice for pilgrims was full that September with severely handicapped patients from a Lancashire home. I was the one destined to hear their confessions. For some reason Monsignor was not available. The problem was they did not know where to begin or where to end; some of them did not know where to kneel. Some could not see, others were deaf, and some could hardly speak. At the end of two hours I was emotionally exhausted. Within a couple of decades confession would become rare and Communion would become frequent, but in the late fifties the reverse was true.

After Mass and Communion the next morning all the hospice pilgrims would bathe in the freezing waters of St Winefride's Well, men from 8am to 9am and women from 9am to 10am, then they would all climb back to the Hospice for coffee and return to the well for a service at 11.30. The little town nestles at the top of the valley but the well is in the crypt of an ancient and beautiful chapel, several hundred yards down the hill. One of the handicapped men had an epileptic fit. He was completely and frighteningly out of control, nobody knew what to do, I least of all. Eventually, since he was clearly going to hurt himself if not other people, another man and I grabbed an arm each and marched him back up the hill.

Everyday between Whit Sunday and the end of September, I would carry the relic of St Winefride from the Church to the Crypt. Relic! What relic? It was a small piece of bone from her tomb. We are not back in mediaeval times when the relics of the saints were deeply revered, or are we? At that time I was not sure it mattered very much. What matters, I would say as I climbed into the little pulpit everyday, was prayer and what matters in prayer is love. Whatever actions we do that are acts of love link us to Love itself, to God. Why should not the Saints help us on our journey? I acquired a devotion to St Winefride, impressed not by her story which is largely myth, like that of her uncle St Beuno and other Celtic Saints, but by her 'presence.' Something you cannot argue about but only experience, something that does not happen at once either but only gradually, something that belongs to a spiritual world that surrounds us all.

On Sundays there were often bus loads of pilgrims and more services. I became immersed in the history and strange attraction of an otherwise unattractive place. It was not only always damp and cold, it was savagely desecrated by unthinking iconoclasts in the 17th century, and stumps only remain of the stone tracery around the bubbling spring. The beautiful 15th century chapel above had also been desecrated and in the 18th century was used as a school room.

Bridget often joined the bathers and encouraged me to do the same. It was a gruelling routine. You entered the inner bath down narrow steps, submerged yourself, exited by another flight of steps and repeated the process three times. Speed was essential because of the cold but I had to do it in slow motion when I carried a crippled woman from the hospital through the water. She had hoped for a miraculous cure. It did not happen. There have been many apparently well authenticated cures at the well over the centuries. It was still a time when the nuns in particular believed they should still be happening. Sister Gemma would go down with demented Hospice folk. She would stand well-wrapped up, saying her rosary while a poor woman with Paget's disease was immersed in the pool. When the woman cried out that she was freezing and could she get out please, Sister Gemma was heard to shout, 'Not yet, you can't expect to be cured in five minutes and without a bit of pain.' She was not cured.

After passing through the inner well three times and submerging completely each time, a custom which related to the way baptisms were carried out centuries ago in the Celtic Church, you are expected to kneel on a rock called St. Beuno's stone in the outer bath and continue your prayers with your head just above the water. John Gerard, a Jesuit priest, hunted down and finally captured in the reign of Queen Elizabeth 1 wrote in his Autobiography in 1593.

> *'Once I was there on 3 November, St Winefride's feast. There was a hard frost at the time and though the ice in the stream had been broken by people crossing it the previous night, I still found it very difficult to cross with my horse the next morning. But frost or no frost I went down into the well like a good pilgrim. For a quarter of an hour I lay down in the water and prayed. When I came out my shirt was dripping, but I kept it on and pulled all my clothes over it and was none the worse for my bathe.'*

He needed to be better for his bathe. He was put in the Tower of London, tortured no less than ten times and still he did not betray anyone. He was finally condemned to be hung drawn and quartered, apart from crucifixion the most barbarous form of execution invented by man. Incredibly, he managed to escape, managed to climb through a small window in his cell and down a rope to a little boat in the Thames, and so back to France. Many of his fellow Jesuits, Henry Garnet, Edward Oldcorn, Nicholas Owen, the conspirators in the Gunpowder plot and many more, were not so lucky. They all came on pilgrimage to the well and they were all executed. Nicholas Owen, nicknamed 'Little John,' died on the rack. He had been responsible for constructing numerous hiding places in large houses up and down the country and saved many priests from capture when the houses were raided. He could have given the murderous Richard Topcliffe, whose special task was hunting down priests and torturing them for useful information but this time he only pulled the wretched man's body apart.

In quieter mediaeval times when the whole country was Catholic even kings made pilgrimages to the well. Edward 1 on his way to subjugate Wales, Henry V in thanksgiving for his victory at Agincourt, and finally James the second with his Queen, Mary of Modena in 1686. The king gave money to repair the well chapel and the Jesuit priest at Holywell gave him part of the shift that his grandmother, Mary Queen of Scots wore at her execution. The Queen prayed at the Well to ask that she might be blessed with a son but this proved a disastrous idea. When her son was born in 1688, the event caused a revolution. The idea of a Catholic heir to the throne caused panic among the powerful protestant landlords, many of whose ancestors had done well out of the dissolution of the monasteries, and William of Orange was invited over from Holland. He arrived in November with a squadron of expensively equipped cavalry and 200 black men from the Dutch plantations in Central America to attend to the horses. But he did not forget to bring the rest of the army as well. By December, James the second, aware of the unfortunate end his uncle, Charles 1, had suffered, fled with the Queen and their little son to France.

It was, despite the risings of 1715 and 1745, the final blow to Catholic hopes of a return to the 'old faith.' So many miscalculations had been made, the Pope's foolish excommunication of Elizabeth, a provocation that led to the execution of Mary Queen of Scots (1587) and the Spanish Armada (1588). All that and much more had caused mayhem for Catholics, especially for priests trained abroad, entering Britain disguised and considered traitors. Many died. Some of their brave lives seemed to linger on like friendly ghosts in the house and chapel where I slept.

The well became famous beyond Britain's shores in the Middle Ages but the story and life of St Winefride dates back to the seventh century. It was strange finding myself in charge of a Shrine, one that had seen unbroken prayer and penance over centuries, cures of mind and body. But if the prayer and penance disappear, as they have done to a large extent today, the healing, support and joys of another world go as well. In my view that is an enormous loss. It was not like that in the late nineteenth century. A Jesuit priest obtained permission from the Clerk of the Peace for Flintshire to open a chapel at 'Ye Olde Star' in 1808. Then he began building the first half of a church, completed in 1832. His successors obtained a lease on the Well crypt in 1873 and built bathing cubicles all round the outer bath. The poet, Gerard Manly Hopkins, was living at the time in St Beuno's College on the North Wales coast. He wrote:

> Here to this holy well shall pilgrimages be, And not from purple Wales only nor from elmy England, But from beyond seas, Erin, France and Flanders everywhere, Pilgrims, still pilgrims, more pilgrims, still more pilgrims What sights shall be when some that swung, wretches on crutches Their crutches shall cast from them, on heels of air departing, Or they go rich as roseleaves hence that loathsome came hither! Not now to name even, those dearer more divine boons whose haven the heart is.

I was sleeping at night in the upper part of the 1808 chapel. It had been divided horizontally in half. Below me was the kitchen, a kind of lobby with the big bookcase and a bathroom. It was linked up to the old part of the house, the original Star Inn, an unusual hostelry, the innkeeper in those days was a priest and the guests were pilgrims. I read about the extraordinary history of Holywell through the centuries, the years of persecution, the secret Masses, the betrayals. Emancipation came finally in 1812.

It was now a very busy parish, two convents, two Catholic schools, a Grammar and a Secondary school, youth club, Sodalities, Mothers Union, Scouts and Cubs. On top of that, a substantial amount of mail about St Winefride's well and the Services there. There was no space for a day off.

Chapter 5
Feet of Clay

Christmas came with its splendid celebrations, carol singers, decorations, and a box of chocolates. That last was unexpected and embarrassing.

I suddenly found I had acquired a shadow. I could not attend parish meetings and associations, the youth club, give a Service at the Well or even say Mass without her eyes drilling holes in my back. This was the kind of thing I might have expected, something to bear with, something that by its nature would peter out on its own. It should not have been such a surprise and should not have caused me such turmoil. Bridget noticed the persecution and brought me another Guinness. Later on she brought two more but Monsignor mysteriously discovered them. She must have left an empty bottle around, very careless, the supply dried up. The months went by and at last my shadow gave up. She began to walk out with a teacher at the Richard Gwyn Secondary School in the neighbouring parish. I was relieved but also depressed. There was a pretty serious chink in my armour; indeed I did not really have any.

Throughout the summer, groups of pilgrims would arrive from this or that parish, place petitions at the well, Mass offerings, questions, questions. The busy days were Sundays and several times between Easter and September there were very large pilgrimages. The whole diocese was involved on the Sunday after 22 June when a sea of banners and statues were carried down from the town, the Mothers Union, the Children of Mary, The Knights of St Columba, the Scouts, numerous clergy and altar boys.

A large Polish pilgrimage came every year and sang magnificently and one year a pilgrimage of Eastern rite Catholics came, no one knew from where. A bishop, or perhaps a senior cleric, came to the door of the presbytery wearing a blue soutane. He was bearded and his English was excellent but he was not alone, a little behind him stood a beautiful woman. He introduced himself and then his wife. I could see his pectoral cross was finely worked but plain, there was no crucified man there. He himself looked well fed and I was suddenly and stupidly jealous. We organised the details of his pilgrimage which turned out to be spectacular and became an annual event but I found I was further disarmed. I had not met an Eastern rite married Catholic priest before, though I knew they existed – somewhere.

A year later I began to notice the girl again. She was engaged to be married to a very suitable young teacher, but one day I found this young teacher in tears at the back of the church.

"She has left me and it is because of you, Father."

"What madness," I replied, and then added foolishly, "I will talk to her."

My heart leapt, for the shadow was back but I knew I couldn't, shouldn't, keep my word. She had become a primary school teacher in the parish and on the feast of Corpus Christi, a Thursday in June, the school had a holiday. I said the 10.30 am Mass, knowing she would be there and knowing that I would speak to her afterwards. I was distracted throughout, planning how, when and where to talk to her. At the consecration when I was saying the words, 'This is my body given for you,' I felt that the words were directed at me personally, that I was the object of the words, not the bread. 'This is *my* body,' the words said. It was as though Christ was claiming me and expected me to be one with him and give myself in the way he had. It was a precious insight and yet I remained stubborn.

At the end of Mass the Church emptied quickly but she remained. Could I now keep my rash promise, speak to her? I wanted to, feared to. She was collecting the hymn books, storing them away in a cupboard.

"I have to talk to you," I made it sound like an obligation.

"Where?" It would have been enough to have suggested the Presbytery waiting room, instead I said

"It is a holiday; would you like to go for a walk in the quarries near your house?"

They were old quarries used probably to build Pantasaph Church and monastery and, after many years unused, were covered in short grass and small trees. The suggestion was met with stunned silence.

"It's a free day," I added.

"When?"

"This afternoon. About half past two?"

"It could rain."

"Yes, it could rain."

"I will meet you there," she said firmly.

I told myself that I had to persuade her that she was crazy to follow me around and it had to stop. 'Infatuation is not love,' I was going to say. She was not doing herself or me any good. But a part of me wanted so badly to be with her. The self deception was obvious. I was about to stoke the smouldering cinders into a blaze and forget that I had been called to be a priest.

I drove up to the quarries on my scooter, left it at Pantasaph Church and walked. It was a blustery day, scudding clouds and intermittent sunshine and it had been raining, the grass was wet. I tried to walk calmly, unhurriedly, carrying my gauntlet gloves, a black figure, embarrassed by my collar. I felt sure there were people in the distant houses with binoculars. Jesus loved women, treated them as equals, and broke all the taboos that existed at the time. If he did not marry it was not because he did not approve of marriage. I need not be afraid either.

I could see her distant figure carrying something. 'Boy meets girl,' I said to myself gloomily, 'alone by agreement, in a quarry,' I added bitterly. And then, 'Loosen up. It's not that bad. Talking does nobody any harm.' We met coolly.

"Let's go for a walk."

I spoke with energy about the virtues of her boy friend and the importance of a steady relationship, how difficulties have to be overcome. She listened ecstatically without hearing anything. She carried a book with her. She thought it would interest me; it didn't. It began to rain again.

We sheltered under a small gnarled oak tree. She sat on my gloves. The shower of rain stopped and knowing that I had said all that I could possibly say and knowing too that she had not listened to any of it, I said limply,

"I must go now." She did not get up.

"Let me have my gloves." She looked defiant and did not move.

I sat down again and struggled to dispossess her of the gloves and ended up kissing her. You would call it a peck on the cheek but at that moment I heard great shrieks of laughter. Was it my imagination? I can only say I heard it, my collar seemed to throttle me and my blood froze.

"If you don't give me my gloves I won't see you ever again."

She laughed, knowing it was an empty threat, having secured something of mine she was not going to give it up. I stomped off; my hands froze on the scooter. Worse still I feared what use she might make of the gloves. I cursed myself, feeling an utter fool. Bridget asked what was wrong but I was too ashamed to tell her.

The next morning I was due to take Communion to several people in the hospital. I had to be there by 6.30 am and back in the Church to say Mass by 7.30 am. Instead, I found myself driving a red sports car through the countryside with the young school teacher at my side. We found an inn crowded with people but managed to get through them to an inner room where we were alone. There were windows all round but they were covered in thick brown paper. No one could see in. This was a relief but it did not last, someone began peeling the brown paper off the windows.

"Time to go." I said.

Back in the sports car I suddenly remembered the hospital.

"You have made me miss taking Communion to the sick," I cried bitterly.

I had been dreaming, of course, and was amazed that I could blame someone else, even in a dream. The red sports car was the same one that the beautiful secretary had driven over from Liverpool to tell me about her marriage problems some months earlier. I did not realise I had envied her that vehicle so much.

Then the alarm went off. It was exactly six o'clock. I was not late but I was in a confused state and very nearly lost my life. I knew something was going to go wrong and the morning began badly when I gave Communion to the wrong man, not entirely my fault, the screens were

29

round the wrong bed. When I left the good man, who seemed perfectly happy to receive Communion, the right man called out,

"Father, what about me?"

That meant another unscheduled visit to the hospital.

I was still distracted later that day, trying to find a family in Pentre Halkyn. I had gone the wrong way and found myself in Pantasaph instead, the very last place I wanted to be. Returning from Pantasaph, passing the quarries again and driving too fast, I came to a crossroads. I imagined I had the right of way, it was a straight road but I was wrong. A white van appeared from nowhere and was immediately in front of me. There was no time to brake, no time to do anything. I smashed into the side of it. I was wearing my new duffle coat which had a hood but one that would be completely useless at saving my head in an accident, but since I was travelling at speed, I took to the air and made an elegant loop over the top of the van, landing in the road absolutely flat, my head pointing in the direction from which I had come. If I had managed to brake and had been travelling more slowly, I would probably have killed myself. A woman came out of a cottage with some brandy, which was very welcome, the local Vicar stopped by and then an ambulance arrived on some other mission. The ambulance took me back to Holywell, but apart from bruising, I was unhurt. The Vespa was a write off, but I realised I had a remarkable guardian angel who had not yet given up on me. Nevertheless, no more risqué visits to disused quarries. Monsignor made no comment. We seemed to live entirely separate lives.

St Winefride's Well

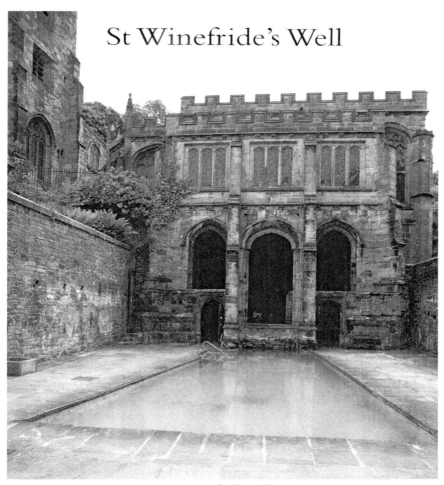

St Winefried's Well

Chapter 6
A Surprising Joy

I had learnt to ride a motorcycle in Bushfield camp, Winchester. Norton 350s were part of the equipment of a modern rapid deployment regiment. The whole company had a splendid week riding round the countryside led by an instructor. Everybody passed except three of us. One fell off his bike every time a fly got in his eye. Another could not cope with a bumpy cross- country ride and a third, riding just behind the instructor, could not stop when he stopped. I was the third. The memory is vivid; the instructor leapt from his bike in a fury. The penalty for our inefficiency was an extra week on motorbikes, what bliss. The rest of the company went on manoeuvres, sleeping on concrete floors in empty pigsties, while we had wonderful days out on our bikes and slept in our beds.

Riding my Vespa likewise had been good fun and now I was reduced to a bicycle, even reduced to pushing the damn thing when it got a puncture. This is where the divide comes, the gulf between me and ordinary people.

"You can't do that Father, here let me push it."

I did, but I could not explain that I did not like being on a pedestal. Briefly without a bike, I had to walk to Lluesty hospital. It was quite a long walk and I was deeply depressed, although the work itself was as satisfying as ever. I knew it mattered, that it was right that I continue. There was no time anyway to worry about myself and then an extraordinary thing happened. One day, at the same time as the depression, I had a strange experience similar to one I had read about in the life of St Teresa. After the usual morning Mass and returning to the sacristy I found I could go no further, I felt myself transported. There is no other word for it. I had to make a huge effort to go into the dining room for breakfast, I was just so happy. I was not interested in food and I am sure I did not look any different. I knew I had to behave normally but the experience lasted all day. Do not ask me to explain; that would be impossible but the experience took away the depression I suffered, at least for a time.

News reached my family and friends in Monmouth of the demise of the Vespa. There was general consensus that Vespas were dangerous and four wheels were safer. A few weeks later a present arrived, it was a dilapidated 'Deux Chevaux' and Monsignor did not like it at all, though he could do nothing about it. It was already there at the bottom of the garden beside his elegant garage. It made a wonderful noise and I had a moment of euphoria. Its battery was rather weak and it had to be cranked but so what. It had canvas bucket chairs, a canvas roof that could roll back, and one key. That was its greatest weakness, it had only one key. I was so delighted I skipped all the tasks I was supposed to do and went for a trip round the Dee estuary and into the Wirral. I stopped in a little village and went into a sweet shop for some chocolate to celebrate. When I came out, the key I had left in the ignition had gone.

There was a man on the opposite side of the road regarding me with particular interest and I felt sure he had taken my key. He was obviously fascinated to see what I would do next but how do you go up to a stranger and say, 'have you taken my key?' I went back into the shop instead and consulted the proprietor. He showed no surprise, came out to the car and pulled out a lead from the steering wheel. He then separated three strands, joined two together to switch on and then the third to start the motor, and so it did. I was amazed and expected the man on the other side of the road to clap, and wondered how many car keys he had collected and whether the two of them would have a drink in a bar together later. It was a strange event and rather spoilt the pleasure of the chocolate, but I got quite used to joining up the leads to everyone's amusement. It was like a new toy and gave me great pleasure, a gift from Peter Kelly, a family friend, in Monmouth.

Back to work: I used to visit every bed in Lluesty hospital and spoke to every patient no matter who they were at least once a week. It was still a time when the various ministers looked after their own, so my efforts were not much appreciated by the Vicar, or the Baptist Minister. The cancer wards were the most distressing. The patients there were just waiting to die and some were quite young, men and women, their children would come to the bedside. That was peculiarly distressing. I visited the wife of a young man who had just died in that ward. She had two children and could not come to terms with the fact that now she had to bring them up alone. In the living room there was a note on the mantelpiece for her husband. She looked completely wild.

"I know he will come home."

The room still stank of tobacco smoke and she continued to smoke herself. There was no awareness in those days of the connection between smoking and cancer.

I do not think one can do anything more important for people than visit them in hospital. The clerical collar, which I had reduced in size to a small white patch, was useful at the time and usually met with respect but not always. As I entered one ward a woman cried out;

"Who are you?"

"A Catholic priest."

"I didn't ask to see you."

"I didn't come to see you specially; I've come to see everybody."

"Nonsense, you've come to see me. Well you can go away."

The next time I saw her she said;

"Take that collar off, I can't stand it.

"I'm not the only one who wears a collar."

"The others don't come and see *me*."

I was not going to make any progress with the lady though she was a Catholic. On my third visit I dared to ask her.

"Why did you put yourself down as a Catholic since you clearly don't want to be one?"

"If I die somebody will have to bury me, I suppose, and my mother will want to be there. Damn her."

"You are not likely to die in this ward...but you could be an exception."

She actually smiled, grumpily.

"Why don't you take your collar off? You would look much nicer?"

As you know I did not like the collar myself, though it did give me free rein to wander round the hospital at almost any time. I made no effort to explain my hang-ups to this lady. She was recovering slowly from a stroke and gradually she got used to me and became less aggressive. We talked more each time. She had been badly hurt and was pretty unforgiving but one day she said;

"I'm so glad to see you. I had a terrible dream. You won't believe this but I dreamt I was trying to get into the Church but round the pathway leading to it there were horrible wild animals trying to stop me. I had to fight my way through them. When I finally got into the Church I found you. You were not only *not* wearing your collar; you were lying on a couch with an empty bottle of whisky beside you. You were drunk." she looked at me, "do you drink?"

"Hardly ever, but are you telling me you tried to get into the Church in your dream?" I took her hand. I felt so strange.

"I'm so pleased to see you," and now there were tears in her eyes.

"When I'm out of here I *will* go to Church."

I was happy, not because one has to go to church to be a Christian but because she had been released from something weighing heavily on her mind.

That Summer I encouraged my parents to drive to Rome. We stopped two or three times in France then in Genoa and eventually found a convent with rooms for us close to the Trevi fountain in the heart of Rome. We were going to see the Pope. We did not know it at the time but it happened. He was opening the newly built Beda College Seminary close to St Paul's on the edge of the city. They let us sit in the sanctuary of the new chapel and then suddenly there was a great buzz and security men and Cardinals trooped in and John the 23rd sat almost opposite us. He bounced up and down in his chair delivering a prepared speech and ended up with hesitant English. The best bit was seeing him slumped back in his chair with a 'that's done' smile on his face. We did not know then he was just about to call the Council and transform the structure of the Church itself.

Chapter 7
Antony and Anna at the Well

I had my noisy French car now but then my mother turned up with a huge piece of furniture, a record player and a heap of records. Yet another diversion was on the way, my youngest brother, Antony, had recently married Anna, from Australia, and the two of them took over St Winefride's Café and Guesthouse, which was immediately opposite St Winefride's Well. Neither of them had any idea how to run such a rambling establishment but they were ready to learn. A large pilgrimage from Bolton, 60 people, booked in for lunch and my parents hurried up from Monmouth, to help carve the beef. It proved impossible to keep the meal hot and worse was to follow. A woman found half a slug in her lettuce and did not keep the matter to herself. It caused consternation, everybody examining their salad, women getting up and prowling round the kitchen,

"Eh, luv, it's not laik it used to be, new to the job are yer?"

The most lucrative side of the business seemed to be the ladies 'loos' which required guests to spend a penny before they could gain admittance. I remember going down to find Antony counting the day's takings, but the Lancashire lasses got wise to it and held the door open for each other. Antony was an artist and this was really not his scene. In his first week he had to chase a rat down the stairs and kill it with a poker. He found another in the cutlery drawer where it had died. Antony had seven white rabbits, destined for rabbit pies, but they all mysteriously died as well. The house had been a dormitory once for poor children employed in the factories down the valley. It was divided into rooms by 3 ply wooden partitions which were infested with woodworm and Sister Gemma would often send down her surplus guests, most of whom turned out to be bedwetters. But up in the attic there was a fireplace and space for painting and sculpture which became a kind of art studio for Antony, and Anna played the role of model. Then the winter came and it was so cold they fled south. When they returned the hot water bottle had frozen in their bed.

The legend of St Winefride, (Gwenfrewi in welsh), is that she was the daughter of a local prince. Her uncle was a missionary monk who founded the monastery of Clynnoc Vawr in Caernarvonshire and was revered as a saint. It is said he instructed his niece, Winefride, and she decided to become a nun. Unfortunately, a neighbouring prince had other plans for her and when she ran away from him he cut off her head. The head bounced down the hill and where it came to rest in the valley, a huge spring of water gushed forth. Her uncle was there and since he was very good at raising people from the dead, having managed it six times already, collected Winefride's head and placed it back on her body and, 'having prayed long and earnestly,' she woke up as if from sleep. Her uncle was St Beuno and there is plenty of evidence for his real existence and death in 640 and for the subsequent life of St.Winefride. She was buried in the small convent she founded at Gwytherin not far from Holywell but in 1138 a casket of her bones was taken to Shrewsbury Abbey where the contents remained undisturbed until the Reformation. Prior Robert of Shrewsbury and others, undoubtedly, embroidered her story. Hagiography at the time was much more concerned with spiritual values than material facts and not ashamed to create a few miracles to inspire (or scare) the people. For example, the angry suitor fell dead at Beuno's rebuke and 'disappeared into the ground.' The trouble is there are still gullible people today who believe the blood of Winefride still stains the grass red. Anna had to push a visitor up the hill to collect some of this blood-stained grass and when another guest found similar grass way down the valley he asked Antony in all seriousness:

"Did the head roll down that far?"

Meanwhile I went on with my own strange life and even now it is the hospital rather than the schools, the weddings, the baptisms, the funerals, the muddled up lives of the parishioners, even now it is the hospital I remember best.

It was difficult to know what to say to people who were quite obviously dying. Do you pretend that they are not dying, that they are going to get well again? Death and dying, like politics and religion, were taboo subjects in the army but it must be better to face reality in the end. In the hospital the ward nurse tells you which patients have registered themselves as Catholics and also which patients are terminally ill. It was my job to help people (if they would let me) make a peaceful exit from this world so I told a lady, who seemed to me amenable to the suggestion, that she was dying and....I got no further. The result was blood curdling screams which brought the nurses running.

"The priest told me I was dying," shriek, shriek.

"Of course you are dying," said the Ward Sister. "We're all dying."

I was grateful to the Sister for that intervention. The woman stopped yelling but continued to struggle rather desperately not to die. For that reason she was in no mood to accept 'Extreme Unction' as it used to be called, the anointing with oil of chrism, eyes, ears, nose, mouth, hands and even feet. The words too were final, 'May the Lord forgive you whatever wrong you may have done through your sense of sight' etc. Nowadays the emphasis is different. The anointing seeks to heal and postpone death. It was introduced in the very earliest Christian communities and represented Christ healing the sick. It brought comfort sometimes to people, to a woman for example who remembered nothing of her childhood except the second half of the Hail Mary prayer, the part which ends, 'pray for me now and at the hour of my death.'

My ministrations in the hospital were, however, too successful. An embarrassing number of chronically ill patients wanted to become Catholics. After receiving 3 or 4 of them into the church I realised they could just be saying 'thank you for befriending me.' But I was not sure. The Vicar, however, was quite sure, a nice mild man. He did not often appear in the hospital but now he went to see Monsignor about it. Well, you can guess how sure Monsignor was. He made his usual comment,

"You are wasting your time."

That did not deter me altogether but I did say to the next man, who was half paralysed and had become a good friend, that he had to tell the Ward Sister that he wanted to become a Catholic. I regret that now. He could not bring himself to do that but what is there in a name? It is only desire and love that will count in the end.

A shy young nurse also stopped me one day in the hospital and said she wanted to become a Catholic. She, at least, could join the Church community which is really what it is about, so one afternoon, on my way back from the hospital; I called at her house to make arrangements for her instruction. She answered the door and then kept me waiting in the front room. When she came down the stairs she was wearing a ballroom dress with a plunging neckline, a revelation uncommon at the time and rather startling for me. It was a beautiful full length dress in deep blue with gold trimmings. I was glued to the chair, speechless. I was so naïve I really thought she was interested in becoming a Catholic but she, clearly, had a different agenda. She wanted to interest me in herself, and that was not difficult, she was attractive. I could see that returning to her little house on the pretext of giving her instruction could lead to more than a ballroom dress with a plunging neckline. She was not quite as shy as I had thought.

"Don't you like it?" she asked. "I bought it last week in Liverpool".

"Of course," I replied in a flat voice. "But you are not interested in becoming a Catholic."

"I am, I am" she replied bright eyed.

But though I was sorry she had gone to Liverpool and bought herself a dress for my benefit, I made no arrangements. I was being told something about myself, something I was beginning to understand but could not share with anybody.

Lluesty was more than a normal hospital. It was also a hospice for the dying and had psychiatric wards as well. It even seemed to have a possessed woman in the old part of the building, the old workhouse. She was not the only mad woman there but she was the worst. I could never go near her. She did not just begin to scream, she shouted abuse and blasphemies. The most unnerving aspect was that she sensed my presence even when I was nowhere near her, even when the anxious sister had put screens around her. Taking Communion to that part of the hospital was a nightmare. She was of course demented and could not have been actually possessed by a devil as was thought possible in the past. On the other hand she probably needed a really good psychiatrist or maybe she was beyond that too. Another woman mystified me. She could be quite reasonable one day and cursing the next, using the most obscene language. On those days no normal communication was possible. Only one of those mental patients was always the same, she could neither see, nor speak and neither could she hear. She could only feel. I was always astonished by her smile when I took her hand, it was innocent and simple as though she understood and valued the contact. Somebody was in there, imprisoned, waiting for release.

Chapter 8
Return of the Shadow

My shadow was back now and became a menace, even though it was still term time, I dreaded the holidays. I was crazy enough to write to her at the school; it was a serious, even brutal, letter. Among other things I demanded the return of my gloves, even though with no scooter, I did not really need them anymore. The result was an embarrassing interview with another teacher who came hesitantly to the Presbytery shortly afterwards and told me, equally hesitantly, that the girl had boasted to the staff about receiving a letter from me. Worse still, they were all given to understand that a close relationship existed between us. I was seriously worried. I read George Bernano's account of the same thing in 'Diary of a Country Priest' and oddly enough Cardinal Heenan (he was the Archbishop of Liverpool at the time) told a few of us after a conference how he was being harassed by a woman who even discovered his foreign trips and would get there first. He described arriving in Amsterdam to be greeted by the lady on the tarmac. When the hilarity had subsided, I did wonder if she would have bothered had he been wearing the blue soutane of the Eastern Rite and accompanied by a beautiful wife. Naturally we found the staid Archbishop's embarrassment amusing and also enlightening, as I think he meant it to be. The collar can be a target instead of a protection. I had seriously enhanced my target possibilities and after Mass had to retreat into the house, even the sacristy was not safe any more and, if Bridget was not around, I had to watch who was at the door before answering the bell. I could not succeed indefinitely but on school days at least I could walk up the street. A little girl sitting on a doorstep called me.

"Why are you not at school?" I asked.

"I have a cold, are you coming to see Mummy?"

I had no intention of seeing Mummy, but agreed I would. She led me into the house. Her mother was Irish, a formidable lady. The children were violent, passionate, seldom in church but die-hard Catholics, the kind who might join the provisional IRA, since they were really nationalists rather than Catholics. There was a feud between the mother and the eldest married daughter. It had gone on for months and I knew the daughter suffered. Dare I bring the subject up? We were alone. There was no loud TV programme on, which was the normal welcome you got when entering a house, I had to admit it was often more interesting than the priest, but this time the house was quiet, no TV and no rows taking place. I wondered if I dare mention her daughter. It was worth a try.

"I went to see Hilary last week…." She did not let me finish.

"I'm not having anything more to do with her. I have had enough," and she began a tirade which went on and on.

I regretted having brought the matter up. Her daughter was a hopeless girl, pregnant again; eventually she would have twelve children eleven of them boys. The husband never seemed to have a job and possibly Social Security made it possible for them to live without one. The little girl reappeared.

"Get out, Sophie," the mother screamed but the child had a message in her hand.

It was from Hilary. The mother looked at me suspiciously. When she realised I had nothing to do with it, wouldn't dare to organise such a thing, she was quiet. She read the note. Sophie and I waited in suspense, but her mother looked at me calmly now.

"You have made me very happy," she said and gave Sophie a £1 note to take to her elder daughter.

"I have not heard from Hilary for months," she added, and I realised that she too had suffered, the old battle axe!

Christmas came round again and we made the most elaborate crib ever. I forget who took part but somehow a large canvass was obtained, draped over boxes to make hills and painted to make a country scene. Somebody made little carts, houses, a windmill, the stable itself. Finally a large number of animals, people, and shepherds were collected. It was the kind of Christmas scene they are used to making each year in Italy and Spain. The Child was kept back and carried down from the altar after the Midnight Mass to be put in the empty crib. The 3 kings on their camels would not appear on the dusty track leading to the stable until January 6th, Epiphany. Everything was ready and in place on the altar steps of the Lady Chapel. The lighting was switched on and the curtain drawn back on Christmas night. It was a great success, but during the twelve days of Christmas the animals and figures began to disappear, even Joseph and Mary looked as though they were on the way out. I thought it would probably be happening in the afternoons and so watched from the organ loft. A small boy from a wretched home on Pen-y-Bryn came in and filled his pockets rapidly and greedily with animals and figures. This was clearly his biggest haul but I did not stop him. That evening I went to his house. His father was in prison for theft, not for his real crime, repeatedly beating his wife and abusing his 15 year old step-daughter, his wife's illegitimate child. For that indeed he should have gone to prison but they would not dare testify against him. When the mother heard that Michael had been stealing, she burst into tears.

"Not again!" she shouted.

"Michael, come here." Michael came out of his room and stopped when he saw me.

"I didn't do nuffin,"

"What didn't you do?"

"I didn't take them figures."

"What figures?" His mother raised her voice to a high squeak.

The daughter, Sarah, came in from somewhere, hit the boy over the head and said,

"Tell the priest the truth".

"It's alright Michael" I said. "I don't mind you having some of the animals and some of the people too but I must have the shepherds back and a few of the sheep."

He went silent. His sister was about to hit him again. He made a last attempt,

"Ow did you know it was me?"

"I saw you, Michael".

He went into his room and brought out a box. They were all there. I selected some sheep, a donkey, three shepherds and let him keep the rest.

Monsignor was not at all pleased. He decided that creating a novelty crib each year was not worth the hassle. So, he had a young architect design a stable that could easily be assembled and taken down each year. It lacked all originality but is still in use to this day.

Michael, however, had prompted a visit to his home that I needed to make.

"What are we going to do about Sarah?" I asked bluntly.

"Nothing, I can't send 'er away. Where can I send 'er??"

But we found somewhere eventually. She was just sixteen and we found her a living-in job in Chester. After six months her stepfather came out of jail. I called at the house when I knew he would be out drinking. He never had any regular work but he could still find money for drink.

"What did your husband say when you told him where Sarah was?"

"'E was angry at first, wanting to fetch 'er back. Then he calmed down. I think 'e knows tis for the best."

"'E's not a bad man really," she added hopefully. "'E's 'ad no chance in life."

This was pretty generous I thought for a battered wife. She made some ghastly tea, brewed too long. I drank a little. I remember her now, thin and drawn, unattractive, the big attraction in the house spirited away, and wonder still how he treated her when he came home full of drink.

Holywell was not a city parish but it had a surprising number of broken homes and marriages on the edge of breaking down, sometimes holding together solely for the sake of the children. A woman abandoned all three of her small children and left her husband devastated. The priest in those days was either treated as a friend and welcomed, or looked upon as a policeman and unwelcome. 'It's the priest,' I sometimes heard the children calling. Silence followed. I never knocked again. Today the pressure of work and the shortage of priests has probably made home visiting impossible but when it is possible it can have enormous value. One discovers the needs and worries of people. I was constantly discovering Catholics on the fringe, disgruntled, upset, ready to drop out of sight but often ready to come back.

The parish extended into the hills, to Halkyn and Pentre Halkyn. Once a month I took Communion to five housebound people there. One year I organised a minibus to collect them from scattered farmsteads and cottages and bring them into Holywell for the Palm Sunday procession and celebration. The operation was a success and could have been repeated for Good Friday but apparently I had sabotaged the work of Fr. Aloysius Ward, a bouncy young Franciscan, two years my junior, who was in cahoots with Monsignor and running a mobile mission at Halkyn. He arrived on the Monday morning and was jabbering away to Monsignor in the inner sanctum. I could hear a raised voice even through the double doors. After a while I was called in for consultation. The idea of gathering together the scattered sheep on special occasions was dropped and Aloysius Ward went on to become the Archbishop of Cardiff.

After the morning service at the well I went to see my brother, Antony.

In the dining room a man had removed the ham from his sandwich and was thawing it out on the teapot. Antony was painting a frieze on the wall.

Chapter 9
The Benefits of a Fire

Monsignor suggested that I should not sit by the windows in my room.

"You can be seen from the road."

Has it come to that, I thought, that I have to move my desk in case the girl sees me? I liked to have my desk by the window and write there. If she did see me and if she did call, Bridget would still protect me. She would say:

"Go away, he's not in," and wave her arm dismissively before the poor girl had even opened her mouth.

I felt more sorry for her than for myself, having dishonestly raised her hopes. She took to writing letters and even found my breviary one day and left a note in that.

"I need to talk to you," she kept saying, "just for a few minutes."

The problem was I did not need to talk to her, not even for a few minutes.

One day I was writing something at my desk when I smelt smoke. Smoke was seeping in under the door, what horror! When I opened the door it came billowing up the staircase, dense, black, choking smoke. I closed the door hurriedly. I had feared something like this might happen. Bridget only felt confident frying food and since she was becoming absent minded this was a recipe for disaster. It was already a disaster gastronomically. Monsignor seemed to have an iron digestion but mine suffered. Water! I turned a tap in the basin and filled a tooth mug. Ridiculous, I emptied it. Perhaps if I soaked a flannel with water and held it over my nose and mouth I could get down the stairs. I tried that but it was quite hopeless; when I opened the door the smoke billowed in blacker than ever. Wet flannel or not I was choking and could not see a thing. I slammed the door shut and stuffed a blanket round the bottom of it, coughing uncontrollably. The smoke continued to trickle in round the sides and I was now beginning to panic. The windows in the room were the top half of church windows, as I have already mentioned, windows belonging to the original chapel which did not open. At some stage, after the new church had been built in 1842, the chapel was divided horizontally in half and a staircase put in. It was a steep staircase, difficult to negotiate at any time, impossible now.

The only window that would open was behind a chest of drawers on the west wall, a sash window that opened at the bottom. I used to open it at night; the chest of drawers obscured a view of anything from outside. I hauled the heavy piece of furniture away and opened the window wide, planning to make a rope ladder of sheets and blankets, but that proved unnecessary. There was an iron balcony there, it was certainly ancient and rusty but it was there. What a relief! I climbed through, it shook but did not collapse and even more wonderful it had a metal ladder. Clearly somebody had realised the room could become a trap but nobody had painted the ladder, it had been rusting away for a long time and looked dangerously fragile. No time to consider that, it could still take my weight. I climbed down and ran round to the garden door of the house. Monsignor was in the hall, several doors firmly shut between him and the inferno. Bridget was nowhere to be seen. She had carried the flaming frying pan from the cooker towards the back door but never got there, dropping the pan, one slipper on fire, she got out of the house but could not rouse Monsignor who was not accustomed to leaving his study to answer the bell. Franticly, she broke a window and at last Monsignor, perplexed and annoyed by the endless bell ringing, had emerged from his study. He was just in time to hear the glass breaking in the dining room which did not help matters at all. By now the fire had taken a good hold and was eating up the linoleum and the furniture. You could hear the crackling noise from the hall.

Monsignor pointed to a fire extinguisher.

"Read the instructions," he commanded.

He was far too grand to read them himself. Just then, mercifully, the fire brigade arrived and with their enormous hoses destroyed what was left of the kitchen and dining room. Next an ambulance turned up and Monsignor asked the men to take a protesting Bridget to hospital.

She had been hopping about, howling, in the waiting room, it was not her day.

Since there was now no supper and no prospect of any for some time, Monsignor and I went down to the Hospice which was run by two nuns. In fact for the next two weeks we practically lived in the Hospice. It was bliss. Sister Evangelista was in charge, she made you well aware of that. Sister Gemma was her companion and an excellent cook. We probably had V.I.P treatment, perhaps the assortment of pilgrims who stayed at the Hospice did not fare so well. With our roast beef, Yorkshire pudding, well cooked vegetables, dessert, even coffee afterwards, we could have been living in a first class hotel or dining in a top restaurant. I could see Monsignor was impressed and thoughtful. He too had suffered from mushy potatoes, tasteless cabbage and overcooked meat. Bridget did her best, worked all hours in the house and in the Church, was loved by everybody, but quite simply could not cook. The two Sisters in the Hospice on the other hand seemed to have been waiting to show off their skills. Sister Evangelista was ambitious. She had taken risks and got away with them, in fact she had had a dodgy relationship with Monsignor ever since she arrived in the parish several years before. She started off asking permission for making this or that change, making this or that improvement. He always said 'No,' so she ended up making what changes seemed necessary and inviting Monsignor down to see them once they were completed. He could not remonstrate with her because she was always right.

After a fortnight of great hospitality, Monsignor must have wondered what she might get up to next. He did not have long to wait, a major change took place. A wall came down, a load bearing wall that would have frightened the life out of Monsignor. 'On no account,' he would have said, with absolute conviction. But the indomitable Evangelista had a steel girder put in place, a new window cut in the wall, extended the lounge to a really decent size and had it all decorated. Somehow or other, Monsignor, driving back and forth to Wrexham, had not noticed the building works, the noise and rising dust, or perhaps he chose not to notice. When everything was finished, she invited Monsignor down. He could not have been anything but impressed but he did not say a single word. Evangelista found it very funny and poured me a whisky.

PART 2
Seeking something more

Chapter 10
Crisis Times

I had not bothered with the Hospice until then. It was the kind of enterprise that went on quite happily on its own. The pilgrims were always on time for the 11.30 service at St Winefride's Well. Three hours earlier they had all been immersing themselves in the freezing water. Later on they would all be at Benediction or praying in St Winefride's Chapel before a marble statue of the Saint, which had been blessed by pope Pius IX and brought all the way from Rome. The pilgrims came from Catholic parishes in Lancashire and were keeping up a tradition that had lasted for centuries. Their own forbears had left the pile of crutches, leg irons and surgical supports that cluttered up two corners of the Well crypt. Ugly perhaps, but witnesses all the same to gratitude, and the occasional cure. It was not called the Lourdes of Wales for nothing.

Monsignor did not like clutter and he did not like emotional attachments of any kind. He could not even bring himself to visit his faithful gardener who was on his death bed. He had had to kill the affective side of himself and become a machine which is one way, perhaps, and for some the only safe way, to be a secular priest. There was a downside to this as Monsignor could not see the part that emotion plays in worship, nor the support that emotion can give to belief. He ordered the caretaker to remove all the crutches etc. and burn them. This was sacrilege as far as the caretaker was concerned, and he hid them away until the 'persecution' was over, as he described it. But there was worse to come, round the outer bath there were lines of bathing cubicles on all three sides. They were all needed when pilgrimages were at their height and bathing at the well was a principal activity. The hours for bathing were not then restricted to the morning but continued all day from 6 am to 6 pm. Jesuit fathers cared for the holy well in those days and from 1873 when they obtained a lease from the Town Council, until the beginning of the Second World War all the activities of the town, including its economic activity, revolved round the well. When the Jesuit fathers left during that war, their missionary spirit left too, bathing declined and most of the cubicles were gradually dismantled. I do not believe this would have happened if the Jesuits had stayed. They understood and valued the spiritual power of the well, but Monsignor would visit the well only once a year when the bishop arrived for the annual procession. He knew the economic value of the well and appreciated the income received from sales in the shop, which he authorised and encouraged, but beyond that he appeared not to see. He would become the final executioner of the cubicles and bathing would decline even further through neglect. He did not need to discuss his vision of things with anybody, least of all with me. He was the Vicar General, he could just give orders.

"Pull down the bathing cubicles," was his command to the hapless caretaker who had only just given them a fresh coat of paint.

He had no option but to obey. Monsignor had the architect who had designed the Christmas stable to design two collapsible bathing cubicles. They were clumsy and a great deal uglier than the original cubicles, but they could be assembled when required and dismantled after use. They would be required less and less. The caretaker was aggrieved, what was wrong with my wooden cubicles, he asked everybody. There was nothing wrong with them, they were perfect for changing in and their very existence was a witness to the ancient practice of bathing. The old guard of devotees were demoralised and, since I was the one who took all the Services at the well, I suffered their protests and was sick at heart. There was no parish council in those days and no way dissent could be easily expressed.

I was distracted at Benediction that night, the evening devotion that was so popular at the time. I arrived at the altar with two altar boys and began 'introibo ad altare Dei,' the introductory words not of Benediction but the Mass. There was no response though the boys were well rehearsed. I looked down at their kneeling figures,

"Benediction," one of them hissed.

I climbed the altar steps hastily and the choir began 'O Salutaris Hostia,' but I remained in a daze and after the prayers forgot to give the blessing. The altar boys behind were poised to sound the gong, shake the cluster of bells, raise a cloud of incense with the thurible, ritual that today has almost entirely disappeared. At last I woke up, held the jewelled Monstrance high, gave the blessing, slowly, solemnly, bells, incense, all was well, but it was not going to be well for long.

When the altar boys had gone and the church emptied I was alone in the sacristy. Was there anything I could do? Bridget was as upset as I was. She was often down at the well early in the morning. I began the weekly chore of rinsing out the purificators, napkins of linen used for wiping the chalice dry after Communion. The nuns were not allowed to wash them until the priest had rinsed them out first. It was a strangely scrupulous world at that time. Marie Jennings, the organist, was still practicing music for a wedding and was alone in the organ loft. The church was otherwise empty, or so I thought. Suddenly the door opened, I froze.

"You are not allowed in the Sacristy."

"I have to talk to you."

"I cannot talk to you, you know that."

She came closer. I backed away. I retreated down a passage to the boy's sacristy. The charcoal embers were still smouldering in the thurible and a strong smell of incense hung in the air. She followed, but I was making for another door into St Winefride's Chapel and from there I intended to get back into the church. The organ went on playing, the chapel door was locked. Panic.

"For God's sake get out of here."

There was real pain in her face. She had me cornered and I could not bear it. I grabbed an arm and threw her to the ground. There was a cry. I leapt over her and fled. Still the organ played.

I could not eat Bridget's supper, nor return to the Church to lock up. Eventually I told Bridget what had happened. She said something unrepeatable, checked the sacristy, locked up the church. There was nobody around, nobody, but next day the girl appeared again, her arm heavily bandaged. She shouted at me, something that seemed ludicrous at the time, yet hit home,

"You have broken my watch."

Bridget was limping a little, a bit daunted by the new kitchen but with her old indomitable spirit. She needed that spirit. Monsignor had recently announced that he had asked another woman to cook the midday meal. He failed to tell her that the new cook was also bossy and black. There is no reason why the woman's colour should matter but it did to Bridget at the time. I felt her distress. It was really hard for her to be considered inadequate as a cook and denied her kitchen 3 or 4 hours a day. She made herself scarce, scrubbed the church porch, polished everything in sight, she was heroic. It has to be said, however, that the meals, were good. Fr. Jim Mitchell from the neighbouring parish of Abergele began to come regularly for lunch. He was a natural comedian and always had a story to tell. The black lady lasted only a few months, she did not find the work congenial and left abruptly, to Bridget's great relief. Father Jim stopped coming to lunch. So, a better plan was devised, we began to eat twice a week at the Hospice, 'to give Bridget a rest.'

Bridget was a wonderful friend to me and a great character. It was bad luck she could not cook. I thought back to the army fare at Bushfield camp, it had been considerably better. I had looked forward to getting a commission but wondered about the lifestyle it would lead me into. When the day came it was indeed an honour. We assembled on the parade ground and waited for hours. It was very hot and one of the cadets fainted. The band played and played. A General came eventually with his adjutant and the Battalion commanding officer. He did not look at our shining boots, as the Queen is said to do, but paused and said a word to each of us in turn. And that was that, we were commissioned. The next day we dressed up in our new officers' uniform, exchanged the beret for a cap, wore the Sam brown and carried a small baton covered in black leather. The dress uniform was bottle green in colour with numerous buttons, quite magnificent. It was impossible not to be proud of ourselves. After the passing out we all had three weeks leave and would then be posted to one or other of the Battalions on active service. But it never happened.

No, it never happened. Was that by design or not? Was there a plan I did not understand? Whatever the answer to that I seemed to have a different kind of mission that I could not endlessly put off and now I was wearing a different kind of uniform and riding a bike through Holywell town. And then to my delight the old 'Deux Chevaux,' arrived, which, of course, had a practical value, I was able to get to the outlying areas of the parish and I found the strange malformed car had another endearment. It could be heard arriving at the hospital ahead of time. 'I heard you coming,' they would say.

In the parish hall, next door to the Hospice, the scout room and the meeting room just below it were badly in need of decoration but there was no money. There was a veto on raffles of any kind in the parish which, like the veto on putting down rat poison, was understandable. Raffles might jeopardise the parish football pools which were a big money raiser for the church. Money was needed for the upkeep of the church and to keep the Catholic schools going but there was no money for improvements elsewhere. David Lloyd, the scoutmaster knew that and organised a raffle despite the veto. He had little scouts running around everywhere which made it a great success. Both the scout room and meeting room were re-decorated. If some raffle tickets had not floated out of the scout room window and landed on Monsignor's car, he would never have known about it. He plonked the tickets down on the hall table to let us know he knew but said not a word.

The meeting room was no longer dingy and dark and we moved the Legion of Mary meetings there. I went down early to check that the heating was on and to my surprise the table was already prepared. The 14 inch statue of Our Lady in white, with a blue veil and arms outstretched, was already standing on a white cloth flanked by candles. The meeting would be at 6 pm. It was now only 4.30 pm and I was about to leave when I heard steps on the stair and turned. She was there. I still cannot understand how it happened, how she had managed to walk into the club and climb the stairs just at that moment. I was scared stiff, I did not want another confrontation with her, she had nothing to do with the Legion of Mary, and even had she wanted to belong she would not have been accepted.

"It's alright," she said, "I won't come near you," and, presumably, to give me confidence, she sat down at the other side of the table.

I sat down too, alarmed, guessing the questions she might ask and knowing I would have trouble finding answers.

"I have to get something straight," she said, coming to the point immediately. "You don't like me chasing you because you are a priest. Of course not, but why are you a priest?"

My stomach knotted up. I looked at the statue. I thought it might just be possible to talk. I really do not think it is just a belief, an odd conviction of Christians, that Mary has influence still in the world. It is not so long ago that there were statues and images of the mother of Jesus all over Britain. More than fifty churches and chantries were dedicated to 'The Mother of God,' along the 215 miles of the River Thames.

There was an awkward pause.

"Why am I a priest? You might well ask. I can only say it is because I believe God wants me to be a priest."

"How do you know that?"

"How can any of us know what God really wants? I was only 7 or 8 when I first wanted to be a priest."

Long pause. I felt uncomfortable, wishing I did not have to try to defend myself.

"Two things happened which affected me very deeply as a child." I began awkwardly.

"The first was a dream. One night I dreamt I was falling into a black hole and returning to nothingness. I was in extreme panic and then a Power which I did not know rescued me, and after that experience as a child I have always known I was loved and safe."

She looked at me puzzled and I realised I had started off rather badly. She could not possibly understand me. I was silent and embarrassed – but in case it is of interest, years later I found this reflection from the writings of Thomas Merton:

> 'Somehow out of all this comes the miracle,
> the unbearable lightness of being, as you
> might say; the recognition that my reality
> rests like a feather on the breath of God. It
> is because God speaks, because God loves
> and it is for no other reason. And if we
> want to know what it is to say that I am,
> the only answer is I am because of the love
> of God.'

"Loved and safe? You are not telling me that is why you became a priest?"

"Not quite, but from then on I became aware of God."

"You said two things happened to you as a child?"

"I don't talk about these things. They are very personal."

"Try me. I need to understand."

"Why?"

"Because, if I don't understand, I can't go away."

"Go away?"

"Yes, if I know that you ought to be a priest and should stay a priest, I will have to go away."

It was getting dark and the heating had not yet made much difference to the temperature in the room. I did not know whether to continue or not.

"I will try, though I am not sure this will make any better sense than what I have said already. The second thing that changed my life, if I dare say that, is that I discovered prayer, not saying prayers but prayer itself. I was given an experience of prayer which needs no words and is like the experience of being in love. We were living at that time next door to a Benedictine school and monastery called Worth Priory in Sussex. I went to the school and my father taught there. One day there was Exposition of the Blessed Sacrament in the Chapel and among the mass of candles and flowers were all the chalices of the monks. I found myself unaware of anything else around me and stayed there a long time. I knew I wanted to be a priest, not a monk but a priest who would look after people."

"Could you have known what was involved?"

"Of course not, I simply told everybody I wanted to be a priest."

It was indeed true that I had no idea of the consequences. When I did have to think about it, particularly when I began to fall in love with people, I wobbled badly. At that time I thought celibacy inevitable, believed I had to stay apart from the 'world,' saw myself as a kind of sentinel on guard while the people played games. A bit ridiculous, but I did feel that was, or ought to be my mission. I went to see the bishop. He sent me a list of clerical gear I was to buy in London and booked my passage on a steamer which would take me from Southampton to Santander. I was to join the English Seminary at Valladolid in Spain.

I was in a panic and agonised before a small picture of Mary, standing on the world with her hands outstretched, clothed with the sun, the moon at her feet and round her head a crown of twelve stars. Suddenly I had the absolute conviction that I should accept and go to Spain…. but in the end I did not have the courage.

In that particular crisis I had to write to the bishop and, of course, he cancelled everything. Then I took another boat and went in a different direction, across the Irish Sea. I went to Galway University to study medicine. I could not say any of that to the girl sitting opposite me, all I said was:

"I did not study to be a priest to begin with, I studied medicine."

"But you never became a doctor?"

"No."

"Why didn't you become a doctor?"

"I couldn't go on with medicine. I fell ill with TB. It was not the first time."

I could see her face in the failing light was worried.

"Perhaps it is just as well you know this. The first time I was seriously ill, I was nineteen, the war was still on and I had just been commissioned in the Rifle Brigade but found myself in hospital and had to have a kidney removed. Since that did not finish off the TB, I had to spend a whole year in bed. You only realise what it means to be healthy and able to walk when you cannot do so, especially when you fear you may never do so again."

There was silence, I was telling her things she did not want to know.

"So that's it, is it? You are not going to change?"

"No."

"Then I will have to go away."

Her face was tense now. "I will go far away but may I write to you?"

"Yes," I said.

"And will you write back?"

"Yes," I said, impulsively.

She got up quickly, and left as silently as she had come. I sat a long while very still. It was now dark outside. Occasionally a car climbed the hill noisily. I had to think of a homily to give at the Legion of Mary meeting and felt drained.

Interview at the Well for the BBC program "Down Your Way"

Chapter 11
That other Life

I had arrived in Galway in the west of Ireland in October 1947. In those days there was hardly any traffic. Every Friday the centre of the town was taken over by a cattle market, horses too were being sold. There were no pens for the animals; farmers just haggled over prices in the street. Children ran about everywhere. There were thatched hovels in the countryside and when the circus came to town, tousle-headed urchins clamoured round you for a sixpence to get in. I rented a room in the centre of town and lit a peat fire in the little grate. It was October and already cold. Galway was a wonderful experience and I was very happy there. After a month or so I moved into Sarsfield Hotel with two Polish students. It was higher up in the town and overlooked Galway bay which had unbelievably beautiful sunsets and the good Mrs. Sarsfield fed us royally and spent much of her time behind the bar which, after closing time at 10.30 pm, moved downstairs to the basement. Coming home late we would sometimes find the bar empty except for one of the Garda and Mrs. Sarsfield, the two would be talking quietly while she plied him with whisky, his reward for turning a blind eye and a deaf ear to the noise in the basement. At the end of the first year three of us were awarded honours and became tutors in biology, that is to say we helped new students pin anaesthetised frogs to boards and open them up to see how the heart pumped the blood around and we earned £3 a term, in those days a princely sum. At the same time we began anatomy and biochemistry. I bought a huge Boilue Grant atlas of anatomy and a skeleton for £3. The skeleton had lost an arm and a leg,

"In the war," said the student who sold it to me.

"Which war?"

"Jesus, I don't know. I bought it from a geezer who said he dug it up."

Every bone was perfect and the skull as well. I had conversations with 'Seamus' and imagined his life. Whatever happened to him cost him an arm and a leg. Eventually, taking into account inflation, I sold him for £5. Now began the bizarre bit. The anatomy lab was like a large hospital ward with beds on either side, except that all the patients were naked and very dead. They lay under mackintosh sheets and smelt of formaline. Four students attended each 'patient.' They had become nameless and were referred to as 'stiffs,' which was more than accurate, they were just that. Our first task was to go to the mortuary with a trolley and collect our 'stiff.' They were all floating in an enormous tank of formalin which made your eyes sting. The attendant provided us with a boat hook and after several attempts, that is to say several efforts to select a reasonable specimen, we landed a lady. We trundled her back to the lab. For weeks and months we worked on the lady and discovered a great deal about nerves and lymph, arteries and veins and how the muscles linked up with cartilages and bones. She, poor soul, became more and more disreputable. We carefully put all the bits into a metal bowl which were to receive, we were told, a decent burial, a bit difficult to imagine.

As much as I enjoyed the mental stimulation of the study, we had a great time socially as well. We all managed somehow to get hold of bicycles, went off through beautiful Connemara to Clifden, waded out to the lighthouse and swam back, watched the salmon leap at Colonel Cross's Bridge, watched the fly fishing gentry at work. They were charged £2 a day for a rod and were allowed to keep half the fish they caught. Sometimes we took a boat and rowed around the Corrib. We didn't drink much but we danced a lot and I wrote ecstatic letters home.

At the end of my second year in Galway University I was ill again. Just imagine, I was completely shattered and I was back in bed.

Maybe I was meant to learn that my life was not really my own. I did believe I belonged to God and should do what he wanted, one day at least. My year in bed four years earlier had been a frightening experience. I lived in a summer house then, on the top of a hill with a wonderful view over Monmouth town. I had TB ulcers in the bladder which did not clear and I had to return to St Mary's hospital in Bristol for more treatment. Then I began to walk, slowly, slowly. Now, back in bed again, what was going to happen to me?

I thought back to that earlier disaster and the long, slow climb back to health. I had spent a whole year getting stronger and during it was given charge of a flock of sheep, 50 ewes and one ram. I learnt how to treat their ailments, foot rot, worms and maggots, watched the lambing, moved the flock from field to field, came to know each sheep by sight and all the lambs. In six months the flock had doubled in size to 106. One of the sheep was wilder than the rest, always breaking through a hedge into a different field, its ears torn by the brambles. Many times I had to round it up separately when moving the flock. It had two lambs and was teaching them to behave just as badly. It was early spring and still very cold. All the sheep were in a distant field, up a muddy track beyond a wood. One dark and windy night there was a noise at the back door. It was the sheep with the torn ears which stood there trembling in the light from the kitchen. It was ill but had found a way out of the field in its usual fashion, come down the muddy track through the wood, negotiated more than one gate, and found its way into the backyard. It was swaying from side to side. I let it in, put down sacks for it to lie on and gave it warm milk. It had very bad mastitis and I could not save its life but in those doubting years of mine, it seemed to carry a message. Perhaps I was really meant to be a different kind of shepherd. I had gone off to study medicine but was I stopped in my tracks because I was going in the wrong direction? Impossible, the TB would have been lurking if I had gone to Valladolid instead of Galway and then I might have been returned to England labelled unfit to continue as a seminarian!

The shock this time was not just landing up in Rookwood military hospital, Cardiff, (The army was still keeping an eye on me), the shock was losing the excitement of study and the company of many friends. After weeks there and another operation, my parents sent me to convalesce with the Blue Nuns who had a convent at Fiesole overlooking Florence. I had a balcony to myself and a wonderful view over the city. The nuns brought me breakfast in bed and I amused myself painting and going into Florence by tram. It was a great experience and I made friends with one of the young nuns who used to bring me my boiled egg and found myself gently scolded by an older nun.

Staying with the Blue Nuns at the time was en elderly priest who urged me to go on to Assisi and stay in a convent there. At the time I was not only bewildered about my own life, wrecked as it seemed to be, I was also very worried about my sister, Priscilla. I loved her dearly. She had a job in Baker Street, London, working for the herbalist, Hilda Lyall. She was in an emotional state because she thought she wanted to be, or ought to be, a nun but could not make up her mind. Perhaps I could discover in Assisi an answer for us both. I am not sure anything matters so much in life as seeking the answers, painful though the process can be.

St. Francis

Chapter 12
A New Direction

I found a convent of the 'Poor Clares' in the Borgo San Pietro and was given a little room above a potting shed that you could only reach by a ladder. There was one bed in that loft, a very small window, and no other furniture except a chair, a small table and a washstand. The rafters were low and there were chinks of light through the tiles and lots of cobwebs. I had arrived wearing plus fours, an overcoat and trilby hat and looking like the perfect English gentleman. In Fiesole it was in keeping with the surroundings, in Assisi it was not, I felt distinctly uncomfortable. I climbed the ladder in my plus fours. A small nun in a brown habit, an extern or lay sister, climbed the ladder too and put a tin hot water bottle in the bed. I never actually saw the community of nuns, though you could hear them singing like distant angels in a side chapel of the church. The silent little nun put a jug of cold water by the washstand.

I resolved to make a novena, nine days of serious prayer, and imagined myself in the limbo of waiting between the Ascension of Christ and the wind and fire and transformation of Pentecost, not hoping to be enlightened myself, but hoping Priscilla would be. It was February, very cold and wet. I was determined to play the martyr and began by removing the hot water bottle from the bed and setting an alarm clock for 5 a.m. It was not that sensible. I was not that well.

By 5.30 I had climbed the narrow streets to the basilica of St Francis and was in the semi-darkness of the crypt serving the first Mass at the tomb of the Saint. I stayed there, serving Mass after Mass for two hours each morning and emerged blinking into the daylight with a huge appetite for the coffee and bread which the nuns provided. The rest of the day I wandered up the narrow streets from one shrine to the next, even in the rain. Most shops and restaurants were closed. There were few people about and the old town was mysterious and beautiful. It had scarcely changed in 800 years. I walked from St. Clare's body kept in a glass shrine in an enormous basilica, to her convent in the valley, preserved in its simplicity exactly as it was. It is a very peaceful place and St. Francis wrote his hymn of praise there, to sun and moon, fire and water. All the other places connected with the life of St Francis, in the town, on the mountainside, in the valley, the chapel where he made the first Christmas crib, were all within walking distance. I ended up each day in the chapel where the Blessed Sacrament was exposed among candles and flowers and where it was warm. It was nine days of solitude. My French was weak and my Italian non existent so not talking to anyone was not difficult.

The over weight Franciscan Sacristan in the crypt gave me a small card with the blessing of St Francis which I treasured in my missal, but when I wrote to a girl in Cardiff whom I had met in the hospital there, I enclosed the blessing. When I opened my missal again, to my great surprise, there was the same blessing. He must have given me two and it gave me a strange joy to find it safe.

On the 8th and 9th days the weather improved and on the 10th day the sun came out and I walked down the hill to the Porziuncula, the ancient chapel unchanged since the day Francis and his followers made it their HQ. In those days it stood in a wood but now it was covered by a vast basilica and looked minute when you first saw it. Wearing my absurd plus fours, I shuffled forward on my knees across the huge empty nave, imitating the peasants and feeling an utter fool, but in that mosaic-frescoed ancient chapel, where St Francis cut off the hair of his beloved Clare and dedicated her to the religious life, is a peace not of this world.

The whole ten days is still unforgettable, an enormous grace, and if it did not do anything for my sister, it changed me. I discovered the difference between being happy in Florence and the deeper joy of Assisi and realised for the first time that the greater happiness is joy of the spirit, which is not dependent on pleasure or pain. Indeed, can be greatest when pleasures are denied. It is a paradox. One loves one's pleasures so much and rapidly returns to them but I understood the secret and real motivation for the religious life. It is not possible to outdo God in generosity, but he does tend to string people along sometimes and play a game of hide and seek.

I wrote an enthusiastic letter to the bishop. I said I wanted to go to a seminary at once. He showed no enthusiasm at all and did not reply for several weeks. When he did write, he said he could accept me if I could manage all the funding myself. The government had given me a grant for medical studies and amazingly they were prepared to continue the grant to cover four years of seminary studies in Rome. So, I went to Rome, I was 24. The bishop thought I might not survive a normal seminary so he sent me to the Beda College.

The College, the oddest in the world, occupied an ancient palace four stories high that overlooked the Piazza Barbarini. From the roof you could see down the Via Tritone to the Corso and the centre of Rome. It was full of middle aged and elderly gentlemen, a few of them ex-Anglican Vicars, most of them just late vocations, as they were called. The head boy was Colonel Schomberg in his sixties. His aides were more military men, majors, captains, lieutenants and there were two pilots. The oldest was 'Pop' Norton who was 72. He had had two wives who gave him several children and 13 grandchildren. He did not want to marry anymore so he decided to become a priest and since he was able to pay for himself he was accepted. As it happened he would have liked to have spent his whole life as a priest and regarded it as an extraordinary blessing to be allowed to get there before he died.

The students at the Beda were a motley crew indeed. As well as the military war veterans there was a precise French diplomat, an accountant, an artist, an excitable actor, a Quaker pacifist and a Welsh chemist.

The speed of a convoy is determined by its slowest member and the regime at the Beda was regulated in much the same way. It suited me well but I have to admit it lacked the excitement of Galway University. They were all rather serious and important and I managed only one successful prank. Edward Leen was a kindly man, a good friend, an ex-Anglican vicar, but very serious indeed. I put it around the building that a lady had been looking for him. I arranged the theatre props owned by the college such that it appeared she not only found his room but his bed as well. Her golden hair flowed over the pillow, other pillows traced her ample form, and her dress and stockings hung on the chair.

He was so shocked and came out of his room in such haste he nearly had a heart attack. It was funny at the time but not in retrospect. He later played the butler in 'Make Hay while the Sun shines' which, with no experience whatsoever, I inexpertly produced that year. After the first act Edward Leen had a real heart attack. He climbed two flights of stairs to his room and that was that. It was hard convincing the grave diggers that they had to go down six feet for an English man. The local custom was two feet down with the prospect of getting dug up after a year or two and put in a box which was then placed in a wall. You might need a ladder to reach the box with your flowers and candle.

The Rector, Monsignor Duchemin, was not having any of that. He insisted the grave diggers go on digging. At first they misjudged the coffin size. Mr Leen was a portly gentleman, a perfect butler. Then they failed to disentangle the ropes and after lowering the coffin had to go down themselves. The Rector, white haired and short sighted, had not noticed. So, after intoning the prayers, he began shovelling the earth on with enthusiasm, he did not want them digging Mr Leen up again. The patient diggers put up with the first shovelful but after that began to shout aloud. We found it difficult to contain ourselves and maybe should not have tried. He would have enjoyed the joke.

In Rome my happiness was real but different; the lectures were often less than inspiring. Philosophy was good but the Theology lectures were lifeless monotone deliveries and we rejoiced when the Vice Rector became ill and Alan Clarke, the Rector of the English College came in his place. He livened things up and deserved to become a bishop which duly happened. The cassocks we all had to wear were uninspiring too; I sat on my bed for a long time before I could bring myself to put on the garment the Rector gave me. You felt such a fool, the wide brimmed soup bowl clerical hat was even worse.

It was fantastic to be in Rome yet impossible to be other than enormously sad over the poverty. It made anti-clericalism inevitable and a constant rebuke. How compare the bitterness of the desperately poor with the pomp and ceremony of the Church, much of it inherited from imperial Rome. I often walked the narrow streets alone, aware of the ugly contrasts, the inequalities obscuring the Gospel, there is such history, such art, such magic in the older cobbled streets, fountains, palazzos, ruins, catacombs, museums, churches. It was an absolutely unique opportunity to learn some Italian and explore Rome and in the holiday breaks, Naples, Siena, Orvieto, Loreto, Foggia and several times back to Assisi. In the college, Monsignor Witty was the Vice-Rector and law-enforcement officer. The Rector, Monsignor Duchemin behaved like a very kind grandfather and even slipped you a little extra pocket money from time to time.

But I had never seen such poverty. You could buy an Easter egg for the equivalent of £60, an enormous sum of money in those days, and ignore the hundreds of beggars, the prostitutes with their painted faces in the Via Tritone, the backstreet hovels. I would sometimes walk in those backstreets in my clerical garb and the men would spit as you passed by. It was not surprising. The Church was rich and Rome was full of well fed Seminarians. I visited a family living in a wet subterranean vault under the ruins of the Carracala baths. The man was emaciated, his wife sick and lying in bed. There was no other furniture. There were two small children looking like urchins and the man confessed there was another on the way. He could sell in the market, he said, if he had a barrow to push. I had no idea what he might sell but I gave him the money for a barrow. I returned some weeks later but he still had no barrow.

Jean Charles-Roux, the ex diplomat and I, took round half our breakfast each day (a filled roll of some kind) to the 'bone yard' a few streets away. It was a Franciscan monastery and they gave out food to the poor, but they did not like burying their dead or if they did they dug them up again. Brother Leo, Brother James and all the other brothers, sat upright in the crypt. That is to say their skeletons sat upright, or if they had been sitting upright for some time they were dismantled to leave room for later arrivals. Then they became part of an elaborate pattern round the walls and ceiling of the crypt, everybody was jumbled up, so tangled in fact that any kind of resurrection was clearly going to be difficult. It was a kind of exposé of death, macabre, but people came to look at the dead monks in their dusty cowls, and, no doubt grateful not to be there themselves, slipped the silent monk, slumped in a chair a few lira. That is when they had made quite sure *he* was not dead too.

In my fourth year in Rome I contracted TB yet again. The Pope's physician, Dr Rocchi came to see me. It was January 1955. I was due to be ordained in April. Dr Rocchi sent me to stay in a Convent at

Bracciano. It had thermal springs and some of the elderly Beda students with rheumatism would go and sit in the baths on their days off. Dr Rocchi had a different remedy for me. Streptomycin was proving a wonderful new drug and he prescribed an injection every day for a month, plus Nicotobin tablets every night. I presented alternate buttocks to the good Sister's syringe every morning, and rested and rested. Every day was quiet except Sundays when hordes of shooters surrounded the orchards and massacred small birds. Three weeks went by and nothing happened. I spent time in the chapel which was beautiful but the singing of the nuns did not raise my spirits. I was in despair. Then suddenly, at the end of the course of injections, I was cured.

Chapter 13
Palestine

It was worth a celebration, an enormous thanks giving. That Easter break, scarcely on my feet, I went to Palestine, that is, I tried to go to Palestine. I joined an old 'puffer' train which left Mussolini's great marble station early one morning heading for Bari. I was in high spirits until I discovered I had left my boat tickets behind, a catastrophe, I could no longer enjoy the view from the train. In the port of Bari on the Adriatic coast I went to find the tomb of St Nicholas in the Cathedral. He was the original Santa Claus and spent some of his time throwing coins down chimneys which fell neatly into stockings hanging up to dry, thereby rescuing distressed maidens from penury. But I had little time. I prayed hurriedly at the tomb while the foghorn on the ship kept sounding its unnerving message, 'hurry up.' Afterwards I hurried to the quayside past numerous hovels and small boys with very brown bodies diving or jumping into the harbour. I was the very last one up the gangplank and began the difficult task of explaining to the officer what had happened to my tickets. There was no way he would let me on board. The ship sounded its siren again. At that moment a young boy ran up waving my missal which I had left behind in the Cathedral. The boy would not part with it and I was only too glad to give him a tip. The officer laughed and let me board.

I shared a cabin with Walter Kullmann, an Israeli businessman who lived in Haifa, and made friends with his family which gave me a view of Palestine through Israeli eyes. At Alexandria we disembarked to see abject poverty far worse than I had seen in Rome but were rushed off quickly through the hot desert to Cairo to climb a pyramid, see the Tutankhamen treasures and sleep under mosquito nets. Walter landed at Haifa but I went on to Beirut for a weird experience in a Maronite monastery.

My company changed. Three boisterous Frenchmen and a dour Australian joined me in a taxi. They were all seminarians. We went north along the coast, through a series of garlanded villages celebrating a Marian feast, to a monastery in the mountains. There we were entertained with little cups of jet black coffee and some strange liqueur. Their revered and saintly Abbot had died but not really died. He appeared at the back of a group photograph looking like Moses and we were given copies to prove it. Then they took us into the chapel for their strangely beautiful Syriac liturgy.

Baalbek was the next stop. We stayed together now and walked round the ruins of Roman temples and palaces, built on a grand scale but never completed. Baalbek deserves its fame, it was awe inspiring but the over spiced cafe meal, some kind of polenta, was revolting. We reached Damascus in the evening, stayed with the Jesuits and slept under more mosquito nets. The French seminarians had organised things really well. Outside the principal gate of the walled city they were still baking bricks in the hot sun and the first street was called "straight" and whether or not the house they showed us was really the spot where Paul recovered his sight was of little consequence. It was the same city. Two thousand years ago might have been yesterday.

The next day we boarded a train to Amman. The station in Damascus was crowded not just with travellers but with every tradesman imaginable. It was a market as well as a station. I bought an awful liquorice drink from a turbaned Arab who poured it out of an elaborately carved coffeepot, it was undrinkable. Then the splendid steam engine straight out of a western cowboy film, shunted, hooted, hissed and began to move. The traders followed along the platform completing their sales.

The carriages had corridors open to the air and the rear carriage had a kind of open balcony where you could stand and watch the countryside go by. It was hot, the land parched and rocky, peasants, donkeys, goats, occasional odd dwellings, nothing more. The land of the Decapolis had hardly changed since the time of Christ.

We reached Amman in the evening and ate supper in a restaurant. I was still not wary enough of Middle Eastern food and ate chillies. The result was dramatic and the bus journey up the tortuous road from Jericho to Jerusalem which might have been fascinating was a nightmare. Dismounting unsteadily at the Damascus gate and feeling horribly ill, I let a small boy carry my case. 'Casa Nova' I said and the boy disappeared down narrow streets so fast I had trouble keeping up with him. I was alone and lost, one adventure too many, as the boy disappeared round a corner I was forced to run. But out of breath we got there and I was mercifully sick. Meanwhile the others had been far more sensible and ordered a taxi.

The Casa Nova was a Franciscan house in the old city; we were welcomed by the friars and stayed a few days. The most moving places in Jerusalem were not exactly beautiful. They were first of all, Lithostrotos, the vast pavement forty feet below the Sion convent with its crude games carved by Roman soldiers, and the ruts of chariot wheels. It is almost certainly the forecourt of Pilate's palace where he washed his hands. The Way of the Cross through the narrow streets is made every Friday, but when we were there it was suspended to allow the body of a young melon seller to be carried the same way shoulder high, through a totally silent crowd. He had been shot from the Israeli side and lay outside one of the gates to the old city for several hours before anyone dared to collect his body.

The suffering of the Palestinians was abundantly clear. Many thousands had been driven out of their villages and from their land in the War of Independence in 1948, only seven years earlier. One of the Israeli commanders was Ariel Sharon whose Alexandroni Brigade quickly acquired a reputation for ruthlessness. He was promoted to command the Golani Brigade, and then the elite 101st unit which destroyed the village of Kibya killing 69 civilians in 1953, revenge for the murder of an Israeli woman and her two children. The village was in Jordanian territory, and the soldiers crossed over from Israel by night. The Friars in the Casa Nova told us about the Israeli atrocities and the huge refugee camp outside Jerusalem confirmed what they said. We went into Samaria and climbed Mt.Garizim and looked down on another enormous refugee camp, a mass of white tents occupying the valley where Jacob dug his well and watered his flocks. The camps were a bitter rebuke to the world and the bitterness remains to this day. The Egyptians attacked in 1952 but were routed. Meanwhile Palestinians and Israelis remained in a state of permanent conflict; there was frequent gunfire at night. The UN Refugee commission organised food for the refugees but no serious effort was made to remedy the injustice.

Returning to the Casa Nova in Old Jerusalem, the French students organised a walk through Hezekiah's tunnel. The city had been besieged by the Assyrians in about 800 BC, and the tunnel was cut through a hill to bring water from a spring that was outside the city to within the city walls. Thus was created the pool of Siloam. The tunnel was started from both ends and bends abruptly in the middle where the miners linked up. Two of the Frenchmen took their sandals off and sloshed through the water into the cave like entrance and the rest of us followed. You could only walk bent double and once in the tunnel there was no turning back. The water was pleasantly cool and the floor of the tunnel not too rough but we were groping our way for what seemed an eternity in complete darkness until we rounded the double bend and could see light. We emerged into strong sunlight to meet startled women washing clothes in the pool and none too pleased to see us.

This was the pool to which Jesus had sent a blind man to wash. He spat on the ground, made clay with the spittle, placed it on his eyes and told him to go and wash in the pool of Siloam. Jerusalem is the most marvellous old city in the world but, like the events that happened there, it is still full of tragedy. Jesus wept over it, foreseeing the destruction it would suffer at the hands of the Romans in AD 70. He would weep today, little has changed. The bitter struggle for control and possession continues.

Gólgotha, which means a skull, was once a small hill just outside the old city walls where criminals were crucified. A large basilica covers it now and little of the original hill remains. It was where Christ died and close by was a garden where his body was laid. That cave-like place is now included in the basilica. It has an outer chamber and a small inner one with a shelf on which the body was laid.

There has been conflict for centuries between different Christian traditions for a foothold inside the basilica, even for a few yards on the roof. The uneasy compromises seemed to be reflected in the way the building was shored up with enormous timbers, and bored looking soldiers stood on guard. That day we heard Mass in a fine chapel owned by the Franciscans close to the tomb. The friars sang the Mass but it was interrupted half way through by little more than caterwauling from the Copts on the roof. The Franciscans continued unabashed, clearly used to the situation.

Since the Arab and Israeli world were still in a state of conflict we had to cross no-mans land between old and new Jerusalem on foot carrying our bags. It was a wasteland and on the Israeli side there was a customs hut riddled with bullet holes which was not very comforting. Our luggage was taken away to be scrutinised and we were left sitting on a bench with plenty of time to examine the bullet holes. Since I had illegal dollar bills in my bag it was an uncomfortable wait but they were not found, or if they were they were prudently not noticed. The economy of Israel and Jordan depended on visitors.

We caught a bus to a Franciscan Monastery in Nazareth, 70 uncomfortable miles north, several days on a donkey when roads were still dusty tracks. They showed us a house where Jesus lived, with back rooms cut out of the rock in the hillside. It could have been like that. More convincing was the brow of the hill where the enraged citizens of Nazareth tried to kill Jesus by throwing him over. They showed us the synagogue and old parts of the town that still had open drains running down the cobbled streets, and you walked with care, all too conscious that slops could still empty from upper windows on to your head. It was a shock to discover in Nazareth the power of propaganda, in old Jerusalem the Franciscans spoke of the Israelis as the demons, in Nazareth it was the Arabs.

The next day we walked from Nazareth to Mount Tabor. You could get there by taxi but we climbed the hill laboriously and stayed in the monastery there. The huge buildings obscured the summit where Christ's dramatic transfiguration is said to have taken place, great buildings instead of three tents as Peter suggested. We climbed the mount of Beatitudes and stayed in a convent, sleeping out on the balcony and watching the twinkling lights of fisherman's boats. Yes, they still fish at night. It is usually a waste of time in the day, 'we have toiled all night, Master, and caught nothing,' was Peter's response to Jesus but then he obeyed, threw out the nets and landed a huge catch in the middle of the day.

In the morning we walked again, this time over the hillside, where the crowds gathered and were mysteriously fed, but it was bare of flowers and grass, and a shadow of anxiety hung over me once more. This time I had lost my passport, having got into Palestine I might not get out. We bathed at Tabgha, where the shore of the lake was shaded by date palms.

It was wonderfully warm. Peter may have landed his big fish there and discovered a shekel which paid the temple tax for himself and Jesus. The lake was perfectly calm but nevertheless a boatload of children ran aground in the bay. We swam out and pulled them clear and were invited to visit their kibbutz at Ginosar. I alone accepted, driven now by the need to return to Nazareth and search for my passport. Thus, unexpectedly, I experienced the mystique of a kibbutz, a collective farm that had a beautiful position on the lakeside and was highly organised. While the parents worked the land, growing citrus fruits, grapefruit, bananas, avocadoes, pineapples, the children were cared for separately and even had a little house designed for them where all the furniture was small. They gave me grapes, so they must have had a vineyard too. To-day, much more of Israel's land is being irrigated with water taken from the lake with the result that the river Jordan looks more like a stream and the dead sea has sunk lower and become even deader.

The Friars in Nazareth put me up for another night and gave me the same room that I had stayed in before. When I shut the window something fell out, my passport! Only then did I remember that I had put it there to act as a mirror in order to shave. I went back to the mount of Beatitudes by bus via Tiberius and khaki-clad women soldiers carrying automatic weapons stood at the bus stop. One of them boarded the bus, a security guard. She did not look friendly.

I rejoined the others but it was time to leave the 'holy land,' where the Man who came to bring peace is least loved and still largely rejected. Abraham is revered as the Father of Judaism, Christianity and Islam. Each religion has given treasures to the world and each has hated the others. Palestine as a whole but Jerusalem in particular is the heart of the conflict, the crucible where peace can be made and the treasures shared. But this will only happen when humanity learns that each man is his brother, irrespective of religion, and the blood of each one is his own.

Chapter 14
Last Hurdle

I returned to England on 1April, intending to go to Llantarnam Abbey on a pre-ordination retreat. That was the joke, one of the many failures of my life. I went down with 'flu' and was only on my feet again a day before my ordination to the priesthood on the 12th of April. It took place in St Mary's Church, Monmouth, but that too had been difficult to achieve. It was in the diocese of Cardiff and I was being ordained for Menevia which covered the rest of Wales. Archbishop McGrath of Cardiff preferred candidates for the priesthood to come from his native land, Ireland, and did not think I was suitable. He had become a fussy old man and refused to allow ordinations for another diocese to take place within the borders of his own. It required persistent lobbying and visits to his house in Cardiff in the August of 1954, visits at random since he refused to allow an appointment, visits which brought me face to face with his formidable unsmiling housekeeper, with whom I left messages. But my efforts eventually caused the Archbishop to make an angry 'phone call to my own bishop, John Petit of Menevia, who successfully mollified the old man and wheedled the permission out of him. It was all a bit sad. Where had such a culture and use of Authority come from?

When the day came it was full of joy. The Church was packed and afterwards a horde of friends and relatives made their way up the hill to Callow, my family home and in the sunshine of a beautiful day, spread themselves over the lawn. My sister, Priscilla, made me a chasuble with her own hands, and I gave her my bottle green officer's dress suit, out of which she made a skirt and jacket. A little while later I was the new curate in Holywell town.

But now it was 1962 and I had been working as a priest for seven years. They had not been easy but life had become more peaceful. I used to visit the primary school once a week and had noticed with relief that the girl had kept her promise and left. But then the first letter arrived, a long hilarious description of her new job in Liverpool, and I replied, careful not to compromise myself or give her any hope. I hoped time and distance would gradually weaken a link that I believed could never be other than a dream.

In the hospital at Holywell I came to know a retired Sergeant Major in the regular army. He was gruff and uncommunicative; I was too young for him. 'Can't they send me someone who knows a bit about the world?' he seemed to say. Months went by and he was getting gradually weaker, in pain and no longer able to walk. The Legion of Mary organisation I had started not only requires its members to attend a weekly meeting but also to carry out a weekly task. I sent two legionaries to visit the Sergeant Major and they began to care so much for him that they even broke the rules and took him flowers on his birthday. Quite unexpectedly he said to me one morning:

"Come back next time as a priest." It was a command.

He had already told me part of his life, how he used to march his men to church but he would not go in himself.

"I couldn't," he said, "I'll tell you why one day."

It seemed the day had come. I returned early one morning. He made a confession and I was able to lift the burden from that man's heart that he had carried for a great many years.

I brought him Communion the following day, the rest of the ward was still sleeping. He whispered,

"I had a dream, I dreamt I was part of a huge crowd of people waiting outside the gates of heaven but no one could go in because no one knew the password." He paused, "I knew it," and his pock-marked face had a wry smile.

"What was the password?" I asked, but he couldn't remember. Before I left he called me to his bed again and whispered:

"I remember now, it was Elm."

It did not matter, but the Legion of Mary had kept up their visits and prayed for him and it was obvious to them that if you try to make a word out of L.M. for Legion of Mary you could not get closer than 'Elm.' They were encouraged and all ten of them went to his funeral. He was a 'prodigal Son' who maybe had wasted his gifts but when he returned home would be welcomed by his 'prodigal' Father. It is the most comforting story in the Bible.

The Sergeant Major grew steadily weaker and towards the end I could do no more than sit with him and hold his hand. He was quite different towards me, a friend I will always remember and miss. His landlady was astonished when told that he should have a Catholic funeral. He had lived with her twelve years.

"Very private man 'e was. Kept 'isself to 'isself 'e did."

She herself was always in Church and seemed disconcerted that her lodger could get there too at the eleventh hour.

The church, meanwhile, supposed to be built on a solid rock was finding itself on shifting sand. Rules, customs and even beliefs, unchanged for some hundreds of years, were being altered bit by bit. It certainly needed to happen. The erosion began with changes in the fasting laws. No food or liquid must pass your lips after midnight if you wished to receive Communion the next morning, even washing your teeth could be a cause of anxiety. Suddenly the rules changed, you need only fast for 3 hours from food and one hour from drink. Even more revolutionary, Mass could be said in the evening as well as in the morning. For centuries the evenings had been reserved for Benediction, a time for prayer and adoration before the Blessed Sacrament. At first Benediction was retained and followed by a Mass but soon it became an anachronism and virtually disappeared. The older folk moaned, traditional pieties were being undermined, and worse was to come. The impetus for change had been gathering momentum for sometime. Why should Sunday morning shift workers not have the chance of going to Mass? Reluctantly evening Masses were allowed, first on Sundays and then on Saturdays as well. Why should night nurses have to fast from midnight? The Law was relaxed for their sakes and it was as though a small breach had been made in the dyke. What next? The people should understand the scripture readings, some said, but they have missals with the translation, others replied.

The argument for no change had always been that wherever you travelled you would find the Mass said in the same Latin language and feel at home in the universal church. For a decade or more, eminent liturgists had been knocking the theory. They began by asserting that the Mass was not a liturgical celebration reserved for the priest and watched by the people. The people themselves should take part. The Latin responses that the server had to make were now extended to the people. They had to be taught 'et cum spiritu tuo' and join in a so-called 'dialogue Mass.' This was not a total success. When more radical changes were mooted the rumblings of alarm and discontent, grew louder. English could be on the way in and Latin on the way out, and, if that were the case, the Protestant reformers would be proved right after all. The horror of this possibility caused the bishop to pale at the annual clergy conference. The Canon, at least, he declared vehemently will always be in Latin. He was not to know that soon the central prayer of the Mass would not only be said in English but aloud for all to hear. Even more devastating the priest was going to turn round and face the people. The mystery that went on at the alter in total silence and the worship and awe it inspired in the faithful, most of whom did not have missals and did not try to keep up with the priest's rapid Latin, was going to end. 'Hoc est Corpus Meum,' which became a derisory 'hocus-pocus' for the reformers, would become quite simply, 'This is My Body.'

But the long struggle over several years would not end easily. 1961 had been a year of preparation before the planned opening of the 2nd Vatican Council in October 1962. Hans Kung with remarkable insight wrote a book, 'The Council and Reunion.' Pope John the 23rd not only wanted to revitalise the Church (aggiornamento), he also wanted to promote Christian Unity. Kung made a powerful case for doing exactly that. I showed the book to Monsignor. He was not interested and suspected heresy.

That Autumn I continued the Enquiry Talks that had taken place each year, with some excitement about the new direction the Church might be taking. We had just completed a census in the parish; a substantial number of dormant Catholics had been discovered. When I began to add them into the parish registry Monsignor was not amused.

"You are wasting your time," he said.

What I feared he meant was, you are increasing the number of Catholics in the parish, which would swell the numbers but not do the finances any good. Every parish had to pay a tax to the diocese based on the number of registered Catholics. It was called the schools quota and was raised to pay off massive debts incurred through the building of new Catholic schools.

The survey carried out jointly by the Legion of Mary and the Children of Mary, using a carefully prepared questionnaire, unearthed no less than 202 people who said they were interested in the Catholic Church and would like to be informed about the next 'Enquiry Talks'. They all were, though only two had the courage to turn up. Fortunately, we had not changed the invitation to Catholics to bring along their non-Catholic friends. The ten week course was a success and ultimately led to the reception of 7 more converts into the Church. Somehow, the impending ferment in the Church was a help rather than a hindrance.

In the autumn of 1962 the bishop with 3000 others from around the world was called to Rome. The 2nd Vatican Council opened on October 11th. Monsignor, the Vicar General, became effectively bishop of the Diocese.

"You have to take full responsibility now," he said. "You will not have any time for Enquiry Talks this year."

'Nor next year,' he might have added.

I was disappointed. It was an opportunity for the informal instruction and discussion which was stimulating for me and helped both Catholics and non-Catholics understand the Gospel a little better.

Monsignor was an administrator, not an evangelist. No poison, no raffle tickets, no bathing cubicles, no talks, no discussion on anything. It was disappointing but it was the Church of the time. However, I have to admit in retrospect I was over zealous, over active, and believe now I was hiding from my secret anxieties. At the same time I was longing for the Church to lose its fortress mentality, to be less clerical and less triumphant, claiming in practice too much infallibility. If you attended a non-Catholic service, a wedding or a funeral, you were not expected to join in the prayers. Catholics kept their distance. The Youth club was strictly denominational, intended to foster Catholic marriages. If any young Catholic suffered the misfortune of falling in love with a non-Catholic there could be no wedding in Church, it took place in the Sacristy. Even that could only happen when solemn promises had been signed to bring up any children as Catholics. Exclusiveness had its consequences. The Youth Club Socials were frequently under siege and I was the unhappy policeman. The excluded clung to the lamp posts peering in, ran around the building shouting, hammering on the doors. The parish priest of Ruabon did things differently; he excluded nobody but Fr. Owen Hardwicke was ahead of his time. When I progressed from a black suit to a grey one, wore a duffle coat and a strip of white plastic in a black shirt instead of a dog collar, Owen Hardwicke scandalised his fellow clergy by giving up clerical dress altogether.

If my talks to a mixed Catholic and non-Catholic group had to end, debate among the Grammar School sixth formers became more lively. If it was no sin any more to eat meat on a Friday why was contraception still a sin? If one law could be changed, why not another? Should we have English in the Mass?

"Yes" they said, "It makes sense."

"Should the priest face the people?"

"Why not?"

But older people generally did not want the changes and some converts particularly were shocked. They had entered a Church that they thought would not, indeed could not, change. Bridget was different, her loyalty was above the arguments going on, but she would mind, she said, if priests were allowed to marry.

"They couldn't love everybody equally if that happened." On so many things Bridget's instinct was right but perhaps not on that one.

They gave you a good breakfast in the Convent parlour after your Mass. Reverend Mother would come in to see if you needed more toast. One day I asked her,

"What has happened to Sister Margaret?"

Mother replied;

"She has gone back to Birmingham."

"A pity, she was such a good teacher."

I visited the school every week and tended to delay in her classroom, it was sad to realise that quite innocently I could upset things. More upsetting, however, was the return of the girl. She had stopped writing which made me uneasy and with good reason, she re-appeared in the parish.

"I could not bear it," she said.

"You know what is going to happen now?" I replied.

"*I* will have to go away."

Bridget was misty eyed.

"You can't go," she said. "You are needed here."

Indeed it was where I felt most needed and where I had the strong support and protection of Bridget. I should have suffered the harassment which would have petered out sooner or later.

I left Holywell in 1964. By that time Antony and Anna had left as well and nobody risked taking on St Winefride's Guest House and Café. The sign over the door had sagged and Caradoc's sword cut into the neck of Winefride. It could only be raised up when the door opened and it fell when the door closed. It was my contribution to Antony's venture and meant to encourage visitors, but it could easily have put them off. The sword had fallen permanently for a whole year and now it fell, not only on the Café, but on my life at Holywell as well.

Chapter 15
The Rhyl Presbytery

I suffered a kind of bereavement on moving to Rhyl. I was leaving behind so many people I had come to respect and many I had come to love. I missed Bridget badly. Her dedication gave me a strength that I lacked in myself.

I felt a failure too in my constancy and in my relationship with Monsignor, especially when I disagreed with him and did not say so openly. It would probably have led nowhere but I should have tried, not just for my own peace of mind but on behalf of the parish and on behalf of the pilgrims. The result is that I have caricatured him. He was a good administrator, as loyal as he could be to his own lonely destiny. Bridget told me that he too went through a crisis once over a woman. She could not help noticing the regular appearances of this person and how, after each visit, he would go into the church and light candles before the statue of Our Lady.

"I have never seen him do that before," said Bridget and laughed – or rather giggled - but not unkindly.

I was disorientated in that gloomy Rhyl presbytery. My window opened on to the main street which was noisy all day and most of the night. It was no help that I was living again with a totally uncommunicative Rector. He was small, even wizened, and never seemed to have shaved successfully. He looked at you with sharp eyes under bushy eyebrows and gave the impression he had broken through the 'sound barrier' and all the other barriers that anchor us to the earth. He was not neat and respectable like Monsignor but careless and almost shabby. He seemed to have both feet already in heaven, for which good reason he was not much bothered about what went on around him.

Monsignor said bluntly when I left Holywell,

"Don't keep in touch with any of the parishioners here."

It was almost conspiratorial but in keeping with his idea of the priesthood as a profession which should not get muddled up with people, so parishes had their boundaries and you were not supposed to poach. Rhyl was a holiday resort, the presbytery was late 19th century and like the church, an ugly pseudo-gothic building on the main street. The inside was equally ancient and equally grim. There was only one colour scheme and that was dark brown, and only one kind of picture on the walls, pious oleographs of simpering Saints. There was nothing congenial about it but that had never been part of the deal. My room was large and overlooked, as I have said, the main street and the noisy life of the town. There was no green and tranquil garden to look out upon while pondering the next sermon or planning the next parish visit. It was a busy parish. I was not followed there but one day a big parcel did arrive.

"A young lady left this for you," said Mary, the housekeeper.

I recognised the writing and found it was not a box of chocolates this time but a large wooden box for housing slides. My slides were indeed in a mess, dozens of them about the well, pilgrimages, the life of Christ, catechetical slides and so on. The old projector was a good teaching aid. There was no message, and though I made use of the box I did not write to thank her. She was obviously doing her best to be brave herself. I was unhappy and felt quite unjustly and wrongly that Rhyl was awful.

I was acting chaplain to Kinmel Army camp, a few miles away from Rhyl. It was full of apprentice boys and in the passing out parades I had to march on to the parade ground and read out the Oath of Allegiance in as loud a voice as I could muster. Afterwards, in the officer's mess the Commanding officer would invite me to escort his wife into the Regimental dinner. I sat beside her, it was an unexpected honour. The occasion was glittering, the wines good, the chatter idle. But I was in the wrong uniform, in a black cassock and I did not feel entirely at home. I was also embarrassed by the lady on my right, an Italian married to a senior officer, she had accosted me earlier.

"I have to talk to you," she had said in a conspiratorial manner. The phrase echoed menacingly in the recesses of my mind, a Regimental dinner was not the time or place.

"After the Mass on Sunday," I replied.

She remembered and remained in the Chapel after the Mass and we sat together, she wasted no time.

"I have to leave my husband, he has been unfaithful to me," her voice quivered and I could actually feel her suppressed fury.

"How long were you away in Italy?"

"Three months."

"Three months! That was far too long. You should forgive him."

"*I* forgive *him*?" She was indignant, about to explode.

There was no point in arguing with her. I just got up and walked away. She seemed to want me to take her side, to let her go back to Italy with a clear conscience.

"You have to forgive each other," I said making for the door.

The organist was waiting to be taken home. I liked taking her home, she was a stunning young blond, far too attractive for the job but she did it very well. She had responded to an advert and as far as I remember was the only one who did. I picked her up in town every Sunday and took her to the camp.

"Where did you find *her*?" they all asked, goggle eyed.

She was another one who lived in a house all alone waiting for a white knight to arrive. In the camp she played the organ brilliantly but ignored all attention, she was on duty, earning a paltry sum, but in Rhyl the young men hovered round her like bees round a honey pot, and eventually she selected one of them.

I was surprised at the number of Catholics in the camp. The Chapel was filled with officers, NCOs and their families, not to mention the boy apprentices. I had the chapel enlarged, that is to say we took over the hut next door and joined it up, gaining a vestry as well in between. The second hut served as a classroom for officer's children preparing for their First Communion. I brought along a nun on Saturday mornings, but one day I hit something on the road. It was another car in fact but we need not go into details. Her door flew open and she tumbled out into a ditch. It was such a pity, she was a lovely elderly podgy nun who made the children laugh but she soon decided she had better things to do on Saturday mornings. Our YCW (Young Christian Workers) meetings also took place in the hut. We studied the Gospels with a 'See, Judge, Act,' handbook. About six young apprentices would turn up but one of them in particular could not see or judge anything correctly and ended up in Bristol jail. He was like the sheep with the torn ears, always in trouble, I went to see him in jail and realised how useful the clerical collar can be. A warder with a huge bunch of keys led me through a maze of security doors and gates to the boy's cell. Years later, when he was back in Civvy Street, he came to see me. I think his dishonesty was not something he could cope with but a kind of illness. He was in need of psychiatric treatment rather than prison. While in Bristol, I took the opportunity of calling on Monsignor JC Buckley in the diocesan Curia offices, he was far enough away from my own diocese and said to be a wise man. He was very kind but genuinely surprised when I told him I was deeply unhappy. I must have attempted to tell him why because he suddenly said, and I remember the question clearly:

"Did you never feel released by celibacy, proud to be able to give your life totally to God?"

I can see him now, sitting behind a huge desk, a large man, plump and seemingly satisfied, and I realised how very different the problem can be for some. No doubt, the victory could be hard won but the resultant peace looked very real. I thanked him for listening and for his encouragement, for he did indeed try.

Bridget had turned into Mary in Rhyl and the menu was no improvement. Mary was as selfless a character but an equally bad cook, to be fair the standard was not good in Britain at the time. The parish priest, Canon Collins, spent hours in the Church every morning before visiting every bed in the large Alexandra hospital, his compassion for people was real and the people loved him. He was literally not interested in food and did not expect me to be. Of course there was never any sign of drink, whereas in Holywell there had been *signs* of drink though they were carefully locked up which was almost worse. In the evenings, when we watched the six o' clock news together in his crummy sitting room, Canon Collins nearly always fell asleep.

By now the Second Vatican Council was really shaking up the Church. There was a revolutionary decree on Ecumenism which acknowledged the work of the Holy Spirit in other Churches. Wow! The Council had deliberately opened the door to dialogue and the aim was Christian Unity *now*. I felt motivated and, with the help of the Legion of Mary which was stronger in Rhyl than in Holywell, we organised inter-faith discussion groups. 30 to 40 people from the Church in Wales, non-conformist chapels and the Catholic Church met to study gospel texts in small groups. One member in each group made notes and summarised the conclusions reached by the group. It was very rewarding. Once a year we took over a Rhyl cinema for a shared service but the euphoria and hope was short lived.

Moving to Rhyl was no panacea and my depression became serious. I knew people depended on me, a lot of people, but instead of being freed to serve by my collar I felt imprisoned by it. I had the worst malaise for a priest, a divided heart. There were women who loved me in the same way as they must have loved Jesus and I owe a lot to them, they were a great support. There were others who reverenced me which I could not stand and there were others again who loved me differently. It would happen so innocuously. I had to attend a dying man over several months. He was being cared for at home by his wife and daughters, married though they were they took their turn. I became aware of one of them who seemed always to be there and who would pass me like an electric current on the stairs, giving me a slight shock. Eventually, the man died peacefully and the funeral was not a sad one. The vivacious daughter invited me to visit her which I did, and then again.

"I will call in on my way home," I said, wanting to appear casual.

I knew perfectly well that I shouldn't call on her again. On that next 'casual' visit I almost turned back. The house was a bungalow and all the rooms opened on to a small entrance lobby.

"Come in," she called and then appeared, straight out of the bath, in a towelling dressing gown.

We embraced for several minutes without speaking. It was of course, satisfactory, intoxicating no less. There was no need for words. We were still in the lobby when a key turned in the front door and we were jolted back to reality. With a husband hovering, it was quite inappropriate for me to stay and I left, although, for a short while, I still felt the intoxication and remained on a high, the longed for physical intimacy glimpsed for a moment. The world was briefly beautiful until the implications dawned on me: she was vulnerable to infidelity but then, so was I. We met and shared the trauma in anguished looks but I made no more visits.

I spent my next holiday trying to regain some balance. I flew to Rome and took a train to Foggia on the Adriatic side of the Apennines. From Foggia I caught a bus to San Giovanni Rotondo. It was an ancient bus crowded with peasants, live chickens, a small pig and masses of bulging sacks and packages, even so there was just enough space for most people to sit down. I sat next to a large woman and did my best to ignore the strong aromas which emanated from her and the other pungent odours all around me. We climbed, creaked and jolted our way up the mountainside, jettisoning people, live animals and packages on the way. The higher we went the colder it got. Only the chickens and a mixed bag of elderly peasants stayed to the end. We alighted in the Piazza of San Giovanni Rotondo as it was getting dark. The mountain rose in a dark mass high above the village. The few people about were well wrapped up, but wearing drab if not black colours, the women and children, thick woollen stockings. There was a very definite air of poverty. A young girl of about twelve begged me to go to her parent's house and I followed her. She led me through the older part of the village to a small but, to my surprise, a newly built house. I was told later the family had been re-housed from a cave; it was certainly a very primitive and very poor family. The woman showed me my room which was clearly her own room with a large double bed. I paid her more than I would have done to stay in a pension and when I left she asked me for my alarm clock. She had never seen such a thing before.

The living room was the kitchen; it had no furniture beyond a range, a couple of tables and a number of chairs. There was no electricity, just one lamp and a candle by the bread, but the house seemed wired for electricity. Sitting round the board with the rest of the household, I remember only the cold and the small relief to the toes of burning charcoal in a pan under the table. If it was a new house their customs had not changed, it was semi-dark and the only food was watery cabbage soup with hunks of bread. There was an older man and his wife and a younger couple with the 12 year old. The men seemed glad to cut off endless hunks of bread from a huge loaf. I tried to eat with them each day, but there was never any meat or equivalent in protein and at the end of three days I was famished. I sneaked into a primitive trattoria in the village and gave myself a steak.

I was on a pilgrimage. I had come to see Padre Pio, a friar who was said to bear the five wounds of Christ. It is difficult to imagine a stigmatist as being other than a saint and certainly Padre Pio was revered as such. He spent hours hearing confessions each day and giving advice. Hundreds of people came to seek help from him. The huge Franciscan monastery nestled in the side of the mountain. One of the friars took me round on my first morning there, and suddenly we met him, he was at the end of a balcony with arches. You could look down over miles of countryside to the Adriatic but there was a mist that day and I suspected there was a mist most days. Padre Pio wore mittens to cover the wounds in his hands. We spoke only briefly, he was very gentle. I asked if I could serve his Mass and when we parted I kissed his hand, that is to say the mitten covering his hand, it smelt of roses. How could that be, I wondered. I could not believe he was using a scent.

Padro Pio's Mass began at 5.30 am. While he was vesting, he suddenly knelt down and I could hear the tinkling of the sanctuary bell in the chapel next door. It was the moment of Consecration in someone else's Mass. I have never known a priest vesting in a sacristy do that before, but Padre Pio seemed to live totally on another plane. His Mass was punctuated by long periods of contemplation, particularly after the consecration, and lasted about two hours. Time stood still, and seemed to stand still for the whole packed monastery church as everybody seemed caught up in his prayer. It was a very moving experience. Lots of people gave him money which he spent building a hospital for the people of the town, the first ever.

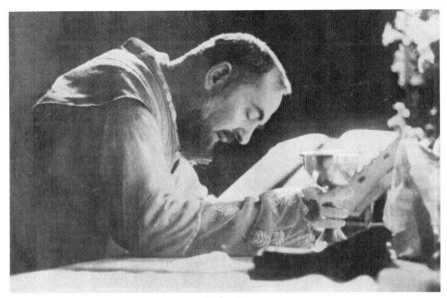

Padre Pio

I returned to Rome and went on to Turin. I wanted to see the 14 foot long burial cloth known as the Turin Shroud which had been kept for three centuries in the Royal Chapel next to the Royal Palace of the Dukes of Savoy. It was in a magnificent silver casket above the high altar. Overhead was the fine Guarino Guarini dome. Behind the altar were life size photographs of the body on the Shroud, both front and back view, positive images and negative images, the former blurred but the latter dramatic and shocking. It was clear that what one would see if the shroud were on display would be the blurred and largely incomprehensible image, only the blood would show up as dark stains. In the negative, the body both back and front takes shape; above all the face becomes clear. The eyes are closed but the features are strong and unforgettable. The whole body had been scourged back and front and the injuries that showed up on the negative photograph as white flecks and on the positive picture as dark blood, corresponded exactly to the fearsome Roman scourge. This had two thongs tipped with dumb-bell shaped pellets which tore the flesh. There were blood flows too from the multiple wounds around the head which indicated not so much a crown as a bunch of thorns, long trickles of blood from the wrists, a lot more around the feet and darker globules of congealed blood from a gash on the right side of the chest. The astonishing clarity of the body image was only discovered in 1898 when the first photograph was taken by Secondo Pi

"On the glass negative there slowly appeared before me, not a ghost of the shadowy figure visible on the cloth as I had expected, but instead an unmistakable photographic likeness."

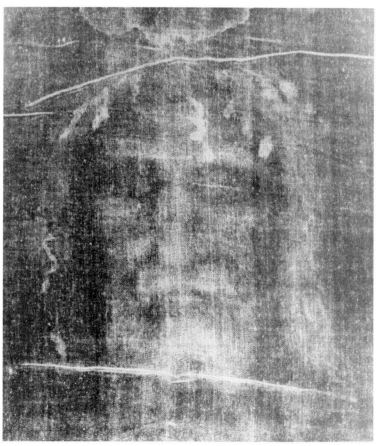

Turin Shroud

It was a huge shock to Secondo Pia. He was the first to discover that Christ has left a portrait of himself that no one can explain nor needs to try.

I was more than blessed by the experience of meeting Padre Pio and by the experience of seeing the Turin Shroud. Seeing it was like reading a personal Last Testament, an unimaginable record impossible to fake. That at least is my experience. I believe Carbon dating from a sample of polluted cloth was ill advised, unnecessary and faulty, but it is not the place here to argue the case or quote the experts.

Chapter 16
An Escape

Since 1960 I had been a schools' inspector in the diocese of Minevia. Religious instruction for Catholics was linked in those days to questions in the penny catechism and children still learnt the answers by heart, but the Vatican Council was changing traditional thinking and catechetics was taking the place of religious instruction. Corpus Christi College in Notting Hill, London, had been founded for the purpose of translating the documents of Vatican 2 into a new catechesis, a newly liberating proclamation of the New Testament. It was to have rather different liberating results but I did not know that at the time.

The idea was good. I asked the Bishop if I might go to Corpus Christi to study for a year and he agreed. Dear Canon Collins did not notice my departure but he had scarcely noticed my arrival. Tom Shepherd took my place. It was 1967, the year the future of Israel was made secure. At the beginning of June the Arab countries, Egypt, Syria and Jordan joined forces to attack Israel. The threat was obvious and imminent, the intention was clear, to eliminate the cancerous growth in the Arab world that called itself Israel. But Israel, armed with the most sophisticated American weaponry for years, saw the threat coming and struck first. Early on the morning of the 5 June, Israeli planes attacked 11 airfields and destroyed most of the Egyptian air force on the ground. Then they had a fine time destroying the Egyptian army, 50,000 killed, thousands more captured, including several generals. The rout was total. After that they could turn on the Jordanians and the Syrians, capture the impregnable Golan Heights, old Jerusalem and the whole of the West Bank, and continue their triumphal march across Sinai to the Suez Canal. Ariel Sharon was prominent again, commanding armoured divisions and (so it was said) reluctant to take prisoners. In six days the chosen people had recovered the Promised Land. Of course, the struggle would go on but Israel was essentially secure. The call from the Arab countries now would not be, 'no negotiation ever, no recognition ever,' but 'please, Israel, go back to the 1967 borders and we will make peace.' But given Israel's belief that they are only taking back what was taken from them, that will never willingly happen.

During this dramatic six day war, on June 7 in fact, my father died. He had been playing chess with David Blackburn, one of the boys my parents were caring for, when suddenly he stood up and collapsed. He was 64 and his going was a catastrophe with unforeseen consequences. No one quite realised what a linch pin he was for the whole family, a truly good man who would disappear to his room each day and find strength that was not his own. We buried him on a knoll overlooking the lawn and placed a praying monk on his tombstone carved by Hubert Van Zellar, a day of immense sorrow.

I now had my distraught and wayward mother to look after; at least that is how I thought of it at the time. I would be studying in a College in Notting Hill, so I rented a flat close to the Portobello Road. It was No.2 on the ground floor of a huge block, several storeys high. Next door in No.1 lived the Swan family, nobody ever emerged from No.3 but a whole world lived above us. The owner of the property arrived in a chauffer driven Mercedes and was wearing an expensive overcoat that almost touched the ground.

He asked 'Were we comfortable?' We were, but I complained about his toad-like agent who not only took our deposit and rent in advance but demanded an extra £10 before handing over the key.

"He is very badly paid," said the rich man.

Whose fault was that, I wondered.

"How about splitting it," said the rich man and he gave me £5 back.

The Swans were quite friendly, or rather, she was friendly and her three children ran about everywhere very happily. His occupation, like that of several others in the block, was dubious. He was often away for days at a time. When he was home, strange men would arrive wearing raincoats and dark glasses, carrying packages. One day his wife was in hysterics. He had arrived home with a badly gashed wrist. 'Would I bind it up for him?'

"It's a doctor's job" I told him. "You should go to the hospital."

"Later," he answered tersely.

I bound up the wound as best I could. I wanted to ask jocularly if he had fallen through a skylight but did not dare. The air was tense, the children shut away in the bedroom. I did not know then how wise I was to say nothing.

"Do you know," my mother said suddenly, "this is the first time we have lived together, just the two of us, for forty years? Forty something years ago, I took a flat in Kentish Town. Aubrey was at sea and you were not quite one."

Mother had a chest full of letters, an extraordinary record of her early years before she married. Reading them, my own existence seemed problematic indeed. She lived in Eastbourne and he was a young petty officer stationed in Greenwich. They had met on the top deck of an open-air double-decker horse-drawn bus. She had only been in London for the day. This unarranged encounter eventually led to my existence on this earth, and after me came a sister and five more brothers, but it was not easily brought about.

The background to our lives does have a lot to say about who we are. There is the genetic inheritance and then all the influences and seeming chances that make up our development. My mother, Phyllis, had been an only daughter with four brothers, the two eldest of whom died in the First World War. She was tempestuous, generous, lovable and wilful. 'You are not to go to Morocco, it is highly dangerous there,' said Sub-Lieutenant Aubrey David before going off on exercises. She *went* to Morocco. Welsh blood flowed in her veins from the Powell's in Carmarthenshire, Quaker blood through the Copes in Yorkshire and Irish blood from the McNeelys in Northern Ireland, but the family had settled in London a few generations ago. Nobody knows how Grandma Cope happened to marry William Neely (the Mc had been dropped), but both parents were hostile to their daughter's proposed marriage to a young and indigent naval officer. They had much better plans for their only daughter. Norman, a respectable Catholic with prospects, sat in front of them in church. He would make an ideal match for Phyllis. Only Aubrey's parents thought differently, they were enthusiastic about the match, his mother, Celeste, wrote to him.

'My darling boy, Phyllis writes me the most delightful letter and Dad and I will go down a little later as she suggests. That is when her mother has got accustomed to the idea of her being serious! It's wonderful being given a daughter whom one can't help loving straight away. Dad and I both feel that already, but you never have given me anything but happiness all your life. I told Phyllis that, and this is going to be the crowning thing. I'm awfully happy about it as I feel quite confident that all the difficulties will melt in time.'

They were not to melt so easily, William Neely was made of sterner stuff and could not bear the idea of his only daughter marrying an indigent wog. That was his unacceptable word.

"But Papa, he's English."

"Rubbish, he's Armenian."

He was in fact half Armenian, a quarter French and a quarter English. His father, Markham David, was the youngest son of Marcar David (Davidian originally) and Elisabeth Manook. The Davidians and Manooks were both descended from the 22 families captured by Shah Abbas of Persia in 1600 and brought to live and work in Isfahan, perhaps the most interesting city in Iran today with its 4 Armenian churches. Marcar David dropped the 'ian' from his name and moved to India in 1851 where he started up a successful trading firm, 'M. David and Company' and made himself very rich. In 1865 he married a very young and beautiful Elisabeth, who bore him 9 children and died at the age of 29. Marcar David was devastated, left his business in other hands and moved his wealth to London, together with 5 surviving children. Our grandfather, Markham David, was aged two. Marcar's mother-in-law, Erin Manook, came to live with the family and Armenian remained the language of their new home in 11 Princes Square, Bayswater.

Phyllis made sporadic efforts to change William Neely's mind but he could not be crossed. On every occasion he threatened to fly into a rage which always precluded any kind of rational discussion.

"You are not to see that young man again," he shouted, "and I'm not going to tell you that again."

In order to be more independent of her father and mother and more available for Aubrey, who was not allowed access to the house and where no letters could be sent, Phyllis got herself a job. She wrote to Aubrey:

'Darling, oh my dear, our beautiful castle in the air is all knocked on the head. You were perfectly right, darling, not to be so sanguine. I can hardly write you the disappointing news. It isn't that the matron of St Mary's won't have me. Everything was settled. My application was accepted. Then the bomb shell was sprung on me this morning as I was making a bed with mummy. She suddenly said: "We're going right away from here, Phyllis."
"Oh" I said, "where are we going to?"
"We're leaving England, all of us, shutting up the house next week, perhaps going to the South of France."
"But I'm going to work in the hospital in February."
"No you aren't" she said. "We are not going to let you."
Oh my dear, I can't explain everything to you in this letter. Granny is a dear, letting me write to you as usual in "Merrington" (20 Grange Road) but I must be off in a minute to meet mummy in Church. The only thing I can think of dearest, is for you to disguise yourself and come to Dolly Burn's fancy dress party. I shall be there, next Friday, beginning nine o'clock at 11 Beaufort Gardens, Kensington. Tel. 6565. Disguise yourself because of Jackie. I'll make it alright and tell Dolly about you.

We can dance and dance. Give your name
as Mr Malcolm and disguise yourself with
a beard. Borrow, beg or steal your dress.
Thank you thousands for your ripping
letter.'

Aubrey got to the party dressed as a pirate
and smelling strongly of glue. They danced
all night and mother's younger brother,
Jackie, never twigged who Malcolm was.
Almost the next day she was taken off to
the South of France for two months. Her
mother now had a chance to work on
her. She nearly succeeded but not quite.
She was threatened with no inheritance
whatsoever, if she did not accept Norman
who was altogether suitable and clearly
very much in love with her. Fraught letters
followed between Phyllis and Aubrey but
finally she made up her mind, once and for
all, and married Sub Lieutenant Aubrey
Cyril Markham David in the Brompton
Oratory, London, on July 21 1925. All
the Davids were there, our grandfather,
Colonel Marcar David, his wife, Celeste,
with her English father and French mother,
great uncle Cyril and great aunts Grace
and Maude, the pair of them exotically
dressed. Not a single Neely turned up. It
was just as well. William would surely
have had a heart attack and found it quite
impossible to shake hands with people he
considered obvious Orientals, much less
give his daughter away to one of them. An
enraged William wrote to his daughter:

Phyllis, your fatal marriage against our repeated warnings, against our most urgent wishes, against all our appeals, have made the last years we have left full of sorrow and bitterness, and very nearly killed your mother.

The reason was not that Aubrey was scarcely 22 and Phyllis 27, the reason was that in William Neely's eyes he was not an English gentleman. As far as William was concerned, he was a dark-skinned Armenian whom he viewed with horror and did not allow across the threshold of his house.

In fact, of course, he was a quarter English, a quarter French and only half Armenian, nevertheless he could never be the spouse of an only daughter brought up in the shadow of the empire and the remnants of Oscar Wilde's Victorian world, 'with the utmost care.'

Mother took a flat in Kentish Town and was pretty poor. She tried to sell things in an antique market and had a bit of luck when the lights went out and she was able to sell a lamp for two pounds, a prodigious sum. Then Priscilla arrived and seemed to take exclusive control of my mother so I stabbed my sister with a pair of scissors, leaving a scar on her leg forever.

But jealousy quickly turned into the deepest affection. The Kentish Town flat became too small and mother was pregnant again. She pushed the two of us, sitting either end of a huge pram, in one of London's parks and met up with Norman.

"Oh dear," he said, looking at us, "I could not have been doing with all that."

When Bede arrived it was crisis time. Dad moved the family to 22 Bury Rd., Gosport, where he was stationed, but three children so close together was too much for mother. William Neely softened, he really had little choice. Clare, our grandmother, was so agitated she insisted on taking charge of Bede. The crisis was heightened when almost at once dad elected to be posted to Hong Kong for three years. He realised he was not providing enough income to support the family and became second in command of a submarine, much to mother's dismay and Grandpa Neely's relief. Bede was born at the end of 1929 and dad disappeared in January 1930. We lived on at Gosport without Bede, but made frequent trips to Eastbourne where we would all stay in Grandpa's house, Ruxley, 25 Southmead Rd. He had designed and built it himself in a strategic position, overlooking the park, Beachy Head looming large and magical in the background. We would climb over the wall at the bottom of the garden into the park, Priscilla and I and later Bede as well, but there was a disappointing notice; 'No ball games on Sundays.' Grandpa, with flowing white hair to his shoulders would wander off to his golf course up the road or to a neighbour for Bridge while Grandma sat upright on a hard chair by the fire, wearing black, her eldest sons in their smart uniforms staring down from huge pictures, their lives snuffed out in the Great War. This was her great tragedy from which she never really recovered.

There was a big terrace in front of the house, overshadowed by a huge greengage tree and there was a rocking horse and a tricycle to play on. Eventually Grandma persuaded us all to live with her for a while and we did not object to that, the mortgage had been high on Bury Rd.

The return of Dad in January 1933 was carnival time but mother kept saying, 'never again.' She persuaded him, now a Lt. Commander, to retire at once. I think it was not just Mother who needed him, it was all of us. They both had impractical dreams of the 'good life' and contributed to the 'Soil Magazine' which said you did not need insecticides if you dug round fruit trees and nourished them with manure. So they started doing that in a small way at Ditchling Common where the guru and artist Eric Gill had started a 'Back to the Land' Community. The place was buzzing with real and aspiring artists and calligraphers and dad aspired with them, spending hours on lettering which mother kept carefully and later framed. I was six by this time and the three of us children did not seem to get to school at all, we were far too busy exploring and 'helping,' and once I wielded a scythe injudiciously and gashed my sister once again. Not a happy moment, she was rushed to hospital and it began to rain, heavy rain that continued through the night as a kind of punishment. I remember anxiously waiting for them to return from the hospital, protecting the bed from a dripping roof with an umbrella.

Mother's older brother, Uncle Guy, thought we were all crazy and decided we had to be practical. He discovered a job that could suit dad at Worth Priory. It did not really suit dad but it suited the rest of us and that was important as mother was pregnant again. Eric Gill had retreated to a mountainous retreat in Wales. He was a shadowy figure and we did not miss him but we missed the Cribb family. He was a sculptor and gave my mother a carving that stands today on my desk. I remember they lived in a warm and lovely cottage with beams and an enormous inglenook and had a blazing log fire.

Worth Priory had been the home of Lord Cowdray and called Paddockhurst. It looked Elizabethan, high gabled roofs and tall chimneys, leaded windows, decorated ceilings, an enormous ball room, and polished parquet floors everywhere. Not the kind of place to be infested you would think by small boys. Our new home overlooked it and was called 'Old Paddockhurst,' a dower house for Lord Cowdray's mother. She could sit under her cedar tree and survey the long drive with gates as impressive as those of Buckingham Palace, and smell the huge banks of azaleas that bordered the drive.

I cannot imagine why we should have been so lucky as to find ourselves living in a beautiful house, surrounded by a vast estate, an unimaginable luxury. We could wander into bluebell woods, areas of heather and streams, go down to the ornamental lake with its iron bridge and shoot at harmless voles with an airgun. It was all because the monks accepted us and became our friends, monks who were almost as new to the place as we were. Six of them had arrived from Downside in 1931 to start a monastery and a school. We arrived when the school was beginning to become popular which was why they needed dad.

The dower-house was magic too. We had two large empty rooms to play in at the end of a long corridor and created an elaborate war between the English and the French. They had a fortress with innumerable men on the battlements and cavalry on the ground. The British troops were lined up 3 metres away, but we pretended the war was going badly and we had to bring up reinforcements by train from the first empty room. In fact the war was going well because we had the only howitzer. This was a gun with a wheel which elevated the muzzle and a spring which hurled missiles into the air, missiles which looked exactly like large shells and, when we got the trajectory right, devastated the enemy lines. Instead of bringing up more troops, we spent much time collecting mangled cavalry and headless French soldiers and returning them by train to an emergency hospital in the back room. It was great fun.

Dad taught Physical Training, boxing (he got some medal for this in the navy), games and mathematics. I climbed down the bank to the school for the first time aged seven, and remember receiving panic instruction from mother on how to write my name. She thought it important that I remembered who I was. Bede joined me in the school a year later. Monks are different from ordinary teachers, perhaps because they have different priorities; certainly they were a lot of fun. They became family friends, especially Simon and Hubert Van Zellar, Julian Stonor and Wulstan Phillipson, who was a Shakespeare enthusiast. Maurice Bell was a little more pompous but then he was the headmaster.

But they were years of stress in the family, babies kept coming, roughly every 18 months, and though every time a girl was expected, it always turned into a boy. We had hardly arrived at Worth when Julian was born, and we had hardly got used to him when Nicholas turned up. Before leaving Worth, (on account of the Germans who were supposed to be invading us) Robin arrived and, I am not sure of the arithmetic, but Antony must have been on the way. Dad tried to ease the situation for mother by employing a small army of helpers. Bonny arrived to cook at two pounds a week, a substantial wage but she was a prodigious cook. Of course she had to have a scullery maid. A governess arrived who had to have a nurse maid and there was some strange lady, a major-domo of sorts, who organised everything. Mother reclined on cushions in the drawing room and we were invited in to bid her 'goodnight.' It was not the kind of relationship we really wanted.

The idyllic Worth Preparatory school could not last for us. It was the longest bit of serious education Bede and I were ever to have, and it was the longest growing up time we would ever have with Dad.

Worth Priory, Now Abbey

Chapter 17
The Aurora Borealis and the War

There was a remarkable 'Aurora Borealis' in the sky one night in 1938, a kind of portent. War was declared on September 3 1939. It seemed to create quite unreasonable early panic. Evacuations began. Worth school was evacuated to Downside Abbey, Stratton on the Fosse, Somerset, and we went there as boarders but dad had to return to the Navy. To start with he was at Chatham and then put in command of a naval training establishment on the Isle of Man. This irked Mother, she did not know what to do, and finally decided to move all the family to the island. Bede and I only spent about a year at Downside. The headmaster was Christopher Butler who later became a splendid bishop. I had only one encounter with him when I was requested to bend down while he wielded a cane. The misdemeanour had been defacing a desk during a boring French lesson which irritated the French teacher and there was no alternative to joining the queue waiting for the cane. But Christopher Butler could not see very well, he peered down at you and clearly did not like his weekly task. He was far too kind a person to want to hurt anybody and was soon to be put in charge of a diocese instead, so he made no effort to strike accurately or hard. Priscilla meanwhile was at The Priory, Haywards Heath, Sussex which is where mother had been educated. Suddenly all of us were to be evacuated to the Isle of Man. There were definitely seven of us when we collected on the quayside in Liverpool. Priscilla, Bede and I arrived by train. The 'four smalls,' as they were referred to habitually, were driven to the waiting ferry by mother while dad arrived from nowhere and we all boarded the ferry. It was certainly an adventure. The weather was kind and when we arrived in Douglas we all sat on the beach, while dad rushed off to find somewhere to stay.

He found a dreadful boarding house at Laxey with crumbling floors at every angle and smelling strongly of carbolic soap. We stayed a night there and then moved into Ballahowin, Major Duckworth's house, in the country which was beautiful and we even had a stream at the bottom of the garden. A maid arrived, probably Lou, and dad rushed off to take command of his little bit of the navy. Serious education came to a complete stop. I think at such a time of crisis mother did not want any of us out of her sight. Haywards Heath was clearly going to be bombed and Downside too. So she advertised for a Tutor and hired three elderly retired teachers in succession, the last one, a Mr Law, survived longer than the others but even he would not leave his cottage up the road if it was snowing or too cold.

We spent a year at Ballahowin but it was memorable. Dad was relocated back to England and became 2nd in command of HMS Andania, a merchant cruiser patrolling the North Sea. We all arrived once more at the Liverpool ferry, this time with a whole salted pig hidden beneath blankets. My small brothers sat innocently on top of the blankets in the back of the car. We had all nurtured the pig to its great size over six months and mother was not going to leave it behind. But the customs men found it and ordered it to be taken out. We retreated to a safe distance and mother took it out but put it back again.

"Have you taken it out?" asked the customs men.

"Yes," said mother, which was true.

We drove on to the boat and then from Liverpool south to stay in an Admiral's house at Alverstoke, opposite the Isle of Wight, decamping hurriedly when a bomb fell too close. Mother rushed to the nearest hotel in the middle of the night to order taxis. She found the hotel in a state of panic, everybody moving out, but she got her taxis. Next morning, she moved us all out, seven children, two maids and Mr Law, the tutor. The first objective was to get us to the railway station. Mother led the way in a Morris Minor. At the railway station all the smaller children were labelled together with the luggage, in case anybody or anything got lost. Next stop Petersfield, the Morris Minor arrived there first, final destination was a guest house in Rogate, Sussex. It was a big place and William and Clare Neely, now beloved Grandma and Grandpa, came to join us. Even Eastbourne was considered unsafe. We moved three more times before the war ended. The most exciting time was watching, entranced and awestruck, dogfights in the sky during the 'Battle of Britain.' We were then living at 'Byways,' a house on a crossroads at South Harting. Every time we saw a plane shot down we jumped on our bikes in the hope of getting to the crash before the police. We succeeded (that is Priscilla, Bede and I) only once, bringing home a twisted machine gun and reels of ammunition from a Junkers 88. The plane had come down in a wood and was still smouldering. We stepped carefully round an airman's boot which stuck up in the air, quite unaware of the human tragedy, of families bereaved.

After that we moved to Towngate near Wadhurst. Tutors had given up or been dismissed and Bede and I walked each day across the fields to Mayfield Xaverian college. It was now 1942. We hid our Wellington boots outside the College under a bush. The war went on and HMS Andania was sunk. It was sunk by two torpedoes late at night. Dad described the evacuation in detail, his own last minute return to the ship to rescue his ivory Madonna, the sailors in the Christmas pantomime still in their party gear, some of them still dressed as chorus girls. They all pulled away from the ship just in time to avoid being sucked under but it was a cold night and the sea was icy, anybody falling overboard would not have lasted long. Fortunately, it was also a calm night and the lifeboats stayed close together. When dawn broke six hours later, an Icelandic fishing vessel spotted the survivors and managed to get the whole crew safely on board, standing room only and a stench of fish, but safe. The tough fishermen laughed uproariously to see British Naval seamen dressed up as chorus girls. The pantomime, triggered by months of boring patrol work was never performed but, incredibly, frozen as they were, they all survived. Dad believed in prayer and treasured his ivory Madonna which he reckoned had something to do with their rescue. It was reported in the Reykjavik press when they landed in Iceland, but the dress of the sailors mentioned in the press release was censored in Britain. Back at Chatham, dad was offered command of a destroyer, but mother rushed up to London to plead for the family. She thought destroyers were highly dangerous. They did not take a lot of notice and sent dad with an expedition force to Oran, Algiers, where he became a beach master, and Rommel with his tanks, was too busy fighting somewhere else to upset the landing.

Our Armenian great aunts, Maude and Grace, lived in flats nearly opposite each other in Ashley Gardens, Westminster, and during the war refused to move anywhere else. Grace would give you half a crown and Maude would quiz you first, before giving you the same. They had arrived in London as children, with Sarah, Cecil, Nicholas and Markham, in 1879. Their mother, Elizabeth Manook, died in Dacca, India, in that same year, aged 29. She had married our great grandfather, Marcar David, in 1865 when he was already 35 and she was 15. On her death he moved all the family to London. The youngest, Markham, our grandfather, joined the Royal Engineers and was a Major in the First World War, becoming a Colonel in the Second, but caught scarlet fever and died in 1942.

He left his house to dad and we moved there in the same year. Our grandmother, Celeste, whom we called 'Nona' moved to London. Bede and I started to go to Dixton House School in Monmouth, Priscilla went back to Haywards Heath, but I do not remember the 4 small brothers going anywhere. Mother was 45 and I was 15. Mr Wheeler, living in a bungalow next door, was tending his huge vegetable garden and strawberry patch. He was short and fat and had two dogs, and every evening took them for a walk. A public footpath ran across the top of Mr Wheeler's garden close to his strawberry patch, this was convenient for anybody who liked strawberries. The four smaller members of the family aged from 10 down to 5, liked strawberries very much which displeased Mr Wheeler greatly. His harvest was shrinking. He barricaded the stile which led from the lane to the footpath with large quantities of barbed-wire, effectively reserving the path for his sole use. Since most people at that time were away defending their country against the Germans, the path was seldom used and there were no loud protests but he was creating a little war between himself and our family. Mother was furious, enraged that Mr Wheeler should be sitting in his bungalow when dad was risking his life at sea, enraged that he dared to close down the only public footpath nearby. This account of what happened comes from Antony, the youngest who was 5. The eldest was Julian. He planned a commando raid with the object of burning down Mr Wheeler's house. Julian had discovered a hole in the hedge which was skilfully enlarged. The 4 boys waited for Mr Wheeler's portly figure to emerge from his home, followed by his dogs, and make his way to his now private footpath for his evening walk.

"Now," hissed, Julian.

They all scrambled through the hedge and hid under blackcurrant bushes, *his* blackcurrant bushes. They became distracted again by the strawberries and in no time Mr Wheeler could be seen returning home.

"Don't move 'till I tell you," hissed, Julian, who was already making for the lane.

By the time they did move it was too late, the dogs were barking and Mr Wheeler was shouting and there was a queue of desperate boys at the hole in the hedge. It was an evacuation, Mr Wheeler wielding his stick and the last bottom suffered severely. It was a debacle, severe and humiliating, and Julian's reputation was in tatters. Mr Wheeler strengthened his hedge. He had won the battle but not the war.

Having won so decisively, he must have wanted to offer an olive branch to the boys and gave Julian some pellets for his airgun. Julian was grateful and decided he would give one of them back. He spent a considerable time observing Mr Wheeler's garden and at last the opportunity came. That day the man himself was working among his cabbages. He was within range, and every so often bent double revealing the desired target. The gun fired high and to the right, so it was necessary to aim low at Mr Wheeler's ankle to hit his expansive bottom. Fire! Squeal of pain. Ah, what satisfaction!

The village policeman rode up on his bicycle to see Mother. He explained the purpose of his visit respectfully, almost apologetically.

"Oh dear," said mother, "What a naughty boy, I will see it does not happen again."

But she was not at all displeased and made no attempt to apologise to Mr Wheeler. Meanwhile the 3 smaller boys, Nicholas, Robin and Antony, now joined by Bobby, a short, tough 8 year old evacuee from Birmingham, had other plans to punish Mr Wheeler. Sometimes, the portly gentleman could be seen boarding the small steam train that in those days travelled daily from Monmouth to Chepstow and back. The driver would hoot as he came round bends on the winding track, or entered a tunnel. His black-faced mate would shovel the coal, and the conductor would shout "Wyesham Halt" as the wonderful engine whistled, hissed and screeched to a stop. Then on a good day two or three passengers might alight, occasionally Mr Wheeler himself. It was a splendid way to travel up and down the valley, shutting the windows quickly as you went through a tunnel, rumbling over this bridge and then another, back and forth across the river Wye.

The plan was simple, derail the train with Mr Wheeler on board. Little thought was given to the fate of other passengers, or indeed to the crew. Julian scoffed.

"It is very unlikely fatty Wheeler will be on the train."

Logic does not matter much if you are under 10 and consequences at that age are not foreseen either.

They planted rocks on the line, as large as they could carry, and then listened to the hooting of the engine in the distance. They could even feel vibrations on the line as it neared the last bend. That was the moment to scurry up the bank and hide behind the bushes. The suspense was enormous. The little engine chugged by, slowing towards the Halt, pushing the rocks away effortlessly, what an anticlimax. 'Wyesham Halt,' the well known voice carried down the line, mocking the small boys.

However, they did not give up.

"We must make the train go up and then fall over," they said.

So, the next day their preparations were more elaborate, a metal sheet would encourage the train to go off the rails when it would have to fall over, hopefully with Mr Wheeler inside. They awaited the consequences of this second effort with even greater excitement but the engine pushed the obstacle away effortlessly again and Mr Wheeler was not travelling anyway that day, he was safely in his cabbage patch.

It is not known whether mother ever knew of these escapades; what is certain is that she planned her own commando raid and enrolled me as her accomplice. First, she dyed her hair with henna, then we walked together to the Mayfield Arms and had a pint of beer each, then in the dead of night armed with gloves and wire cutters, we removed all the barbed-wire that impeded the climbing of the stile and use of the public footpath. Mr Wheeler hurriedly picked the last of his strawberries.

Chapter 18
The Demise of Corpus Christi College

All that was a long time ago and now mother and I were together in a London flat. I was able to walk to Corpus Christi College each day via the Portobello Road and saw another side of London life. I was having coffee alone in a small café one evening when two men walked in demanding food and the little man behind the counter rushed off to cook something for them. As soon as he was out of sight, these two hefty blokes began playing the fruit machine and it was a minute or two before I realised they were not playing at all but dismantling the machine altogether. They were using nasty instruments and working fast. They had not noticed me until I began to shout which scared me as much as it did them. They ran off and the little man rushed back to the counter, "Louts," he said bitterly, looking fragile and frightened. The Portobello road lost some of its charm.

The students in the autumn of 1967 were a muddled bunch of religious education teachers, men and women, priests and nuns, muddled in the sense of not quite knowing why they were there. The Principal was Bert Richards, a scripture scholar whose lectures sought to reveal the hidden meaning behind the Bible myths, Old Testament and New. His deputy was Peter de Rosa, a brilliant lecturer, who believed the Church had under stressed Christ's humanity. There were two nuns on the staff, Rena and Ruth, and three more priests, Peter Wetz, John Perry and Frank Somerville SJ. In addition all manner of specialist lecturers came and went. There was a mood of exhilaration and expectation, a sense that the frontiers of reform in the Church had not yet been reached, that there remained much to be done. The College sought to help the Church move forward, away from its protectionism and legalism. It could and should be preaching *good* news to all men; instead of creating so often, anxiety and fear. It was liberation theology, the people of God on their way to the Promised Land. "Original Sin" was not thought of as a particular sin, the crippling effects of which were passed on to all generations, but a necessarily imperfect human condition.

Inevitably, as the days and weeks went by, we became increasingly critical of the way the church was organised in many parishes, aware that too much emphasis had been put on the prescriptions of the law. Christ had not come to impose a series of obligations which, carefully carried out, would ensure salvation. That was the kind of legalism he himself had fought against. It seemed that for four hundred years the Roman Catholic Church had been placed in some kind of straight jacket by the decrees of Trent in the 16th century and was only now through the decrees of the 2nd Vatican Council beginning to shed its fortress mentality and recover from the bitter wound suffered at the Reformation. Only now could we pray with other Christians and accept the common bond of one Lord, one Faith, one Baptism, only now recognise that we have been too triumphal, and believed that we alone were the people of God. The 'Aggiornamento' of Pope John 23rd meant an upheaval in the Church. We had had four hundred years of conservative rule and forgotten that without change there would be no room for the Spirit, no room for the concept, 'Ecclesia semper reformanda.' (The Church always in need of reform).

It was a brave and necessary venture and over the years it has undoubtedly had an impact on the Church in Britain, but Cardinal Heenan became more and more disenchanted. One of the reasons was simple, too many priests and nuns, after a year at Corpus Christi, were leaving their ministry, mostly to get married. This had not been the Cardinal's intention. One of his visits was illuminating. He was the principal celebrant at Mass in the chapel, the rest of us, about 30 priests, concelebrated with him. We all vested together but only the Cardinal in complete silence. I could feel the conflict between his silence and the chatter all around, a clash of values was going on, conservative versus progressive; piety and anxiety before approaching the altar, versus a new found freedom from guilt, a new found joy. I wondered what it was really like at the Last Supper. Did the disciples chatter idly round the table or did they have a presentiment that something dramatic would happen that night and stay silent.(?)

The exuberance of the Corpus Christi atmosphere raised the awareness of living and diminished the awareness of dying. That too was evident. Celibacy demands a kind of emotional dying, it does not have to be like that but it began to seem like that. The College was sharpening criticism of the church as an institution and Peter de Rosa spearheaded opposition to the Pope's encyclical 'Humanae Vitae' in 1968, because of its veto on birth control. I was one of 67 priests who signed a letter of objection printed in the Times. It was a mild enough protest but it was a public act of dissent and many of those who gave their names to it were "disciplined" by their Bishops or congregations and many resigned.

The College did not, perhaps could not, offer spiritual renewal to accompany intellectual renewal. The concelebrated College Masses each day were celebrations of joy, we were living as though we belonged to the world – as indeed we did - where the collar was not needed and nuns and priests were on christian name terms. What could be more Christian than that? It is the right way to live but it overlooked how deeply flawed our human nature is, that is to say if one is trying to live a life on a level that Christ lived, belonging to the world, yet called to witness to values not of this world through the discipline and sacrifice of celibacy.

One weekend mother went off in her Rover 90 tank to The Priory, Haywards Heath, the convent where she had been educated and which she still loved. It still contained several elderly nuns whom she knew and revered. It was the annual 'old girls' reunion and retreat. I was bored and knowing that Mr Swan was out, ventured to call on Mrs Swan.

"Would you happen to have a couple of aspirins?" I asked innocently.

"Come in," she said, rather more eagerly than I had expected. The children were safely in bed.

"Good news" she said, unwisely, after we had chatted for a while. "My husband has just sold £2000 worth of silver to an American."

"Oh," I said.

I thought of his gashed wrist and the joke I nearly made about falling through a skylight. I could not bring myself to share the good news. Was he a 'fence' or a burglar? I would never know. Only the night before I had tried to chat him up, we both happened to be coming in the front door together, he was uncommunicative and, when I started being friendly and asking him questions, his face began to twitch. I persisted rashly and the whole of the left side of his face became convulsed. I hurriedly bade him goodnight.

"Last night," I said to his wife, "I met your husband in the corridor, his mouth began to twitch."

"That often happens. You don't have to worry about that. You only have to worry if the twitch goes up the whole side of his face. If his whole face becomes convulsed then there is trouble. The last time that happened we were in a cinema, the man in front of us was really objectionable, he would not stop talking. Eventually my husband slashed his face with a razor, the man deserved it but it caused a commotion and it was quite difficult getting out of the place. Everybody missed the rest of the film."

"Oh," I said again, and wondered if Mr Swan was about to return home.

She noticed my unease.

"Don't worry," she said, "He's OK really." Then she added, "He's away for a few days."

I did not ask what he might be doing.

"Would he mind me visiting you?"

"Not at all, he wouldn't mind if I had half a dozen naked men sitting round me."

"Oh," I said once more, now totally out of my depth.

"Have some whisky," she said.

The bottle was on a bookshelf which surprisingly held a lot of books. I declined.

Next day she said,

"You had a chance last night which you didn't take."

She said it in such a way that she clearly wished to remind me that her husband was definitely away 'for a few days.'

Lectures continued and the atmosphere in the college became increasingly lively. Some liaisons were forming inevitably and there would be a price to pay. The Cardinal was not happy with the ethos of the college. It was clearly insufficiently respectful of Authority. It was noted that the chief priests and Pharisees were similarly offended by

Jesus. There was an uneasy truce in the following year but in 1970 the axe fell.

The Cardinal attacked from the flank, he picked out and vetoed five guest lecturers whom he thought might be insufficiently respectful of Authority and contributing to the malaise. They were already booked for the academic year 1971-72 and they included Fr Gregory Baum, Fr McDonagh and Dr John Marshall.

This provoked a crisis. The principal, Fr Hubert Richards, and four of his staff, Sisters Rena Boyd and Ruth Duckworth, Frs. Frank Somerville and Peter Wetz, tendered their resignation. Peter de Rosa had already left.

Fr Richards wrote:

> *"There is between us such a divergence of understanding on the nature of religious education that it would be inappropriate for us to remain as a staff in charge of your college."*

Fresh staff was cobbled together and the College carried on, but it could never be the same. It died quietly in 1976, its disappearance almost unnoticed. Hubert Richards, Peter de Rosa, Peter Wetz and John Perry resigned and married. After all what is the point of holding out against the main thing every man wants, the comfort of a wife, if confidence in the leadership of the Church has been lost? Can some of the best brains in the Church pit their strength against the inbuilt inadequacies and even corruption of the institution and hope to bring about reforms from *outside* rather than from within? Perhaps they could only do it like Luther by starting another Church.

Who can like the many things that have gone wrong in the history of the Church? Who can be patient and accept what is wrong today, change the little that can be changed and turn a blind eye to the rest of it? Every society and organisation suffers the same problem. In the case of the Church, the scandal began with the Carpenter from Galilee with his strange accent and gaggle of relatives and followers. The Founder was a failure, his followers were failures, the whole enterprise was a failure, first the gathering of followers, all Jews, then a motley crowd who became despised and persecuted, disappearing underground into the catacombs of Rome like rats, yes, like rats, they were regarded as vermin. In the eyes of sensible people it will continue to be a failure and yet it will survive.

I ended my year in 1968, stimulated and confused. The vision of the Church as expressed in the documents of Vatican 2 was already fading. The hope that the exercise of Authority would be more collegial, involve all the Bishops, indeed all the faithful, was not being realised. The setting up of a commission on birth control by Pope John 23, enlarged to 35 members by Pope Paul 6, was designed to involve the people of God. It was an acknowledgement that the Holy Spirit is at work in the whole Church and is not reserved solely to the Pope. When 30 members of the commission, concluded after two years of deliberations, that Natural Law could not be used as an argument to proscribe all forms of birth control the commission was dissolved. It had reached the wrong conclusion in the eyes of the Pope. So, he exercised his authority unilaterally and we were back to Authoritarian rule as though the insights of the Second Vatican Council as regards the collegial nature of the Church had never taken place.

Bishop Petit came to London and told me,

"I will be sending you to take charge of a new church we have just built in Newcastle Emlyn, in West Wales. You will be replacing Father Joyce. You will also be able to help with Catechetics in the South of the Diocese."

Before leaving London, I said good bye to Mrs Swan. Mr Swan, as ever, was away for a few days. It was in the morning and the three little girls were playing happily. They took no notice of me.

"We would really like to move to South Africa but my husband's business is doing so well we cannot go yet." She kept dropping hints like that and I never had the courage to ask what exactly his business was.

"You ought to see what's behind those books," she said, "I'm not allowed to look."

I began to worry she would one day say too much to the wrong person and suffer for it. I could not bear to think of his anger towards her. She was young, early thirties and he not much older. A burglary had gone wrong in Mayfair; the papers were full of it. A rich bachelor, living alone, had been struck on the head and died. The intruder panicked, stole the man's car and ended up in Scotland. The police caught him there and he was now back in a police cell in London. Who should be going to visit him in prison but Mrs Swan?

"I have to go; his girl friend is frightened of going alone."

I saw the family once more. They were all skipping down the road, all of them literally skipping, the three girls laughing, the two older ones holding the hands of the youngest and I thought of the mother's phrase: 'He's OK really.'

Part 3
Newcastle Emlyn Parish: Loved and Lost

Chapter 19
A Weird Welcome

In September 1968 I arrived in Newcastle Emlyn. I was to live in 3 Castle Terrace opposite the Church. It had been acquired by the Diocese and refurbished but was totally empty of furniture. The key was in the door but there was nobody about and no message. Outside there was a pall of smoke rising from the wasteland that surrounded the newly built church. I explored the house, three smallish bedrooms and a bathroom upstairs, two main rooms downstairs, a small kitchen and back yard.

How was it I didn't know the house would be unfurnished? I had told Father Joyce when I would be arriving and expected to see him. There was nothing left of him except a bonfire that was clearly burning away his bed.

I found the hut open behind the Church; it had served as both chapel and home. Father Joyce appeared to have literally lived in the Sacristy; he had hardly any furniture, there was no room for any, his main possession would seem to have been the bed.

It was an absolutely still day, the acrid smoke from the mattress hung around. I was not sure what to do next as I only had clothes in the car. Then 'Zed' arrived, a large bear-like Polish farmer whose real name was Sieroslawski. His Slav features and shock of white hair endeared him to me immediately. He took complete charge and his wife was equally generous. I was to sleep in his farmhouse. They were the backbone of the parish, he was the vice-chairman of the parish council and she was the treasurer.

They both worked hard to help me settle into 3 Castle Terrace. What could be rescued from the hut was rescued, a table and some chairs. Somebody produced a bed, a carpet, some curtains. Those first few weeks were perhaps the happiest of all, there was such warmth and welcome.

I got £150 out of the Diocese for furniture and spent a large chunk of it on a splendid desk. The back room was now the office, dining room and library. The front room was both a sitting room and available for parish meetings. The front door was always open and George Hemelryk, chairman of the council, often called in. The parish council was the best legacy possible. It ensured that I was introduced to all the needs of the parish very quickly.

Newcastle Emlyn was, and no doubt still is, a sleepy little town, very Welsh and non-conformist. It became immediately important to learn the language which I struggled to do. The Church had been built on the Cawdor Estate land, close to the castle ruins which stood on a mound overlooking the river Teifi. The river flowed round it in a great horseshoe. It was very beautiful. You could watch the salmon leaping the rapids, sea gulls circling overhead, it was only ten miles or so inland from Cardigan Bay.

The Church had only just been completed and had not yet been in use. It was built of red brick, had a high ceiling and fourteen lancet windows, also an entrance porch and a bell tower. Two sacristies had been added, one for the altar boys, the other for the priest. It was stark, imposing and from an architectural point of view, quite out of keeping with the town. Around it was all the mess left by the builders.

There were 200 or so families, one third of them Italians scattered over 200 or so square miles. The Italian men had been prisoners of war and after the war they were allowed to stay and bring their families over, so my rudimentary Italian came in useful. If the weather was bad hardly any of them managed to get to Church on a Sunday and the collection was miniscule.

There was no school and no convent. I managed to get two nuns to come from Carmarthen once a week to instruct the children and began to think the parish did not really need me, not like Holywell or Rhyl.

My mother came to join me as a housekeeper and Antony, my youngest brother, an architect now, came to landscape the grounds around the Church. Together we made lawns, planted shrubs and started a kitchen garden. I began a YCW (Young Christian Workers) group and 35 years later I am still in touch with some of the original members. The parish council organised fund raising for stained glass windows to depict the 14 Stations of the Cross. The subject for the

15th window was to be the Resurrection and that was planned to go above the high altar. There were fir trees alongside the kitchen garden. My mother decided they ought to be cut down but permission had been refused because the parish council considered them part of the patrimony of the parish. I considered the council had a right to care for the parish property and agreed that they should not be cut down. One evening Zed, the deputy chairman, came to see me, he took me out to see the fir trees, they had all been neatly ringed which meant they would all die. I could not at first believe it but when I questioned mother, she said;

"Of course it was me, darling; their roots were ruining my garden."

She was only concerned to produce fresh vegetables for me and resented the parish council having any say in the matter. The dying fir trees spoiled the relationship she had with the parish council and foreshadowed a deeper malaise but I could not send her away. It reminded me of another time and another place, of living in Wyesham House, Monmouth, in 1942 when I was 16. The kitchen garden there was overshadowed by tall fir trees. They were stately trees along the driveway but she had them all cut down. In that desolate time when dad was patrolling the North Sea, she had her hair dyed and behaved like Boadicea. It was her way of hiding her hurt, organising the farm, deciding where the corn should go, ordering the men with scythes, where a hedge laid, a hayrick built. We stooked the corn by hand then, helped with the hay and the threshing, the milking, harvesting. Rats ran around everywhere. She was queen then, nicknamed the Duchess by her cousins and she was still the same at heart in Newcastle Emlyn, and loved me too much to be a humble housekeeper.

I acquired some more Cawdor Estate land, which included a garage, organised a fund raising effort and built a hall. It was still unfinished when things began to go wrong. A Baptist lady who played the organ for hymns at Mass, would also become surplus to requirements. That which was being built up with enthusiasm and joy would falter, not fall apart entirely but never be the same again.

I wrote to the bishop telling him I was under employed and felt marooned on a desert island. He wrote back kindly, in his own hand, but I had not told him I was in an emotional mess and could not cope with isolation from serious priestly work. Nor did I tell him my dear mother was not the perfect housekeeper, that she did not have the ideals and dedication of a Bridget. I did not tell him I had not come to terms with the clerical celibate state and had been even more destabilised by Corpus Christi. If I had told him all that, he might have sent me off to a monastery for three months to recuperate. It is strange but I did not want that either. Having suffered unfulfilled longing for several years, I was now in a much worse state. If the object of one's passion is inaccessible, except by renouncing every principle by which one has lived, then indeed what fate can be worse? And if one continues to fly awkwardly like a winged bird with a heart in such distress, then appearances cannot be maintained forever.

It was winter time and cold. If I tell you about this next event it is because it is true, it is not easy to tell. Nobody likes to be shown up and I could easily leave it out but I would be hiding something that possibly has a wider message than one just for me. Let me say first of all, the details may seem trivial and the whole experience of little consequence, but that is not the point. It had enormous consequences for me and it was obviously related to the emotional state I was in at the time.

I had a small bedroom immediately over the entrance lobby to the house. The main bedroom was reserved for my mother. She was away and I decided to have a siesta and switched the electric blanket on. In Holywell and Rhyl the day was always too busy for that kind of relaxation. Newcastle Emlyn was very different, a suitable parish for an elderly, retired priest! I lay down. It was warm, I had left the blanket switched on, although it was only an under blanket, intended to pre-heat the bed rather than keep it warm. I was completely frustrated and deeply unhappy, and I began to think I simply had to find someone free to marry me. I could not imagine myself not being a priest, and not being married either. Even though I knew that being a priest precluded marriage and logically one should begin by seeking release from the law of celibacy first. The dilemma was that I really wanted to be a priest and believed that was my destiny. How could I reconcile this at the age of 45, and who would want to marry me anyway? Besides all that, I just needed to love somebody physically. One really has to master that one properly to be a celibate priest!

So I wrestled with the problem luxuriating in the warmth of my bed. It was too sensual a situation and too tempting. For the first time I argued with myself as to whether it really mattered. Was the Church more concerned than it need be about sexual integrity? Would a lapse really affect my work as a priest? Could I actually get some relief and even benefit from such a lapse? Would it help me overcome the agony of a misplaced love? I had not argued with myself like this before. I believed any lapse in this area was not only a serious failure in commitment but serious sin.

It was a huge relief, physically and even mentally, but the sense of well being was short lived. The nightmare began. Smoke came from the bed. I ignored it, then leapt up; the bed was actually on fire. It was not difficult to put out but my only electric blanket was ruined. At this point I was not too much concerned, in fact found it rather amusing, but I also realised I had been extremely stupid, no possibility now of preheating the bed in the arctic conditions of winter. There was, of course, no central heating in the house. I was not going to be left long with such idle thoughts.

At that very moment, there was a knock at the front door. How inconvenient! In that sleepy place nobody comes knocking at your door. The wrecked blanket lay smouldering in a corner of the room, I would deal with that later and hurried down to open the door. There was a woman outside carrying something in her hand, at least I think it was a woman, though I cannot describe what she looked like, and certainly I had never seen her before.

"I have something for the high altar," she said, "but I don't know whether it is the right size."

I was bewildered and could not understand why she was offering me a frontispiece for the altar, for that is what she said it was. Why did I not ask her a few questions? To this day I do not know why.

"It is for the feasts of Our Lady" she said.

I could see it had a 'Marian' motif and was finely worked.

"But I don't know if it is the right size," she went on.

"Let's go and see," I answered uncertainly.

We went into the Church and for the first time I felt guilty and worried.

We went up the aisle together and climbed the altar steps. There was a crucifix on the altar with a bronze image. I lifted it down carefully and placed it on the sanctuary floor in front of the altar. That allowed us to try out the beautiful altar cloth for size. It was a very beautiful hand embroidered cloth, or so it appeared. We lifted it together on to the altar and the frontispiece hung down as it is supposed to do, so that the whole congregation could see it, but at that moment, it caught the crucifix and knocked it over. I lifted it up and was so shocked I could neither speak nor move. The figure was broken in half and the face so disfigured it looked as though it was in agony. It seemed to shout at me, 'You are not going all the way with me then?' I knew at once that I was letting down a friend, and more than a friend. The woman vanished and I never saw her again and the altar cloth vanished too. I say 'vanished' because quite honestly I do not know what happened. We had not, as far as I remember, taken it off the altar but that might not be the case. The truth was the church was empty, the woman and the altar cloth had gone. I was left with nothing except the ruined crucifix, the face unbelievably disfigured. I remained alone in the Church, unable to move. Finally I took the broken image out to the river and left it there.

I drove at once to Rhayader to see a gentle bearded Franciscan priest. I did not know then whether I would be able put my life together again. I had received a clear message and knew the Love behind it. It really was saying; 'can you not go all the way with me?' But I had not learnt to abandon myself, my whole being, and was up against a personal wilfulness I thought I could not, should not, and finally decided I could not fight against.

In the parish of Newcastle Emlyn, everything went on normally, on the surface at least. I organised a play at Easter and played the part of St. John myself, not knowing how I dared. I began to think I was not 'safe' as a priest and could easily let the Church down and that would be worse than opting out. Yet I did not want to opt out. I knew I was meant to be a priest. Nevertheless I began, quite deliberately, to look for someone I could love, but someone who would be free to love me. Imagine that task in a remote corner of Wales with a tiny Catholic community. And just suppose I did find someone, I would then have to find a job and make a living. The Church does not educate its priests for any alternative employment. I wanted a life that I could cope with but at the same time a life that would be loyal to the Church, just because I believed and still believe it was founded by Christ, and is an extension in a particular way of his presence on earth. For me, that had to mean release from the obligation of celibacy and permission to marry in the Church.

Meanwhile mother was creating more mayhem in the parish council. She did not attend the meetings but she came in with the tea afterwards. Out of the blue she voiced her opinion on abortion.

"Every woman should have the right to have an abortion," she said flatly.

They were such a loyal group that they accepted her but her rebellious views did not make my life any easier. Every Saturday morning, she would drive over to the tiny village of Tregroes, eleven miles away, to pick up the O'Connell children and bring them back to the church for catechism. Sister Maire, usually with another nun from their Carmarthen Convent, came to teach the children and prepare them for their First Communion. The system worked well but would not have worked at all without the help of the Postmistress in Tregroes village shop. Her name was Gill and she carried my messages to the O'Connells and theirs back to me. She also mothered them when there was a crisis or an accident. For many months I only knew her as the voice at the other end of a telephone. I decided to go and see her. It was 6 February 1972.

Chapter 20
Tregroes Post Office

The Tregroes Post Office and shop was an enormous building, three stories high. It had a large garden and a field bounded by a stream. The O'Connells lived almost opposite in one of four council houses. I felt rather sheepish, I didn't really need to call except to thank Gill for looking after the O'Connells. On the other hand Llandysul people had told me that Gill played badminton and that intrigued me. She came to the door, dressed in blue. She was slim, and I immediately thought, attractive. She led me upstairs to her sitting room which had a large picture window and a window seat. I felt awkward and we did not speak for very long, long enough however for me to discover that she had two daughters at boarding school and was divorced from a husband who had left her eleven years before. Not promising, I thought, yet somehow we had recognised each other. No, I said to myself, I will never seek release from the priesthood in order to marry a divorced woman.

A little while later my mother was preparing supper for Wilson Plant, a Monmouth friend, who was staying at the Emlyn Arms. I invited Gill to join us. It quickly became obvious that I could love Gill and it seemed as if she had just been waiting for me. She was 41. We met a third time and I no longer had any doubts. I went into the Church to thank God. It was very premature.

Bishop John Petit was no longer well and his auxiliary Bishop Langton Fox came to Newcastle Emlyn on a Visitation. Bishops make Visitations to check that all is in order and to rally the troops. That weekend he confirmed all the older children. The bishop was over six feet tall, large and jovial. It was amazing to see him emerge from a very small car. Bishop Fox was a warm hearted, gentle man and he went down well in the parish. I took him out to a distant village to confirm a housebound convert and after lunch he congratulated me. I did not know what to say.

I began to visit Tregroes Post Office and discovered that Gill had been educated in a Steiner school and afterwards had joined the Steiner Community in Scotland and for ten years, in that and other communities, she had looked after handicapped children. She made an unhappy marriage inside the Community and finally left but with two children, the eldest then four years old and now sixteen. The husband married again and went to live in Finland.

That information did not help much and my depression returned. There might not be any future there either, but I went on seeing Gill and became convinced there had to be some way round the problem.

"Was your husband baptised?" I asked one day.

"No, I don't think he was ever baptised because his parents were Christian Scientists."

So, if he was not baptised, Gill could claim the Pauline Privilege, have her marriage dissolved and marry again. It is archaic, a complicated piece of legalism used to justify a second marriage, but when St Paul was making converts among the pagans and some converts were being rejected by their partners, he invented this loophole. To be in communion with Christ, to receive that spiritual presence made possible at the Last Supper, meant everything to me. If I married Gill, separated from her husband for years but still a married woman, I would automatically find myself excommunicated and I could not face that.

However, I could at last see a glimmer of light, a slim possibility. I drove back via Llandysul and the beautiful Teifi valley to No.3 Castle Terrace, opposite the imposing new Church. I rang up Jim O'Reilly. Jim was parish priest in Barmouth and I knew I could talk to Jim. He had not had an easy time himself and had asked to be moved from his previous parish where he had had a housekeeper who had fallen hopelessly in love with him until, one day, he found her naked in his bed. Jim had been severely shaken. He believed should be allowed to marry, but nevertheless accepted the ruling of the Church. He became my 'deep throat,' my guide in the months to come but very secretly. He was the 'Defensor Vinculi' in the diocese. His job was to defend the marriage bond. I told Jim the whole story, the essence of which was that I wanted to marry Gill. Jim was practical.

"Don't move too fast" he said. "It will take time to get the papers together to prove, as far as it can be proved, that her husband was never baptised. It will also be necessary for Gill to receive instruction and become a Catholic."

It has to be said that Gill had no inclination to become a Catholic. I very much hoped that understanding more about it she would realise and share in what has motivated me. I wanted to share everything with her and it did seem to be happening. She was welcomed by the Newcastle Emlyn community and even asked to read at Mass. However, I did not feel I could personally 'instruct' her and told Jim:

"I can't do that."

"No, I suggest that she goes to Father Fitzgerald in Lampeter. If she goes there, Fitzgerald may not only instruct her but also help to start the process of getting her marriage annulled."

She went to Lampeter and Fr. Fitzgerald did exactly that, filling in and signing the first Petition to the Bishop. It was now April 1972.

St Paul allowed converts to the Catholic faith to leave their pagan partners and marry again and Jim was prepared to help me. We were both members of the Diocesan Ecumenical Commission which met regularly at Aberystwyth and knew each other well. It was enough for him that I understood the seriousness of what I was doing and the heartbreak it would be to leave the priesthood, but he accepted that I had nevertheless made up my mind.

The bishop passed on Gill's official application for a dispensation to Fr.John Schikan, (parish priest at Abergele and secretary to the Diocesan Matrimonial Bureau). For a long time there was no response. I was compelled to write to John myself. He passed the buck back to me.

I did not want to carry out the investigation myself and told the bishop so but he said he had to have a statement in favour of the petitioner from the parish priest. I consulted Jim and he replied,

"Go ahead, you tried to get out of it, that's enough."

I was risking everything that Gill would get her dispensation, not only gathering the evidence, no easy task indeed, but preparing for a different life. Here began the second subterfuge for which I cannot be proud. I asked the Bishop's permission to study for a year at Trinity College, Carmarthen, to obtain a teaching certificate. The Bishop readily agreed. He knew I was underemployed and thought I could manage an educational course and run the parish at the same time. I would begin the course in the academic year 1972/3 but decided I could not run the parish at the same time. I found a Jesuit priest, a dry old stick, who had had a breakdown trying to teach in a Jesuit school. He needed a quiet country parish assignment. I promised the parish I would only be away for a year and believed that could be true, that Gill might not get her dispensation, might not be free to marry me. I was very concerned about the Parish Council and found Fr. William Higham SJ, due to take over from me in September, very conservative indeed. He liked Sacraments, rules and the Vatican newspaper, Osservatore Romano, and his enormous dog, but he did not really like people. Would he understand the role that the Parish Council played in the affairs of the parish? Of course he would not. We talked about it and I also wrote the following letter.

With regard to the Parish Council they have complete control of the monies banked at Lloyds Bank and two signatures of members of the Council are sufficient on cheques. I have complete confidence in the elected members of the Council and consider that the Priest's primary duty is spiritual and the responsibility for the material affairs of the parish should be a major concern of the parish itself acting through its elected members.

In September, when Fr. Higham came to 3 Castle Terrace, I moved to Myrtle Cottage, Abergwili, just outside Carmarthen. It belonged to Alice Margit Morris who lived in a mansion called Bryn Myrddyn close by, and she let me have the cottage rent free for the duration of the course. Every so often I said Mass for her in the dining room of her house.

Chapter 21
The Sword that Pierces the Heart

The hard thing now was to conceal an ambition which, after dreadful periods of doubt and much pain, had become firm, the ambition and need to marry Gill. There had to be concealment. The bishop would be reluctant to forward a request for annulment of Gill's first marriage if he knew it would allow her to marry me. Indeed he could refuse to do so. No annulment, no marriage, I would stay a priest, but by going to Myrtle cottage I seemed to be putting that latter possibility almost out of reach.

I chose to live there not only to be close to Trinity College but also to see more of Gill and was digging a large emotional hole for myself that would be difficult to climb out of. Every so often I consulted worthy people, drove over to see a Jesuit father at Fishguard, my Franciscan friend at Rhayader or talked to one of the Passionists in Carmarthen. The combination of lectures, teaching practice, visits by Gill, grumblings of discontent from the parish, made writing essays difficult. But at the time it was the part of the course that I enjoyed most. I was not a born teacher, so achieving some expertise in the weeks of teaching practice was a struggle.

Gathering the evidence for the annulment petition took an age and it was not until 31 January 1973, that Jim O'Reilly could send his report to the Marriage Tribunal in Wrexham. He knew what it was all about and I was touched by his genuine desire to help me. He wrote:

'Having carefully studied the dossier relating to this case, and having personally interviewed the appellant, I can as Defensor Vinculi (defender of the Marriage bond) for the diocese of Menevia , appointed ad hoc for this investigation, see no reason detrimental to the sanctity of the bond why the petitioner's request for annulment should not be granted.

The indispensable requirement in any such case is the establishment of the fact of non-baptism. The parents of the husband in this case belonged to the sect of Christian Scientists who do not practise baptism, and international enquiries have failed to uncover any evidence of christening, and so it is morally certain that he was never baptised.

Secondly, it would seem that scandal is ruled out. The teaching of Vatican Two has stressed the individual's right to live a full and satisfying life, the refusal of the Church to grant something which it manifestly can, would cause a greater scandal than the granting of it. I see no grounds for refusing the annulment.

Gill now completed the process by sending a personal request to the bishop and enclosing all the evidence and papers. He wrote back personally, said he had made six copies of all the documents and sent them off to Rome. There was nothing to be done now but wait.

By March everything changed. The parish had been prepared to accept Father Higham pro tem but they did not do so without a fair amount of grumbling. He was able to play the priestly role within the strict limits and guide lines of the law but found it very difficult to communicate with people beyond rebuking them for talking in church. All was bearable for a time but when rumours began to circulate that I might not be returning to the parish, there was genuine alarm. Letters and visits persuaded me I had to do something about it.

I told Gill I would have to return to the parish early, in fact after Easter. You can imagine how well that news was received. I wrote to the Principal of the Jesuits and he replied on 8 March that he would advise Fr. Higham at once. I knew he too would not welcome the news. At the same time, illogically, I wrote to the bishop asking to be released from parish work so that I could take a job in teaching in September. I also asked him if Fr. Fisher could take my place in Newcastle Emlyn instead of Fr. Higham. The bishop agreed to both requests. I then went to a meeting of the parish council. They had been forewarned and had gathered information about Fr. Fisher who, at that time, was an assistant priest at Old Colwyn. They were not too pleased and I had to admit I had not realised he could not drive a car. I tried to persuade them.

"Fr Fisher will love Newcastle Emlyn and I am quite sure you will love him. I know him well and like him a lot."

"But he cannot drive a car. A priest is useless in this parish if he cannot drive a car."

I made another effort on behalf of the parish and I went to see John Coffey. He was parish priest of Milford Haven, a very good priest but he had been ill. I had the nerve to offer him the little parish of Newcastle Emlyn which would not tax him too much.

Meanwhile I felt reasonably confident that the documents sent to Rome would achieve an annulment for Gill and banking on that I asked her to marry me on 29 March. By chance it was my sister, Priscilla's, birthday. I always felt very close to her and she wanted me to marry. Now, we began to tell close friends but I still hesitated to tell the bishop. This was a mistake. I had not realised the difficulties he would place in our path, nor how much the dishonesty of not telling him, of allowing gossip to reach his ears first, would weaken the request I would have to make for a dispensation from celibacy. I was organising at that time, 13 and 14 April, a two day Ecumenical Conference in Carmarthen. I had been asked to do so because I was on the spot and a member of the diocesan ecumenical commission. After that I told myself I will write to the bishop but it would be too late.

The bishop had received reliable rumours so what defence could I make? It would be trite just to say I wanted to marry. Every normal priest wants to marry. I could not pretend I was an exception and he would not like the idea that I had been planning my escape from celibacy for more than a year, about to acquire a teacher's certificate under false pretences, and working to achieve the release of a woman from her matrimonial vows with no other intent than that she should be free to marry me. It was not a scenario I could easily explain or excuse.

The bishop realised with great sadness that I was going to ask to be laicised, but thought it was far too soon to offer that opportunity. I had given him grounds for believing that I didn't want to leave the priesthood and he was emboldened to make the process as difficult as possible. Before he would be prepared to take me seriously I had to perform 3 tasks, rather like a suitor for the king's daughter in a fairy tale.

I must have no contact with Gill at all for a month. This would be a suitable 'cooling off period,' I must see a psychiatrist and thirdly, go on a retreat. I went to see Dr Jack Dominian in London, an eminent psychiatrist. Dr Dominian sent, in his own words, a careful report to the bishop. The bishop was not satisfied. 'I find nothing in the report which tells me that you cannot continue as a faithful priest,' he wrote. First task fulfilled, first task a failure. Gloom.

There was a Retreat taking place on Caldey Island from 17 to 24 May. On the 17 I drove to Tenby to catch the Caldey Island monastery boat. It was a strange experience and I felt disorientated. The island was as beautiful as ever and the sea was calm. The monastery guest house was being run by Zed and Jo Sieroslawski who had moved from Newcastle Emlyn and recently arrived on the island. I could not greet them as warmly as I would have wished. Not only was it a silent retreat, I was also in turmoil.

I struggled to understand the real issue I had to face. The Mass was still everything to me, still a life line. I was conscious of the enormous intimacy of the Last Supper shared with the apostles, the devotion but also the betrayal elements, the boastful Peter, the 'I know better' Judas, the fears of all the rest. Love asks incredibly much, far beyond our capacity. When Jesus said, 'do this in memory of me,' he was actually asking them to share his life, including the pain of it. 'Can you drink the chalice that I shall drink?' 'Yes,' they said. I could not claim ignorance. I knew what was asked of me. I wanted to respond, to give myself totally, to be one with Christ, and yet I made it too difficult. I wanted that life so badly and yet I wanted, and believed I needed, the support of a wife.

The retreat giver was experienced and the conferences were excellent. Walking round the island was a joy. I knew every track; thirty years earlier, my family had taken a cottage on the island for a month in the summer. We knew every cove and beach, every cave and cliff walk and we caught many crabs at low tide. Every evening we would go to Compline in the monastery church and now once again I was to find myself deeply moved by the haunting chant of the Salve Regina before the monks went off to bed. Their regime was austere indeed but their prayer life created a deeply spiritual atmosphere.

I told the retreat giver what was on my mind. To my great surprise he encouraged me. "Not everybody can be a celibate priest," he said.

For a while I felt relieved but later was overwhelmed by doubt. At 4.30 one morning I suddenly felt certain that I should remain a priest. There is a large cross on a knoll just off the pathway which leads down to the island quay. By five it was already light and I agonised under that cross. I have never known such daggers to the heart. They came because I had already written a desperate letter of renunciation to Gill and would write twice more. They are letters too painful to print as indeed they were too painful to read. I remember writing 'I couldn't have believed in such distress, that is why it would tear me to shreds to hear your voice.' You can imagine what it was like for both of us.

I said goodbye to Zed and Jojo. They couldn't understand my emotion and I couldn't talk to them. I arrived back at Tenby in a daze and knew I couldn't go back to Myrtle Cottage. I went straight to the Passionists house in Carmarthen and saw Father Francis who was in charge there. He was extremely kind and gave me a room at once.

The bishop, of course, was delighted with the turn of events. Fr. Higham informed the parishioners of Newcastle Emlyn that if anyone had heard a rumour that Father David was going to resign from the priesthood and get married they were wrong. This caused consternation to some and bewilderment to others, and the news filtered back to Gill who had not been at Mass that day. Indeed she had fled the area and was staying with my sister, at Priston, South of Bath. The shock waves reached Gill's parents in Minehead who wrote in great sadness. What seemed to be taking shape gradually for their beloved Gill and bringing her happiness now seemed a disaster. Predictably, my mother erupted like a volcano.

"You are murdering her," she wrote.

The tranquillity of St Mary's in Union Street, the tall Victorian Church, ancient buildings, long cold corridors, did nothing for my spirit. The three Passionist Fathers were friendly and invited me into their sitting room to watch the news. I felt somehow disembodied. Resolution wavered.

Gill could not believe it was the end of our relationship. Indeed, at one level, it could not be the end. One's love for someone cannot end just like that. On the other hand I had deliberately ended any hope of an exclusive married relationship such as we had both been working towards for 15 months. That was absolutely shattering for both of us. Nevertheless it became clear to me that if a priest could come to terms with being a bachelor, could love everybody equally, that would be the way Christ lived. That is clearly what the Church is looking for. I remembered the Retreat giver telling me, 'not everybody can do that.' But how does one know what one can or cannot do? Maybe I had gone too far to retrace my steps. Maybe Gill and I should make the decision together and bear the consequences together. That night I had a strange dream. I was in the popemobile, alone with the Pope, and we were travelling down the driveway of Wyesham house (my grandfather's house) at an alarming speed. We could neither stop nor get out and a crash on the main road was inevitable. On 28 May I arranged to see her. She noted in her diary:

> 'I met Christopher at the cottage and we sat and talked for an hour. Suddenly he asked me if I would give him up for the sake of the Church. I felt a knife go right through me. It literally felt like a dagger thrust. He knows he is a good priest. He preached so well last night in Carmarthen and everyone was so happy. Then he said a memorial Mass for Mrs Morris' husband this morning. He just felt he had to ask me this one last question.'

I remember Gill going white, unable to speak. I said I would write to the Bishop tomorrow. I did write but it was several days more before I could bring myself to post the letter. I agreed with Gill, however, that I would hand over all my responsibilities in the parish to Fr.

Higham. That was with a heavy heart. The parish newsletter printed my farewell.

Our Lady Queen of Peace, Newcastle Emlyn. June 3 1973. A message from Fr. David.

This is my last message to you. I would like to make it a personal message to each one. There is no way of leaving you easily or without pain. 1968-72 were happy years for me but they were made happy because we were able to work together so well.

It was an unforgettable privilege to have had the responsibility of being your priest. It was the work God gave me to do and I shall always be grateful. But, without exaggeration, it was because you supported me so well, because we have had such an active Parish Council, because so many in such a small community were ready to work for the Church in a variety of ways that we have been such a happy parish.

May God bless you all.

Fr. Higham invited me to say Mass for the parish that day. There was enormous goodwill and it was an emotional day. It was so hard to leave him in charge but I could see no alternative. The bishop had accepted that I wished to apply for a teaching post though he did not know at the time why I wished to teach rather than care for a parish. In fact caring for a parish was the only work I loved to do. In saying that I hoped Fr. Higham would be accepted as the parish priest, I was only admitting the inevitable. He was happy in Newcastle Emlyn with his great dog.

So there were emotional hugs all round. Everyone knew why I was leaving, although Fr. Higham pretended not to and pretended not to see. Gill continued to attend parish Mass on Sundays and one day brought back a silver tankard inscribed:

'To Christopher, from your many friends of Newcastle Emlyn.' It was a coded message. They had already accepted that I would not be continuing life as 'Fr. David.' The bishop however, was a long, long way from accepting any such thing.

How different the future might have been for me and for others wishing to marry, if Pope John, with his enormous compassion, had lived a little longer. His conversation with the philosopher, Etienne Gilson, was quoted by Father Quentin Hakenworth S.M. in a lecture he gave at the University of Dayton, St Louis, Missouri on July 11, 1967. The subject was celibacy. Gilson suggested: 'There are those who feel that present conditions have increased the burden of celibacy to a practical magnitude that should no longer be required of every priest.' The Pope is said to have replied: 'Would you like to know what distresses me most? I do not mean as a man, but as Pope? The thought of those young priests who bear so bravely the burden of ecclesiastical celibacy causes me constant suffering. For some of them it is a martyrdom. It often seems to me as if I was hearing a kind of plea. I do not mean right here but from a great distance as if the voices were demanding that the Church free them from this burden.'

Ah me. It was a small but beautiful parish. My sad Christmas card included this verse:

It is where Castle ruins catch at December's sun, survey the valley, mist wrapped, shadowed still. Skeletal trees gesticulate, striding the flat, massing in prickly walls, where the river falls. No sound of men at arms, no clink of steel, arrow, halberd, shield, no vestige found. History winters buried in this mound.

A stone's throw away, today's new 'Castle' stands, guarding the corridor of land for peace, not war. And at the low point of the year, when cold night grips, and men are dead in sleep, the garrison will cry: 'Let all men live,' and light will stream from lancet windows high, to glitter in the Teifi racing by.

And so it did at those precious Christmas midnight Masses.

Chapter 22
Crossing the Line

Ahead of handing over the parish and making my farewells, I had written to the bishop. Throughout June and into July I continued to live with the Passionists in Carmarthen. The bishop replied with great sympathy and kindness on 4 June but he refused to take me seriously, in fact his letter concluded with two passages which were rather less than encouraging.

The first read:

> *"I do find it hard to let the Holy Father grant the favour of release from the marriage bond to a person who, while still bound, enters into a deeply affectionate relationship with a priest."*

What I had always feared was now quite clear, the bishop could scupper any chance of marriage in a Catholic Church. You may wonder why I should care so much but it really did mean everything for me.

The second passage read:

> *"The Holy see has asked bishops not to present petitions for release from priestly obligations for which the reason is 'simplex voluntas nubendi (the simple wish to marry)."*

That letter arrived on 7 June and on the following day, Friday, I sat the end of year teacher training examinations. I was so troubled by the bishop's letter that I decided to go back to Caldey and consult the Abbot, James Wicksteed, the next morning, Saturday. I landed back on Caldey Island after a choppy crossing, feeling none too well, physically or mentally. I went for a long walk with Zed over the island headlands, the gulls screaming overhead, the wind bracing. I wanted to ask him if he would mind if I got married but I knew what the answer would be, he would say, 'if it means you can't go on being a priest, the answer is yes.' More than a year ago I had invited Gill over from Tregroes to meet him in the Emlyn Arms; I was unbelievably naïve to tell him so early what might be brewing. The early evening Compline on Caldey, the beautiful Salve Regina at the end, the silence of praying monks living heroic lives, brought peace. On Sunday after the community Mass I saw the Abbot, He said:

"From Bishop Fox's letter it seems clear that he will not take your case really seriously as long as he can claim that you are weary and unhappy. Consequently, I should advise you not to take up the matter with him again at the moment and, instead, simply let him know that you are going away for a month's holiday. It will be more fruitful to take up the matter again with Bishop Fox after that. Also, I strongly advise you to make no reference to the possibility of Bishop Fox's withholding the Pauline privilege. It will be time enough to tackle that problem if and when he does so."

The Abbot thought that, although Rome discouraged bishops from sending in petitions seeking the release of priests from their obligations on the grounds that they wished to get married, it could not be a strict ruling. Bishop Fox would have to be convinced of my sincerity and I should not be in too much of a hurry. I was in no hurry to leave the island but knew, as I gave Zed a bear hug and Jojo a kiss, I would not be coming back.

I continued to stay with the Passionists in Carmarthen and instead of replying to the bishop's letter, I set about finding a job. On 25 June I went to Hartcliffe Comprehensive School, Bristol, for an interview and was accepted for the Religious Education Department. It was part of the Humanities Faculty which included teaching English, History, Geography and Sociology. The head of the faculty was Patrick Eavis, a dynamic and gifted teacher, the brother of Michael Eavis who created the Glastonbury Festival on his farm. The school was huge, 2,200 pupils. It would be a challenge but I was averse to the private sector education system on principle.

On 30 June, Gill and I found an end of terrace house in the village of Shoscombe a few miles south of Bath. The owner of the house had been a miner all his life, working the narrow seams of coal at Writhlington nearby, we inherited his pickaxe, his tin bath and outside loo, but grants were available to modernise. The great joy was an enormous garden and the village itself, nestling in a hollow of hills, was quiet and beautiful. Opposite us was a Methodist chapel and down the road, the village inn and Post Office.

Years later when married ex-Anglican priests were accepted in Britain and running parishes, Bishop John Crowley of Middlesbrough diocese could write:

'Without exception they have been warmly accepted and assimilated into the parishes where they serve. In my experience parishioners look primarily for their pastors to be accessible, kindly, spiritual leaders. Once that gift is given them, the fact of whether it is located in a celibate or married man seems somehow less important.'

I have little doubt that the parish of Newcastle Emlyn would have accepted me as a married priest with few misgivings. They had already accepted Gill.

The dissolution of Gill's first marriage 'in favorem fidei' was handed to her by Father Higham on July 1. It was dated 8 June and signed by Cardinal Brown. When it reached Wrexham it must have caused Bishop Fox misgivings but he consulted Jim O'Reilly who assured him he could not or should not stop the annulment. It was Jim's final effort on my behalf.

The bishop wrote warning me that the process involved in obtaining a dispensation from Rome allowing us to marry could be a lengthy one. At the same time he casually mentioned that the answer could be 'no.' I knew that the answer, yes or no, depended very much on him. Any prospect of a quick reply from Rome had to be given up; waiting made no sense so we began our married life and went on holiday to Rimini on the Adriatic coast of Italy.

It was an odd honeymoon. We did not go alone. Gill's eldest daughter, Angie, came too and so did my mother. It was very hot and we shared the Adriatic Sea with hundreds of other people. Angie found friends and lived much of the time under a boat. Mother, henceforth 'Granma' delayed in the hotel and appeared on the beach like an apparition wearing the most extraordinary dress, sewn together on the hotel balcony from curtains.

"Darling, I left my own suitcase behind and brought Priscilla's instead. Unfortunately, it was full of curtains. I have made some panties as well but I would love to have a bikini."

When Gill bought her a bikini, her very first, she wore it upside down.

In September I began my daily journeys to Hartcliffe School and realised how important it was to live to the east of your work. I drove to school with the sun behind me and in the evening drove back with the sun again behind me. We were very happy. It was extraordinary to be so truly happy. Even so I had managed to get myself excommunicated which worried me. How long would we have to wait before the Church bothered to give me a dispensation? With all those 'caveats' from the bishop, I wondered if it might be forever.

My sister, Priscilla, lived with her history teacher husband and six children at Priston, a small village close by. We had always been very fond of each other, she was only 18 months younger than me and she lived only 10 minutes away by car. She wanted to put the world in order, beginning with me.

"It seems clear to me that the bishop won't release you, he just thinks you are having an affair and will go back to being a priest one day."

"He ought to be able to see that I've made that pretty impossible."

"I don't think," she said, "you should try anymore, just get married."

"It's the last thing I want to do. I would be getting married while still bound by a promise of celibacy. I would like to do things properly and get released first."

"But you have already been getting round the rules for some time and haven't left yourself a real alternative. Gill cannot be your housekeeper."

We talked on and on and round and round the subject. The weather was good and we were outside the Vicarage House where the family lived, she gripping my hand, I, trying not to show emotion. She was fighting cancer and I was distraught.

"OK, I think you are right. There is not much point in waiting."

"Don't worry." Priscilla said, "It's the only way you will get the Church to accept that you really do want to get married. Life is too short to worry." She smiled wanly.

I ached inside, she did not have long to live and her youngest of six children was only 11.

I was struggling with my new life in Hartcliffe School, while Gill was reorganising her Welsh Separates business that she had built up in Tregroes, naming it now 'David Designs.' At one point she had 70 knitters busy knitting cardigans, sewing on buttons, packaging, invoicing, all the business of a small firm. Many wanted to talk about their problems so she turned herself into a social worker at the same time. In our first year at Shoscombe she made a profit on her business of £1.200. Money is not the most important thing in life but it certainly helps.

On Friday, 14 September we went into Bath to buy wedding rings, met up with my cousins Bruce and Sally and had a meal together. They came back to Shoscombe for the night and brought a bottle of champagne. The next morning we were back in Bath at the Registry Office, this time with my mother, Priscilla, two of her children, the whole Czartoryski family from London, Sally and Bruce. It was not planned that way, it just mushroomed. The Registry Office event was a simple impressive decision-making ceremony and unexpected support for it went on all day, first with champagne in the Francis Hotel, then all of us trekking over into Wales and up the Wye Valley to Monmouth for lunch at my family home, Callow. My brother, Bede, was in charge. He had accidentally knocked over three of his neighbours suckling pigs on the drive and made us a feast. Just about everybody was there, including Gill's sister, Daphne, and her husband, Tom. After that everybody went off to Nicholas' house (another brother) at the Skenchill and Robin in high spirits pushed Cousin Sally into the pool. We brought back a disgruntled Sally to Shoscome but she quickly recovered over another bottle of Bruce's champagne. The next morning a letter arrived for

'Mr and Mrs David.' Obviously some people thought that something important had happened which was true.

I thought it would be civil and sensible to inform the Bishop but he wrote back to say that he knew about it already and had sent on the information to Rome.

We were married in Bath, on 15 September, 1973 and kept the anniversary with a meal in the Francis Hotel for years afterwards, but Gill noted that Priscilla looked very ill. I wrote to her, my beloved sister.

Dearest 'Cilla, I took your advice but I have been thinking of you ever since. There are such depths to the sea of life and most of the time we stay on the surface. Our walk round and round the garden touched me deeply. Somehow I felt the unknowable, the deep down presence of God, the love that supports us and that will not let us go. So frail we are, as autumn leaves, so many our fears. But the cycle of life hints at life itself, at a Reality vastly more than we can comprehend. So our love has a double plane of existence, frail and passing yet altogether permanent. Like you, I have glimpsed joy and somehow the mirth of God in his vast creation, yet often the glimpse has been transfigured by pain. It is when one is most low that one can be closest to God. My dearest, you know that all will be well in the end. Our frailty opens us to the power of God, to his enormous love.

Not long afterwards, we stood by her grave quite numbed, but in the Church a butterfly flew down to the flowered coffin and then flew back to a stained glass window.

Chapter 23
Hartcliffe Comprehensive School

It was half an hours drive through the leafy back lanes to Whitchurch, a village now engulfed in the urban spread to the south of Bristol, a mile or two more and I was in Hartcliffe. Driving in, I had time to reflect on the day's programme and going home, on how much of it had been impossible to achieve. Despite the heroic efforts of the staff, teaching in the school was a difficult assignment. Hartcliffe estate had been badly planned. It was carved out of farmland, too far out for those who had lived all their lives in the hugger mugger slum housing and alleyways of the city centre. Now they had nice little flats and bathrooms but the close communities that existed before, now found themselves dispersed and fragmented. They did not care for their brand new utopian housing estate with hills and green fields all around. They felt imprisoned in their skyscrapers. Hartcliffe was provided with shops and amenities but it had no heart. Inevitably the children did not like their new school either but here the planning was, in my view, even worse.

When 18,000 people moved into Hartcliffe in 1952, two schools were planned, one for boys, the other for girls. By 1962 two 7 form entry schools were ready. The boys were enrolled in one, the girls in the other. Each school would have about 1000 pupils and between the schools, which were a quarter of a mile apart, there would be a sixth form building. The residents, now 30,000 in number, objected to all this. It was finally agreed to have two mixed schools, an Upper and a Lower school on the two sites. By the time I arrived to teach, even this compromise had been shelved. Now the whole school of 2,200 pupils occupied both sites. Languages, Science, Mathematics and Art were taught in the East building. Humanities, Woodwork, and PE took place in the West building. As many as 1000 pupils had to cross between the two sites each day for their different lessons, whatever the weather.

This was itself a recipe for trouble but two thirds of the yearly intake had below standard reading ages and half of them were more than two years retarded. At least 30% of the children on the huge estate came from 'broken' homes and were emotionally deprived. Such children needed the kind of intense personal caring a very large school is least able to give. The Local Education Authority was aware of the problem but instead of providing extra teachers to achieve smaller classes, only declared Hartcliffe a 'social priority area' and gave extra money to the teaching staff. I remember a staff meeting at which we all agreed to forgo the extra, so-called 'danger' money for the sake of one or more extra teachers. The head did not agree. Money, apparently, attracted the teachers the school needed in order to survive.

From the third floor in the West building you can see where the pond had been, the concrete floors of the pigsties wired for under floor heating, the chicken run, the horticultural centre, a pen for sheep, the rabbit hutches and green houses. Once there were strawberry beds in the fields around and a nursery of young trees. Production and sale of goods had been business like, profits were ploughed back. The eggs, strawberries and sides of bacon for sale are still remembered. Rural Science had been a subject well liked and was included in the syllabus. This important practical and humanising education, involving the care of animals and the environment, only ended when four rabbits and two guinea pigs were killed in an after dark raid in 1971. The end of such a valuable educational venture which was truly inspired left hardly any trace and now the whole area was out-of-bounds, the pond filled in and the rose bushes dead.

Hartcliffe was a huge testing ground of teacher ability and endurance and because the stress was high, departures were frequent which did not improve stability. In my first term I had lost control completely of a 5th year class. The whole classroom was in uproar. My room was B8, next door to the head of department, Ian Button, in B7. I went out into the corridor to get his help. The classroom doors had glass panels in the upper half so anyone in the corridor could observe what was going on inside. Ian Button's class was also in uproar and I could see what the problem was, above Mr Button's head, stuck on to a ceiling tile, was his board rubber. Mr Button was standing immediately below his board rubber but of course he could not see it. I went back into my own classroom and discovered that they were only trying it on, that they did not really mean to be quite so beastly. Board rubbers, however, were a hazard. I had to remember to look at mine carefully before using it. The boys had a cunning way of secreting matches in it so that when it was rubbed across the blackboard it would burst into flames. It was now evident that it could also be made to stick to the ceiling.

Making a relationship with a class that you only saw twice a week was really difficult, getting to know and remember their names a particular problem. I made a plan of the desks and insisted they return to the same desks each week. Then I could mug up the names before the children sat down. You cannot say to a class of 30 children, "hey, you at the back, put away that elastic band," or "you in the middle, stop talking."

Your tutor group was different, you saw them every morning and they stayed your tutor group year by year. But everybody had to listen to the headmaster's disembodied voice on the public address system - while you were trying to sort out a child's problems - because whole school assemblies were impossible. There were Year Heads but no house system. That was considered contrary to 'Comprehensive' education and equality for all.

> "The most telling criticism of the house system is that it tends to encourage a competitive spirit, with the idea that our house must be the best house which is immature and unfruitful of real educational and social development." ('Comprehensive Schooling' by Margaret Miles).

Another relic of the past considered 'unfruitful' in the new Comprehensive schools of the sixties was streaming children according to ability. This was not allowed except in Maths and Languages. All classes were, therefore, mixed ability which meant they had to be resource based so that the brighter ones could move ahead and they were supposed to inspire the less bright. The important thing was that the less bright should not feel less equal or less valued.

Yet, despite defects in socialist educational ideology, and the fact that I felt ill equipped, walking in the wrong shoes so to speak, I believed in the Comprehensive school objective. It was anti elitist and was helping to create a more equal society in a country still divided by class. Yet, as you know, it was not the work I really wanted to do or the kind of life I really wanted to lead. I felt like a shepherd who had not only lost one or two sheep but the whole flock. In fact, I felt as though I had been given a flock of unruly goats instead. Whereas the odd sheep would stray from the flock but usually came back on its own, this lot seemed to have no sense of responsibility whatsoever. It was a doddle keeping the 'goats' out of the Holywell Youth club, quite another keeping them *in* a classroom prepared to learn something. One terrible girl who constantly disrupted the class had to be exiled to the corridor where she spent her time jumping up and down and tapping on the door. The headmaster happened to be wandering by and took her down to his office. She gave him such a bad time he suspended her for three days. It was exactly what she wanted. Years later she was working in a bar in Bedminster. I stopped by there one evening entirely by chance and she welcomed me like a long lost friend.

There were teachers in the school capable of enthusing even the most hardened switched-off teenager. I was not one of them but I still liked the children and surprisingly they often liked me.

Simon Fisher taught French in the East Building, that is to say he made a valiant attempt to teach French. The lack of enthusiasm among his pupils caused him to reconsider the usefulness of the task and he joined the Social Studies department in the West Building instead. We became close friends and began to hatch plans. He was as concerned as I was that the skeletal sculpture of a man over the front door to the school was falling apart, almost every day another bit was missing. It seemed to reflect the fragmenting school or our vision of it anyway, and it worried us both. Social Studies and RE might work together to create a sense of community but we did not think we could do it inside the school.

The idea of finding a centre, that we could take the children away to, won the support of Berna Fitzgerald, head of Social Studies and even John Simpson, the headmaster. He became enthusiastic and began charging round the countryside with senior staff trying to find the right place to use as a weekend centre. I took them all to Jeremy Sandford's hide away in the hills near Crickhowell. We sloshed around the farm buildings in the mud and melting snow and Jeremy said we could rent it all for peanuts. Jeremy had a strong social conscience expressed in his book, 'Cathy Come Home' and 'Edna the Inebriate Woman,' and really wanted to help, but the project would have cost too much.

Chapter 24
The Dream of Goglwyd

The plot Simon and I hatched together had, in fact, been in my mind a long while, ever since the debacle I could see coming in Newcastle Emlyn.

A friend warned me, 'if you leave the priesthood to marry you will lose your platform.' What he meant was, 'you will have to start creating a mission for yourself all over again.' The dilemma was real, but how do you replace a mission that is altogether right for you, with another?

In that last tumultuous year at Carmarthen I was planning that alternative mission but realized I was not living in the real world from the point of view of the Catholic Church. It was made rather clear, but nevertheless surprised me, that I could not have a mission that was acceptable in the Church if it included a wife. I was facing both ways, wanting to secure an income so that I could support a wife (though Gill was quite able to support herself) and wanting to go on working with children and adults in creating community. I had hoped that if I could find the right place I could start a residential centre. It would promote religion, education and the arts, and it would be especially for children, of all ages. It would serve the needs of Menevia diocese, which covered almost the whole of Wales and would be my alternative parish. Well, I found such a place.

It was hidden in a wood at Llangoedmor, which means 'wooded place', and it was half way between Newcastle Emlyn and Cardigan. It had a drive from the lane which disappeared under trees and climbed up to a steep field, near the bottom of which but still high up, a flat space had been carved out for wonderful farm buildings. There was a U shaped farm-yard, a stable to the left, a line of cow byres, an enormous barn with a high ceiling, great slabs of Welsh slate on the floor, a large grain store with a cellar below, a covered area for wagons, and a potential warden's cottage, and it was all in good order. It was a dream, and the wonder of it continued. Outside was an orchard, and in front a field sloped down to a wood. In the wood was a dingle and in the dingle a stream and lower down a large pond. I could not believe my good fortune, or so it seemed at the time.

Ian and Camilla Beynon-Lewis had bought a large house and farm but this part of their estate was redundant. They invited me to dine with them and when we walked from their drawing room to the dining room I saw the two candelabra were already lit on the polished table and a decanter of wine was ready on the sideboard. It was a memorable evening. Camilla was Italian and a good cook and Ian had retired successfully from a business in London. They were both charming. I bought Goglwyd from them. That name was mentioned in the deeds and meant 'grey cuckoo' but if there was no cuckoo there was definitely a barn owl perched on the great rafters of the barn.

During my first three years at Hartcliffe school, Bishop Langton Fox of Menevia and I exchanged sporadic gunfire on the subject of Goglwyd. He did not like my secret place and he did not agree with my dream. It was not entirely his fault; Fr. Higham in Newcastle Emlyn and Fr. Cunnane in Cardigan did not like my dream either. One or other of them would discover the blissful visits we used to make to our, private, secluded, invisible, retreat, invisible except to the gossipers. The bishop was blunt. If I did not give it up he would not execute the rescript he had from Rome which gave him authority to release me from my promise of celibacy. I had friends who did not believe I should accept an exclusion zone laid down by the bishop. Jean Charles Roux, the diplomat in the Beda College who had had a room next to mine in the College, and had become the parish priest of St Ethelreda's Church in London, wrote: 'You know that I am far less canonically and clerically minded than you are and I feel that, in your position, I would take no account of what bishops want or do not want and live quietly on my land in Wales if it suited me.'

It is, of course, obvious, and yet 35 years ago if a priest left the Church in order to marry it was not just a loss to the Church but considered a threat as well. He should disappear from where he was known as a priest and preferably disappear altogether. I was reluctant to play that game, reluctant indeed to cut off all ties with people I had known as a priest. Jean was a stronger character; he took no notice of directives if he did not agree with them, and baptized children, when the requirements of the Church at the time required parents to be visible members of a congregation. He baptized their children whether or not he had ever seen the parents or would ever see them again. He would marry people with all the pomp and ceremony he thought was right when in some other church they might have been confined to a sacristy, in other words he did not think much of the rules. On one visit to Goglwyd in 1974 we did venture into the wider world of Cardigan. I think we must have been hungry. We went to a hotel on the outskirts. Who should be there but Fr Cunnane? We were already sitting down for a meal but I got up, took Gill with me and introduced her. He was clearly shaken but behaved with due decorum and we exchanged a few pleasantries, all the time aware that we were not actually making contact and repercussions could follow. The heavy guns from Wrexham sounded again, 'it has come to my notice' style, and the expected salvo landed in Shoscombe. Later on a thunderbolt came, this time out of the blue. Gill had been back in Tregroes on a business trip, buying welsh tapestry for her waistcoats and skirts which were then on sale at Heathrow Airport. She turned up in Newcastle Emlyn at the Sunday Mass and was not only made very welcome but invited to read the Epistle. To the consternation of Fr. Higham she also received Communion.

Fr. Higham decided that the bishop ought to know about this unfortunate event and the bishop considered this 'irregularity' worth a letter too, which, in fact, had nothing to do with me. I was not hardened to all this and suffered.

In my battle with the bishop over his exclusion zone, I gathered all sorts of important people on my side, including Abbot Passmore of Downside Abbey, who lived in the clock tower of the abbey church and invited me to his room late at night when the rest of the monastery was in darkness and supposed to be asleep. He was very sympathetic and promised to write to the bishop of Clifton. The good bishop of Clifton, Mervyn Alexander, came to tea and was sympathetic as well. Even Cardinal Basil Hume, who once tried to teach me the art of rugby at Ampleforth College, promised to do what he could. They were all willing but quite powerless. The bishop is king in his diocese.

Meanwhile, with due care not to cause unnecessary upset and further Episcopal missiles, Gill and I continued our wonderful secret trips to Goglwyd but mysteriously the sleuths found out and skirmishes with the bishop continued. It was a rather pathetic and unchristian little battle and one that I could not win. During it, Mike Healy, a young priest in Bristol, invited us to join a group going to Palazzola, a one-time monastery near Rome, for a holiday. That August 1974, we collected my mother and drove across Europe to Rome. We had to drive into Germany surreptitiously because mother had a deep seated antipathy for Germans. She had lost two brothers in the First World War and dad had been scuppered in the second. We crossed the border from France while she was a sleep.

Palazzola was truly a little palace. It overlooked Lake Albano, in the Alban hills, 24 kilometres southeast of Rome. The lake was in a vast crater hundreds of feet below the ancient palazzo and on the opposite side you could see Castel Gandolfo, the Pope's summer residence. There was a steep path down to the lake, and you could climb down for a swim if you did not like the chlorine in the swimming pool, and with a bit of luck you could climb back again. This was where our first holiday at Palazzola almost came to grief. One evening, Gill and I decided on a swim in the lake. We set off after a lengthy lunch, made particularly delicious by Frascati wine drawn from great barrels in the crypt-like cellar. We set off wearing hats, swim suits, sandals, nothing more. We got down via the 'hermitage' without too much trouble, following red markings which showed the way. By the lake we blew up lilos and paddled out, the water was warm and wonderful, but the sun was surprisingly low in the sky, and when we returned to the beach and began the steep climb up, we could scarcely see the red markings anymore. Halfway up the path they had become quite invisible and it had become pitch dark. We blundered on upwards and became trapped, a sheer rock face ahead of us and towering bramble bushes all round. We shouted and could hear cries from the ramparts of Palazzola, in particular the voice of my mother shouting 'darling, where are you?' as loud as she could. We were completely and most uncomfortably stuck. Eventually, around midnight, help was organized; a huge fire engine from Rome arrived by the lakeside but then, mysteriously, disappeared. The firemen had forgotten to bring torches. However, soon they were back again and way down below us lanterns were flickering everywhere and big men with machetes were slashing their way through thorn bushes and calling to us. It was an enormous relief when they eventually cut their way through the wall surrounding us and half carried us down again to where the fire engine was waiting by the lakeside. I had lost a sandal and we were both scratched all over and terribly thirsty. Sitting in the front of the fire engine they plied us with milk, and rang the great bell all the way up to the monastery where my mother gave them the next day's excellent soup. The rest of Palazzola had gone to sleep. It was two in the morning.

When Rome became an oven in August the students in the English College in Rome would retire to Palazzola, swim, go for walks and play cricket, among other more serious activities. In 7 years of study and training they used to go home only once, but now they could go every summer and so their beautiful Palazzola became available for DIY holidays, the best holidays we have ever had. They were organized by young priests, ex- students of the College, and we were early and eager participants. We took with us my mother three times, Gill's father once, our own family, Angela, Merilyn and, later, Jessica and various other relatives and members of the Hartcliffe Humanities department. They were unforgettable holidays with unforgettable liturgies, but the most important and impressive aspect was the way community could be created in two or three weeks of living and working together. We made friends forever and in 1976 organized a mini Palazzola-style holiday at Goglwyd; a whole bunch of 'Geordies' from Newcastle came and stayed in the house or camped in the grounds. They brought with them a priest and a nun, and though there was not a lot of space and we had to turn the kitchen table into a bunk bed, it was a success and there was talk of many more, but how could that be? The bishop was obdurate.

Meanwhile, we had adopted Jessica, who was half Australian and half Indian. She came to us as a two year old, the daughter of Angela's best friend in the University, so the adoption was a private one and took place before a judge.

"Does he take his wig off when he goes to bed?" she whispered to Gill.

"Yes," said the judge in a deep voice.

Jessica was mischievous and beautiful, a real joy. But we feared dark periods in her young life. She screamed when she thought she might be taken back to London and, when she went to play with the little girl next door she would not leave the house without putting a chair against the kitchen door so that she could return easily. Her arrival changed our lives and even the landscape, a wendy house appeared, a climbing frame and even a grassy bank to roll down. Merilyn accepted her generously. She was in the 6th form, one of the privileged girls at Downside School. Angela was mostly away in London or Cambridge.

Rightly or wrongly I gave up the battle over Goglwyd. I was not going to change the bishop's mind and I did not think the venture would work as a residential centre if it lacked the support of the schools and parishes of the Diocese. Thus our situation with the Church was clarified that year and in the summer of 1977, Gill and Jessica went out again to Palazzola. It was September this time and I had to stay behind for school. I was now head of Religious Education and head of 6th form General Studies but, though I wanted very much to be in Palazzola, it turned out to be just as well I was not there. One day in that fortnight Bishop Mullins (who was going to be the bishop of the southern part of the Welsh Menevia diocese) and Bishop Fox lunched at Palazzola. The meal was in the courtyard and everybody sat around the huge table under the trees. Jessica was three and a half and had not yet been with us a full year. She was fascinated by the bishops and took some black grapes to Bishop Mullins. It was a kind of bribe. She wanted to wear his red skull cap and bravely asked if she could. The bishop nonplussed asked who she was.

"Jessica David."

"Oh, and where do you live?"

"Shoscombe, of course."

Bishop Fox, sitting opposite, could hardly believe it.

"Where is your mummy?" he asked.

Jessica took the very tall Bishop to meet Gill who noted in her diary that he was charming and they walked together up and down the garden several times, conversing happily. Back in Wrexham, Bishop Fox wrote to me.

'You will have heard of my meeting with your family in Palazzola. It is a small Catholic world but it is still amazing that through Bishop Mullins asking her where she came from your little daughter revealed her identity. I was delighted to meet your wife.'

Gill added: 'It was just as though no war had ever taken place between us.'

Chapter 25
The Search for Another Dream

By February of 1978, the headmaster of Hartclife, John Simpson, had given up chasing round the countryside looking for a likely residential centre, much to the relief of his senior staff. Simon and I, however, felt staying on at Hartcliffe would be stifling and we had to find another challenge. We were both still intent on finding premises for a residential centre and visited various sites, a run down Mill house, a castle at Farleigh Hungerford, a beautiful site offered to us by Lord Hylton with a magnificent view and woods.

"You can build what you like here," he said, "and lend support to my Ammerdown Adult centre at the same time."

That could have worked if we had created a Charitable Trust and raised enough money. Then Gill and I found a small disused Grammar School with a house attached and a footpath down to a secluded bay on the coast near Truro, in Cornwall, that had real possibilities. It was at a place called Illogan and was a project Gill and I could have managed on our own, an exciting possibility. Cornwall County Council invited secret tenders over £16,000 pounds and I offered £17,000. A local builder's 'secret' tender got it for £17,250.

In the autumn of 1978 Kathy Gabb came to stay. I have no idea why she came. She was ebullient, a feminist, a great character, full of life, and she was on her way to Wick Court. She described the place with both enthusiasm and sadness and said she thought the whole place and conference centre were about to be closed down and up for sale.

"If you go there", she added ominously, "you will want to buy it."

Gill and I went to see it at once and were astonished. It was not yet officially for sale and, indeed, a number of people hoped it would never sell. The residential centre had been created out of farm buildings in much the same way as Lord Hylton's Ammerdown Centre, though that was much grander. We arrived unexpectedly but were shown round the Wick Court 'Tatlow' centre, its huge conference room, large terrace, offices, dormitories which could sleep 50. It could be adapted easily into a residential centre for children and young people.

Wick Court itself was a huge Jacobean Mansion. It was owned and run by the SCM (Student Christian Movement). Rosemary Percival was the SCM president and lived in the Court, caring for a large group of good natured, well intentioned, peace loving folk, who could not cope with the world as it is. They wanted the simple life and lived on couscous and vegetables from the garden and wore weird clothes.

There are numerous histories of Wick Court. One of them begins: 'On the old Roman road leading from Bath to Caerwent, known as the Via Julia, lies the parish of Wick. It is situated in a romantic vale among the wooded hills and winding roads of Gloucestershire and Abson (Abbots town). It was included in the manor of Pucklechurch and belonged to the Abbots of Glastonbury.'

Glastonbury Abbey was one of more than 800 Monasteries, Nunneries and Friaries that existed in Britain in 1536. By 1541 Oliver Cromwell's men had seized them all for the king and 10.000 monks and nuns had been dispersed, many becoming vagrants. The abbot of Glastonbury had refused to hand over the richest and (after Westminster), most important monastery in Britain and was hung for his obduracy on Torre hill, 15 November, 1539. So ended a history which went back to Saxon days and Henry viii distributed the abbey lands among his friends. The nursery rhymes 'Little Jack Horner' and 'Sing a song of sixpence' describe those times. At the same time, a multitude of shrines were pillaged and Thomas Cromwell made bonfires of the images in his garden. It all began in the 27th year of the king's reign and I have imagined King Harry in heaven ruefully counting, not his money, but the final cost. Wick and Abson were given to Sir Edward Wintour who became the first Lord of the Manor. His son John succeeded him and on the death of Sir John in 1664, Thomas Haynes, a wealthy Bristol merchant, bought the property and probably built the house we were looking at. Its appearance with its tripled gabled roof and mullioned windows was grand enough, even if it was only the back of the house.

We knocked on the heavy oak door and Rosemary Percival welcomed us warily. She was in a difficult position, in charge at Wick

Court but responsible to the SCM Trustees. She had invited us to meet the 'community.' She closed the heavy door behind us and we found ourselves in the lobby, a late addition to the house. On the left were the kitchens and on the right the dairy. Immediately in front of us was the original back door which was wedged open and led into the hall. On the right of us now was an ancient oak door which was hinged in three parts and led down into the cellars. Rosemary moved us on faster than I would have wished. We could only glimpse the great beams across the ceiling, the oak-panelled walls, the magnificent staircase, the great front door, the mouldings and panelling on the other doors. The house was even more magical inside than out and through a deep-set mullioned window to the right of the fine original front door; one could just see a beautiful lawn and gardens surrounded by high walls.

Rosemary opened a door to the left of the hall and we went into a very large room also panelled. It had three large mullioned windows, each with a window seat. They were now occupied, and so were the various chairs and settees about the room, all except the three chairs reserved for us. The 'community' was waiting. What kind of possible purchasers would we turn out to be? Would they, as sitting tenants, be included in the sale?

That could bring down the price considerably, I thought unkindly. The community had been told that we wanted to establish a residential children's Centre and they hoped that there might still be room for them in the house.

At that time self sufficient communities were in vogue. The problem was they were seldom self sufficient. It was not difficult to see, looking round the room, why the Wick Court community lacked viability. They were essentially a 'hippy' commune, their alternative lifestyle and dependence on Social Security seemed to mean also that they were neglectful of themselves and of the place. Even so, Rosemary regarded them as her family and was determined that they should not be displaced if she could possibly help it. One member of the community, who lived in an old stable at the bottom of the garden with her two children, was vociferous about the rights of the community and how useful they could be supporting a new project. Rosemary nodded and looked at us.

"What was the project going to be?

"It's a project for young people," I began guardedly.

"I have no doubt of the social and educational value of a residential experience for children," I went on, "especially for those who come from disadvantaged homes."

Damn, I was talking to people who probably all came from disadvantaged homes, and what was I doing trying to explain to this particular audience that the opportunity for children to live together with their teachers for a few days, in a caring and stimulating environment, could give young people an awareness of human relationships and community which no amount of classroom teaching and discussion could achieve. They believed in all that themselves, they were all people in need who had found a home, comfort and community, and they all owed a lot to Rosemary for making that possible.

"I am sure everybody here would be willing to help your project," said Rosemary. Everybody nodded.

After some sporadic discussion which was not going anywhere, I said,

"This house would have to be the home of the people who work in the Centre."

They all nodded again, without understanding what I meant. I tried to change the subject.

"Might we see over the house?"

"No, that would not be possible. There are several people upstairs, including a baby." Rosemary realized there was no point in going on and closed the meeting. As they all shuffled off wearing an odd assortment of clothes, it was obvious they still felt threatened and one could not enjoy the possibility of perhaps, one day, playing the bailiff and turning them out.

The setting for Wick Court was magnificent. The river Boyd flowed 50 yards from the house and you could sit under yew trees and watch the kingfisher flash by, dive for fish and then sit on a branch to eat it. Around the Tatlow Centre were tall sycamores and I could see at once the possibility of an adventure play ground. In the front of the house (for in fact you arrive at the back) is a porch with a sun room above it, no drive now but a great walled garden. The inside of the house itself with its casement windows was very beautiful. We were able later to view the huge carved oak staircase which had a very fine finial on every bend and climbed up three floors. I was enraptured, but it was all in a sorry state, and the problem we faced was serious. Not only was the property for sale, the community was for sale as well. Rosemary made that very clear. She was not going to abandon her indigent flock, and yet at the same time she was under pressure from the Trustees and had to welcome the troops of people we took round to see it, Michael de Leon, a prospective Trustee of our prospective and still mythical Trust, groups of Tutors from Hartcliffe School, Simon and Jane Fisher and others.

Simon and I discussed it all at length and agreed we could make no concessions to the inhabitants of the Court. We offered £90,000 (the asking price) for the property *empty*. It was verbally accepted but Rosemary was seeking an alternative purchaser who might be more co-operative and save the community, and no contract arrived to be signed. At the end of the Spring Term 1979, Simon left Hartcliffe, even though there was still no progress on Wick Court. By July he was becoming thoroughly disconcerted by Rosemary's 'phone calls and being a good compassionate Quaker thought he might be better off working for Oxfam. Rosemary had found an ally in Roy de Freytas, director of Carribean Enterprises Ltd, in Bristol.

"Roy" she said, "had access to Trusts and funds and could raise £100,000 and take on the community as well."

On the 24 July, Gill noted in her diary that Simon had withdrawn. He was not to know that Roy was an impractical dreamer who believed that, if you wanted something badly enough, money would fall from the sky.

My last day at school had been 20 July, an emotional event, a sketch by the teachers and lengthy leave taking. It was a great school in one very real and important sense; it had a number of remarkable teachers who really worked hard for the children. It was a school that would back me and send children to Wick Court, but if Roy was offering £100,000 I knew I would have to offer that too.

Those last months of 1979 were traumatic, filled with uncertainties and fears. Gill wrote every day an excellent diary, that is to say she wrote every day unless she was exceptionally happy or exceptionally sad, so she did not write for a time after we married and she did not write now. Rightly or wrongly we had given up Goglwyd and now, if we succeeded in buying Wick Court, our beautiful Shoscombe home would have to go too, and this would happen just after we had built on a new kitchen with French windows to a terrace facing south, just after we had fenced round our huge garden, built a garage and a wood shed. It would happen before we had got used to our new bathroom and extra bedroom. Those days of wandering down the valley would end, the Post Office lady would not see us again and I would play no more shove halfpenny with my neighbour in the Apple Tree. The wrench would be considerable and there would be no entries in the diary.

Chapter 26
The Wick Court Venture

We did not want to compete with 'Caribbean Enterprises Ltd,' and Roy did not want that either but he did want help. He came to see us on 28 August bringing his pretty young wife with him who said not a word. Roy was voluble and messianic. Would we come and live at Wick Court and be directors of his project? He suggested that we loan the project £15,000 and as directors we would have a salary of £6,500 between us. He was expecting to raise £135,000, enough not only to buy Wick Court but also to refurbish the residential centre.

"I intend to buy Wick Court for use as a Multi Racial Safety Net," he said grandly. "I have no concept whatever of not succeeding. It would be a momentous demonstration of people's belief in a multi-racial society. My only concern at the present time is to get the S.C.M. to agree to sell it to us, and the bank to provide the money."

Roy was good-hearted but apparently naïve. Banks don't lend money that easily but his existing Trinity Church project in Bristol was certainly a lively place. He had successfully begun an educational and cultural programme in a redundant church. His February report that year was convincing, and he had ambitious plans for the provision of workshops and sports facilities. He was in the process of applying to the Home Office for a self help grant of £100,000 and thought his existing debt of £22,500 of no consequence.

"Roy, you have enough on your hands developing the Trinity Church project."

"That's why I would like you to direct the Wick Court one."

But I did not think it would be financially possible and rang up Rosemary.

I told her I believed Roy had his hands full already and I no longer felt embarrassed about competing with him for Wick Court. She simply said:

"You will have to raise your offer to £100,000. Otherwise, if Roy does not get it, Kerry Investments will."

So we made that leap in the dark, or rather *I* made the leap and Gill followed with less enthusiasm. Fresh planning was necessary and this delayed the contract and allowed us time to look for partners. A succession of people came, already running centres or aspiring to do so, people from Oxford and Newcastle on Tyne. I think the sight of the hippy community in residence was not encouraging. Finally my cousin, Hilary, was ready to take the risk. She and her husband, frustrated with London life, came down to see Wick Court. We met them at the Rose and Crown, in the centre of the village, Hilary, very smart and looking eager, Nicholas tall and dressed like a city gentleman. We talked and talked over an excellent ploughman's lunch.

The ancient Inn with its low beams and lockup for drunks was as old as the Court and stood only a few yards from the original and imposing entrance gates to Wick Court drive, but the drive itself had been grassed over. The weather was good and we all walked the few hundred yards down the old drive to the Court and even before the great manor house came into view, behind an avenue of lime trees, Hilary knew it was where she wanted to be. She had been running a catering business in London and her husband, Nicholas, was in advertising. She also had accountancy and computer skills, while he was a craftsman and would supervise the creation of an adventure playground and unsinkable rafts on the river. The house did not fill them with dismay. We disturbed the inhabitants with their mattresses on grime-covered floors for the last time. I remember thinking when we walked down the old driveway to the house, 'here come the capitalists intent on evicting the poor from their home,' but the SCM was in dire straits financially and 'Kerry Investments' was supposed to be hovering in the background.

On 24 October the Planning Committee of the Northavon District Council granted planning permission for a children's residential centre and the SCM Finance Committee agreed to sell to us. It was my 53rd birthday and I was not sure Wick Court would turn out a good birthday present. We now had to enlighten the SCM as to our plans. We had an embryonic Trust organised and several possible trustees in mind. The four of us would buy the house and its gardens while a Charitable Trust would buy the residential centre and its adjoining land and employ us to work there. This alarmed Hilary.

"Suppose the Trustees decide they don't want to employ us?"

"Indeed, but we are going to choose our Trustees carefully."

"So, we actually have to choose our employers?"

"Exactly."

We soon met with our prospective employers: Michael de Leon, a London business man and friend of ours, who quickly became a friend of Hilary and Nick's; Owen Hardwicke, a priest friend of mine, and Bruce Markham David, a cousin to both Hilary and myself and a circuit judge. Thus, unexpectedly, our fathers, the three David brothers, all had a son or daughter involved at Wick Court, which was strangely comforting.

We needed two sets of deeds, one for the house and one for the Centre, which displeased the SCM solicitors but we gave them no choice. The Wycke Foundation would buy the Wick Court Centre, ('Wycke' was the 16th century spelling) and completion date would be 31 January, 1980. On that day Gill moved in and slept on the drawing room floor.

In the middle of the night she woke up and going into the hall stood at the foot of the Jacobean staircase. Waves of welcome seemed to come down the stairs and brought her peace. Hilary and Nicholas's two boys, aged 4 and 8 and Jessica, 5 were wildly excited. They now had a sister and she had two brothers. The boys had grown up in London and all three of them quickly went off on adventures and quickly got lost.

Wick Court was a wonderfully exciting place for children. They could spend hours by the river watching a stickleback making its nest. An abandoned ochre works, woods and fields and numerous farms were all around. We had high hopes city children would love it. We collected lots of animals; a goat, chickens, bantams, doves, rabbits, ducks and, later, two sows and a boar. Sylvester, the drake, had two wives. They would sit together on the weir at night to be safe from the fox. Halcyon days!

The extraordinary good fortune the children were enjoying was shared by their grandmothers. The house was large enough to make two apartments, one for my mother and the other for Hilary's. Both were widows and sisters-in-law, Phyllis, my mother on the ground floor, Muriel, Hilary's mother, in a flat above her. They communicated by telephone and rarely visited each other, both in their eighties, both still driving their cars, but they had very different perspectives on life. Emmie, as Muriel liked to be called, read the Daily Mail while Phyllis, if she could get it, would read the 'Daily Worker.' Emmie must have forgotten that, politically, they were far apart. One day she arrived at Phyllis' door, waving the Daily Mail.

"Darling, wonderful news, we have sunk the Belgrano."

"Absolutely disgraceful," shouted Phyllis, jumping to her feet and, having turned Emmie out, slammed the door.

It was some time before communications were restored and it was fortunate for mother that she did not live directly under her sister-in-law's room. Noisy repercussions continued for some time, in different ways they were both a little eccentric. My mother was often an embarrassment. If she burnt the toast or anything else in her kitchen it set off the smoke detector and she would grab her walking stick and beat it into silence. Nicholas, who was not only warden in the Centre but in charge of such matters in the house, replaced the smoke detector time and again, fearing the whole house would be imperilled, but he could not improve mother's memory or culinary habits. We had a great party for her 85th birthday and another for her 88th as her sight was going and time was running out for her.

My rebellious mother had a passion for the poor. She espoused every Cause, ANC and IRA, and wrote many letters to IRA prisoners from a list of names and addresses given her by Lord Hylton. Eventually one of these prisoners, Pat Docherty, was transferred to Leyhill Open Prison nearby. I went to visit him there and that led to groups of six prisoners coming in a prison van, together with a warder, to Wick Court each week. They worked with Nicholas in the garden and did other things like cutting wood and repairing walls. Hilary and Gill took it in turns to give them lunch, while Grandma Phyllis gave them tea and cigarettes, and even though they were all 'lifers' and had spent 10 to 20 years in gaol, they became real friends.

Meanwhile our children were in trouble again. They had been on an adventure and got stuck in the pig slurry of a neighbouring farm. They got out with difficulty, minus one or two Wellington boots, and stank to high heaven. They were all put in the bath together and Edward the younger boy said to his brother Bisley:

"Poor Jessica, she's only got a slit," to which Bisley replied,

"Don't be silly Edward, all girls are like that."

"Are they?" said Edward wide eyed.

Bisley now had a menagerie in his bedroom. He began with stick insects which at one stage were all over the room. His next craze was garter snakes but he announced one day that one of them had disappeared. It was not seen for several days but eventually emerged through a crack in the floorboards in Grandmother Emmie's bathroom. She happened to be in the bath at the time and came face to face with it on getting out. She was not at all pleased. Bisley moved on to white rats and rabbits and the epidemic was catching. Jessica had two baby squirrels and a chaffinch with a broken wing. When the wing mended it enjoyed pirouetting, flying round the kitchen, picking up crumbs from the floor and when it finally flew away it was like losing a friend. Outside we had a pond full of fish and one day the kingfisher discovered they were easier to catch in the pond than in the river. We allowed it to have five for breakfast and then called a halt. Beside the excitement of little owls nesting in the garden, woodpeckers coming to the bird table and the fox forever prowling around, we had badger sets in the woods and an old quarry full of crystals, fossils and galena. It was an ideal place not only for our children but for city children as well. They did not exactly pour in during that first year but when they came, they had a great time. The old ochre works across the road was ideal for rambles through the woods, identifying plants and birds, finding fossils, and we would climb the hill to the Civil War battlefields at Lansdown or visit the local farms at milking time. In the wood there was a stream; to cross it we fixed up a rope on an overhanging branch. All the children would swing themselves across quite easily, but one day a rather tubby teacher failed to let go of the rope and hung suspended over the middle of the stream. It was only a matter of time before she would have to let go and the children, most of whom had already crossed, were wild with excitement. The drop would be only two or three feet and the water was shallow, but she played her part in the drama, calling for help and waving. When the splash came, she became a heroine and would be able to do anything with those children afterwards in the classroom.

Wick Court was in an area of special scientific interest (SSI) and perfect for nature studies. Gill made worksheets and the children had to find and draw the wild flowers. Our first year was really hard; there were too many empty weeks and empty week-ends. It was hard too, physically, because so much work had to be done and money spent. In the first six months the debt on the Centre went up from £41,000 to £52,000. We could not be sure that we might not meet the same fate as the S.C.M.

Wick Court

Chapter 27
The Challenge and the Joys

"Oh dear, my ears and whiskers, I shall be late for the Duchess", said Jessica on her way home from school.

There was definitely a 'wonderland' side to Wick Court, but a cold one to begin with. February had been bitterly cold and burst pipes in the Centre turned floors into a lake. On top of that, the heating failed and students from the Catholic Chaplaincy who arrived in February had to huddle around fan heaters in the lounge. They had talks from Etta Gullick, who told them that suffering benefits the soul.

The local quarry gave us tons of chippings and we spent hours filling in pot holes in the drive and making a car park behind the Centre, large enough for a bus to turn round in. There was a huge amount of work in the house as well, sanding floors and painting, replacing broken loos, cleaning away the grime and dirt of years. It was actually fortunate that bookings for the Centre did not come in too fast, though we leafleted every school in Avon. The back-up and encouragement we had from the Trustees and Management committee was tremendous and humbling. We could never have succeeded alone. They met together four times in the first year and included the deputy head of Hartcliffe School, as well as an accountant, a social worker, interior designer and director of a World Studies project.

Our three patrons were: Lord Hylton of Ammerdown, the Abbot of Downside and the Bishop of Bristol. Finally, on the 19 September, we all dressed up to welcome the Lord Mayor of Bristol and his wife who arrived in their gleaming chauffeur-driven limousine, a pennant flag fluttering on the bonnet, at 3.30pm precisely. Our children shook hands with them and behaved perfectly.

"I like your chain," said Jessica to the Mayor.

"It is 23 carat gold and worth £80, 000," he said, rolling his eyes and fingering the chain.

We tried to explain what we hoped to do for Bristol city children and what a residential experience in the countryside could mean for them. He liked the river, the landing stage and the fibre glass boat. He was not to know that the boat kept hitting rocks and sinking which was infuriating for Nicholas but highly exciting for the children. Nicholas showed him the adventure playground which was being built round huge sycamore trees with the help of Terry Barter and some Y.T.S. boys. It would have platforms and rope bridges and ultimately a 'death' slide.

We all trooped into the Centre which looked impressive. Hilly and Gill had spent a lot of time buying furniture and new mattresses. The occasional child fell out of the top bunk and would have to be rushed to hospital, but we did not trouble the Mayor with this kind of information. After visiting the large split level lounge, the kitchen, the dining hall, the games room, the tuck shop, the boot room, the dormitories, everybody returned to the Court for tea. The Mayor was satisfied and promised us his patronage too. His wife said Kelston was the only other Centre in the Bristol area she knew and it was not as good.

The embryonic Wick Court Centre was definitely out of intensive care by the end of our first year. We introduced ourselves to the village and neighbourhood at an Open Day on 29 March and about 150 visitors came, and on Saturday 21 June we had a very successful fund-raising garden fete. The gardens suffered but it was a good public relations exercise and we had time in that first year to organise such things. We also had time on special occasions to enjoy the gardens ourselves. We had big wedding parties for Merilyn in the autumn of 1983 and Angie in the summer of 1984. For them Wick Court was a kind of launching pad and the space and beauty it provided was a privilege we could share. We had begun brewing wine and made large quantities of intoxicating elderflower. That effort combined with a lively band was a recipe for success and repeated several times. We had two big parties for my mother when she reached 85 and 88 (fearing she might never make it to 90) and with a group called 'Arran Pilots' playing, danced endlessly on the lawn in front of the great gabled house, moments of splendour to remember for ever. My mother held court from a canopied deck chair, and somehow the weather was perfect every time.

Several events became fixtures. A group of Catholic families which used to go elsewhere came regularly in Easter week and somehow we found priests like Michael Healy, a long time Bristol friend, to do the ceremonies. On one occasion, Paddy, the goat, took the part of the donkey in a Palm Sunday procession but insisted on eating the yew branches strewn on the way and became very ill. On Easter Sunday a week later he staggered to his feet again, but thereafter it took against children and would charge them when they came too near, so, reluctantly, we had to part with him. He was replaced by Seamus, an Irish wolf hound, the size of a donkey, but when he discovered the various ways he could get into the Centre and how easily he could demolish lunch for thirty children, we had to part with him too.

We built up a programme of nature walks, river studies and quarry walks many of which were led by Gill who had always loved nature and knew all the names of wild flowers and local birds and could delight the children by finding fossils, or painting a picture using only colours found in nature. I tended to take charge of the farm visits which became ever more extensive and varied. There was Greenways, where Mr Hooper fed 400 pigs a dreadful-looking gruel at 4.30 precisely by just turning a tap. The children could mount rickety gangways and look down on the unforgettable commotion and suffer the unforgettable smells, knowing now where their bacon came from. The dairy farms were less noisome and more interesting and several farmers went out of their way to teach the children. Jim Nield at Upton Cheyney could hold the attention of forty Hartcliffe children, give them a tour of his large mixed farm, have them sitting on straw bales in the back of his enormous trailer, take them out to fetch the cows and explain the milking. We had a rota of six farms so as not to burden any one of them too much. The farm in Wick itself, Toghill and Bottoms farm were the three easiest to reach, and the farmers' wives produced biscuits and lemonade.

Top juniors, 10 and 11 year olds, from Hartcliffe, St. Paul's and Eastville were the ones who clung on to you on the walks. They had never seen mud before, or the sky at night, never walked through a wood or paddled in a river. They were the ones shocked by the real size of a cow, only seen before on television. On our way to a farm one day with thirty children and two teachers we were crossing a field by a recognised footpath, only to be suddenly surrounded by a herd of cows. This was not unusual, cows are inquisitive, but they rarely let you 'smooth' them as the children say. They are only alarming if they come charging down a field and you wonder if they are going to stop.

"Cows are friendly, they won't harm you," I would say hopefully, but on one occasion we all realised the herd of cows charging towards us were not alone.

They were all heifers, not yet staid, milk-giving cows, but frisky two and a half year olds ready for mating. Their mate, in fact, was with them, prancing around in a hostile manner, lowering his head and snorting. We did not like his particularly sharp horns and the way he pawed the ground, always a bad sign. We were bunched together in the middle of the field, paralysed.

"Don't panic. Keep your eyes on the bull and move slowly sideways."

We edged our way towards the stile which seemed a mile away but the children were heroes and did not panic. It was an immense relief when everyone was safely over the stile, the cows lined up in the field, the bull still prancing. The milking parlour at Toghill our destination that day was an anti climax, despite the fact that it was ultra modern and the children could watch from a balcony a huge turntable with cows coming in on one side, filling each bay and moving round and then out, as the milking progressed, but the performance paled beside the antics of the bull. The farmer claimed that a bull running with heifers was not dangerous as it had other things on its mind. We had doubts about that.

Life is seldom free of conflicting interests. The ownership of the parkland that had belonged to Wick Court for centuries had fallen into the hands of a Mr Dalwood. He now controlled the old driveway, but the deeds of the house contained the right to vehicular use over this old driveway. When Mr Dalwood wired up the gate and added a padlock and chain at the Wick Court end, the S.C.M. students complained. When that was ignored they took Mr Dalwood to court, but the case was dropped when they sold the property to us. Our solicitor, Fergus Lyons, did not want to pursue the matter in court.

"Just saw through the chain," he said laconically.

We told Mr Dalwood that we intended to do just that, and make use of the driveway occasionally. He responded with threats and was decidedly unhelpful. The next day Michael de Leon and I drove up the old driveway; a furious Mr Dalwood jumped on his tractor and prevented our exit at the other end. We did not argue with the man, he was beyond rational discussion and we retired the way we had come. The next day he placed a trailer full of timber across the exit. War had been declared. Students who were staying in the Centre at the time helped to unload the trailer and move it away. Immediately Mr Dalwood, placed a large and heavy chain round the gate and secured it with a huge padlock. He was still furious and tried intimidation as well. The driveway was designed originally to cross the park land diagonally and reach the Manor House after passing through an avenue of lime trees. The lime trees still exist but the driveway had been diverted to end at the stables. Mr Dalwood decided to build a wall on his side of the Wick Court gates. This was unfriendly as it would obscure our view of the original lime tree avenue which had become his property. The policeman summoned to observe this exercise carried out by Mr Dalwood himself with another man, a tractor, trailer, breeze blocks, cement and much swearing, could not decide what to do. Both men eyed him and went on working.

"Whose land is this?" asked the policeman.

"Mine," said Mr Dalwood, "and this is my wall too."

The policeman did not believe him but said he could not be sure.

"Wait until he goes away and then push it down," he said, and got on his bicycle.

So when Mr Dalwood had gone I pushed it all down which clearly exacerbated the situation. He did not try to build it up again, but felt confident that his extremely heavy chain and enormous padlock on the entrance to the driveway would ensure we could never drive again across his land. I took a risk. Mr Dalwood had a large dog and a shot gun and lived only 50 yards from the gate he had safely secured. One moonlit night, I went alone up the two or three hundred yards of the old driveway to the barricaded gate. The dog did not bark. It was an absolutely still, bright night, I needed no torch and began to saw the chain with a hacksaw, appalled by the terrible noise it made, a high pitched squeak enough to wake the entire village, let alone Mr Dalwood.

Still, for some reason, the dog did not bark, and Mr Dalwood did not appear in his nightshirt. I went on furiously, terrified at the same time. At last the chain broke and I carried the heavy thing, padlock and all, back to the house. I did not sleep much that night. The next morning an enraged voice on the phone demanded the chain back. I said,

"It has been confiscated," and put the phone down, my heart thumping.

It was not the kind of exercise I particularly enjoyed.

Purely by chance, a day or two later, we had a Jacobean Evening in the house and gardens. Terry Vardon organised the music and Michael Cockett recited poetry. It was a great success. The Mayor and his wife came and a large number of other guests. So, in order to make enough space for the cars, we parked ours right up to the gate of the old driveway facing in Mr Dalwood's direction. My mother's Rover was first in line touching the gate itself. Emmie's mini came next, followed by the Chiswell-Jones' Volvo and then our car. The next morning all four cars were still in place while all the visitors' cars had gone. This menacing line up was at last too much for Mr Dalwood, he expected an imminent invasion and his heart had been playing up. The Rover 90 looked like a tank and could have easily knocked his gates down, padlocked or not. We agreed a compromise: we would allow a chain on the gate next to his house and a padlock too but with a key for each of us. Occasionally after that we drove up the old driveway and once or twice the right of way proved very useful as an emergency exit from the car park. On Open Days, Art Exhibitions and Book Fairs, the whole area could be choked with vehicles, that was when we used our key to open up the driveway. One could not expect Mr Dalwood to be pleased when he saw from his bungalow window a stream of cars crossing his land, but he made no more trouble.

The pattern of life at Wick Court had become clear by the end of the second year. The autumn term was now almost entirely booked by Comprehensive Schools for first year tutor groups. Primary Schools filled up the spring and summer terms and Bristol University organised intensive language courses in French and German for Sixth form students in November. These two-day courses lasted two weeks and were followed by a four day Art Course for adults at the end of the month. Both the Art Courses and the Exhibition which followed became regular features. All these events depended on Hilly's catering and cooking which was always excellent. Week ends were easy. Most were taken up by self catering Church groups, Quakers, Baptists, Salvation Army, Catholics and Anglicans, who would often invite us to share in their liturgies and celebrations.

Problems came with way-out groups; Exegesis for example who wanted beds for fifty but catering for only twelve. We discovered the group used techniques of interrogation together with lack of sleep and food, to break down the defences that all of us erect around ourselves. When they had achieved this they set about rebuilding their client's fragile and demoralised self. It sounded sinister and did not fulfil the objectives of the Trust. Similarly, 'Education Otherwise' was acceptable in theory but could be disastrous in practice. The new carpet in the lounge looked as though it had been down for years after their visit, a lack of discipline was apparent. The children ran wild, rode bicycles over pillows in the dormitory and spilt hot cocoa on the new armchairs.

"Darling, you've spilt your chocolate on the chair."

"Yes, I know but there was no one sitting on it."

"Of course, darling, it wasn't your fault but we might want to come again."

Hilary and I who heard the conversation from the kitchen hissed at each other,

"No chance!"

The Followers of the Prophet were also a weird group. They didn't do any damage but they insisted on taking their mattresses from the dormitory cubicles into the dining room and sleeping hugger mugger on the floor there. This made serving breakfast difficult. During the day if they were not in deep meditation they walked around in a trance and if the sun came out they immediately took off their clothes. Fortunately the sun did not come out very often that week. One night we could see from the house a number of lights flickering along the bank of the river, they were candles and in the river itself were the followers of the prophet, submerged and absolutely still, their eyes fixed on the candles. Our children were at home at the time and when the prophet led his flock in single file round the orchard balancing paper cups on their heads, the children joined in, first Bisley, followed by Jessica and Edward, very solemnly, with paper cups on their heads, pretending they too were followers of the prophet. Inevitably, the Prophet thought we were unsympathetic and did not understand the serious nature of their activities, so they did not book again.

There is a tremendous reward in giving children an exciting time, children whose lives are often very bleak and sometimes hide great pain. Many have no idea of the countryside and the incredible life and interest it contains. Every expedition was a real adventure, yet we were battling against the odds. Gill recorded this dialogue.

"Are we 'avin' 'ot tonight, miss?"

"Yes, you'll get a hot meal every night. What do you have at home?"

"We 'as 'ot on Fridays."

"Oh, what do you have on Fridays?"

"We 'as Wimpeys."

Teachers said many times that they could achieve more in a residential week away with their children than in a whole year at school. The place had to be interesting but the food too, and Hilly was as good at organising that as she was at running the office.

"We can build up more trust because we can relate to them in a more relaxed way," said the teachers.

This made the remarks of one child entirely comprehensible.

"This is a place," he said, "where teachers become human."

But in order to become relaxed, teachers need to be relieved of their teaching responsibility. Gill and I provided the educational structure, the treasure hunt, the nature walks, farm visits etc. and the back-up resources. Nicholas was responsible for the indoor and outdoor recreational activities; he soon invented unbreakable table tennis bats, an unsinkable raft on the river made out of oil drums, and a death slide. Shared experiences and excitements created a closer bonding in the class and that showed itself in tearful farewells at the end of their stay.

"I would like to stay a whole month," said one.

"I would like to stay for ever," said another, clutching hold of you for the last time. Sometimes it wasn't the last time. Years later, one young man met us and said:

"Do you remember me?" Sadly we didn't. "I stayed at Wick Court three times, once with my primary school, once with my tutor group in the Comprehensive and once on an 'A' level art course."

"And how did you like Wick Court?" Gill asked anxiously.

"They were the best weeks of my life."

It was not difficult, in fact, to give children an exciting week. On one occasion it was too exciting and almost disastrous. A teacher brought along a gorilla suit and suddenly appeared at one end of the dining hall looking very real, and very much as though she had just escaped from a zoo. The children went wild but when the excitement subsided and they had all been happily cuddled by the gorilla, someone proposed a practical joke on the warden. It was never wise to try out a practical joke on a warden, especially on Nicholas.

To the right of the courtyard at the back of the house was a long woodshed, it had a hopper in the corner and had once been the laundry. Over the roof grew an enormous clematis which hung down like a curtain hiding most of the wood. The gorilla hid in the woodshed and the children told the warden there was a large animal in there.

"It might be dangerous, sir."

"It's very big, sir."

There was a pause, all the children hid behind the wall. Nicholas, who was responsible for the safety of the place and took his responsibilities very seriously, came to the door carrying his twelve bore shot gun. The children gasped. The gun was fully loaded and the gorilla could see Nicholas approaching through the veil of clematis and uttered a strangled cry. It emerged hurriedly with its hands up and all was well but it could easily have ended very badly indeed.

Wick Court was and remained for 17 years a wonderful educational Centre and a stimulating playground for children, and schools re-booked again and again. Each time, however, it was different, different children and often different teachers. The experience even for us was never quite the same. Things were going well but at the end of our first four years, Partridge and Love, the printers, who had sold Wick Court to the SCM and who owned all the land across the river opposite the Court, now sold the rest of their property to new owners, Boulton and Noakes, who were consummate asset strippers. They had no interest in reviving the ailing company and began by dismissing all the sales reps. Thereafter it was only a matter of time before they maximised their profits, auctioned off all the equipment in the factory, sold the building, sold the cottages alongside, and put in planning applications for factories and houses on the meadow land opposite the Court. We saw the plans, 4 light industry factories, some 28 or so houses, and a green in the middle which would be a gift to the village. The plan would completely wreck the countryside environment of the Court and we protested to Northavon Council who refused planning permission. Boulton and Noakes, wise to such things, went to appeal and employed a top QC. The hearing was in the early summer of 1986. It took place in a large hall in Thornbury and lasted two days. The solicitor for the Council made the case for refusing permission. He was cross questioned by the QC who made mincemeat of his arguments. We were worried about Fergus Lyons, our solicitor, who followed him on to the witness stand. (It was not a box, just a platform). Fergus was armed with a huge number of letters from heads of schools and numerous other supporters and though he had a difficult time responding to the aggressive QC, he stood his ground. The land was apparently 'white' land and not protected. The council could grant planning permission and were told very clearly that it was their duty to do so. It was an unnerving performance and by the second day we thought we were going to lose.

The hearing dragged on late into the evening of the second day. Finally the QC had the right, apparently, to sum up the arguments at length on behalf of the plaintiffs and demolish those of Northavon Council. The impassive inspector kept making notes. All seemed lost. Then, quite unexpectedly, a storm broke and dramatic peals of thunder and flashes of lightning put all the lights out. There was an eerie silence, except for the thunder which went on rumbling. One could just see the shadowy figure of the QC with his sheaf of papers, obviously non-plussed, the inspector silent too, shadows of other people running about. At last candles came in, but it was too late for the QC to recover the thread of his argument. From being lucid, coherent and impressive, someone who knew what he was talking about, he became dull and ordinary, peering at his brief uncertainly by the light of a candle.

The next morning the Inspector made his tour of the area. We were not allowed to talk to him and he did not talk to us but it was a wonderful sunny morning. The river and the fields beyond looked beautiful. Hayesfield girls from Bath were staying in the Centre and were wandering about with their clipboards on a nature study quiz. About a month later the Inspector's report arrived. It rejected the Appeal. We could breathe again.

Part 4
Wick Court to Crosby Hall

Chapter 28
The Upheaval of Change

At the end of seven years and a dinner party in the hall of the great house for all the important people who had helped us, this story took another twist. We had a visit from Mark and Suzanne Blundell from Crosby Hall in Lancashire. I knew about the family, having read the 18th century diaries of Nicholas Blundell who inherited the Blundell Estates in 1702. The family intrigued me because it was one of the oldest recusant families in Lancashire and had survived the sequestration of its lands, imprisonment and exile. It intrigued me too because members of the family continued to make pilgrimages to Holywell when it was politically and financially dangerous to do so. There was no Lancashire family that interested me more.

Gill and I sat outside with our guests on our small terrace beside the pond. Later we would sit outside another terrace beside another pond, we did not know it then but we were about to exchange the gardens of one stately home for those of another. Mark Blundell was 38 and had just inherited Crosby Hall. The house with its big garden, grounds and outbuildings seemed large and frightening to his Swiss wife, Suzanne, and they thought, perhaps, they could do something useful with the premises and live in just a part of it. They had lived in London for some years, Mark as a solicitor and Suzanne training to be a child psychoanalyst. Mark's parents had retired to the Barn House with its huge walled garden, orchard and greenhouses. All the rest of the estate was now Mark's responsibility, though his father, Brian, still took a great interest in the woods. Pheasant rearing and shoots took place in the autumn and the gamekeeper played a prominent role. Various farms belonged to the estate as did almost the whole village of little Crosby. We learnt a lot that morning and afternoon but a great deal more when we made our first visit to the Hall.

Edward Crouzet, a Benedictine monk, was responsible for initiating these events. He had taught Mark at Downside School. Edward was then chaplain at Bristol University and sent students for week-ends to the Centre. He had suggested to Mark and Suzanne that they should call. I remember them now sitting in our oak panelled drawing room, under the 300 year old portraits of Richard Haynes, High Sheriff of Gloucester, his beautiful wife and next to them a severe looking Tudor matron with a pinnacled headdress. They had been the first occupants of the newly re-built Court, in the reign of Charles II and their dress was exactly similar to that of Nicholas Blundell and his wife in Lancashire. We boldly presented our guests with elderflower wine and Mark sipped it cautiously. We showed them everything, including the noisy children in the Centre having their evening meal.

I wrote to Mark on 9 July offering to take a 'sabbatical,' a year away from Wick Court, in order to help him establish a Centre at Crosby Hall. He invited us for a week-end on Saturday 18 July and we talked 'till midnight about setting up a Trust. The next morning Mark took us on a tour of the estate and the farm buildings. Gill wrote:

"It is an exciting place, a little oasis, 300 acres of privileged ground on the edge of great sprawling Liverpool with all its council house estates and inner city problems."

Unlike Wick Court where the fortunes of the Haynes family foundered and the house never enjoyed the extensions and improvements of later centuries, Crosby Hall became enormous and needed an army of servants. It was punitive death duties after the Second World War that not only decimated the woods of fine timber but also reduced the Hall to a third of its original size. Even so the splendour of the past remained. The Hall was still spacious and grand and the farm buildings were in keeping. We were to see them first, arriving through the back entrance over the cobble stones, and only later saw the imposing main gates and lions rampant holding heraldic shields guarding the main entrance, and the long driveway through the park.

If there was no ballroom anymore, no clock tower or chapel, no extensive kitchens, bake house, dairy or wash house, it seemed not to matter at all.

The farm buildings formed a quadrangle round a large cobbled yard and included a wonderful 16th century barn, hexagonal threshing floor, impressive high-ceilinged 18th century stables, and other farm buildings. We suggested these would be ideal for conversion into a residential centre. The setting was perfect, close enough to the city yet far enough away from it too.

At this point I began to get very cold feet. Mark did not want me to come for a year and then abandon him, he thought such a project would take three years and I had to agree to that. He offered us a flat at the top of the house with beautiful views across the lawns to the 'Vista' wood. It had two bedrooms, one very large with ancient faded tapestries and a smaller one for Jessica. She had already made friends with the eldest daughter Ali (Alexandra) and ridden her horse, Gemma. She had also played the flute with the younger girl Isa (Isabel). The future had a kind of inexorable finality which filled me with dread. I had thought my mission, my substitute parish, was Wick Court, and was now faced with the prospect of giving it up. Gill was forthright and clear in her mind. She knew we had to leave Wick Court and could not understand my indecision. On 30 July she wrote in her diary:

> *"Christopher is in the same position as he*
> *was before we got married. He takes a step*
> *forward and then two steps back. He has*
> *no real faith in Providence, no belief in a*
> *guiding spirit, no knowledge of Christ as*
> *the lord of our destiny."*

This idea of Providence is one I share and yet quite clearly we are personally responsible for the choices we make. They have to make sense to us and be what we really want or think we want. She did not show me what she had written. I had an agonising few weeks but in the end it became clear to me too. I had come to terms with the fact that none of us are indispensable and Nicholas and Hilary would take care of Wick Court. There was no reason to think that what we had achieved together would not continue. The Wycke Trustees and management accepted the new challenge and appointed Nicholas as the director from 1 January, 1988.

It was not only leaving our work at Wick Court that was hard, we would also be leaving my mother and our daughter, Merilyn, with her husband and two small children who had joined us at Wick Court and taken over a share of the house. They were able and willing to take over the care of 'grandma' too. Charlotte, the elder four year old, spent much of her time in her room and even in her bed when it was time to watch the next episode of Coronation Street. Charlotte would explain to grandma what was happening. The prisoners continued to come with their 'minder' once a week and continued to chat and have tea in grandma's large panelled room. Their welfare too became Hilary's particular concern and she ended up becoming a prison visitor for several years.

As a parting gift Gill bought more bantams, Seabrights and Silkies, for the Centre, which delighted Hilly and dismayed Nicholas. "Oh shit," he said, referring, of course, to that aspect of things, and the extra toll on his time.

In February 1988 Mark put in a kitchen in the top floor flat he had reserved for us and on 3 March we moved into Crosby Hall. The kitchen was large and from its windows we could see across the lawns to the wood where a Peregrine falcon, often perched happily on the branch of a great beech tree, happily that is, until several magpies decided to sit beside it on the same branch. The magpies, by devious sideways movements and much chatter would gradually dislodge the falcon from its perch. They considered the whole garden belonged to them and would hold large noisy conventions on the lawns. When they were around, the rabbits kept clear, disappearing into large rhododendron bushes. On one occasion a stoat did a remarkable dance outside one of the bushes, hoping, we presumed, to entice a rabbit out. No rabbit moved and the stoat, pirouetting on its hind legs, eventually gave up. From our windows we could look down on hawfinches in the crown of a large yew tree, they would have been invisible from the ground. We also had a grandstand view of the estate, Charolais cows to the right of the wood, horses to the left. It was an unforgettable sight when the cows lined up behind the ha-ha to watch an open air play, Midsummer Nights Dream, with nymphs emerging from the foxgloves. Opening the gardens of the Hall to such events fitted well with the generous hope that the privacy and privilege of the estate could be widely shared; it just had to be more than a dream.

On our first evening at Crosby Hall, Mark's parents, Brian and Hester, invited us to supper in the Barn House. We quickly realised that although

Brian had relinquished the estate, his influence was considerable. More than anyone else he had to be convinced that the project was worthwhile. The Barn House was in fact the other half of the great barn which would be part of the projected centre, it would be on his doorstep and he would probably be able to hear the children through the dividing wall.

"So you take the children out of school for a week, or less than a week. You give them an experience of a life time and send them back into the city. What good does that do, raise their expectations and leave them where they were before?" He had more worries, especially about the economics of it all.

"You are talking about children from poor families. At the same time you are talking about staffing the Centre with a cook, a director, another teacher, and cleaners. How are the poor parents going to pay for all this?"

We talked about how the Bursary fund had worked at Wick Court, how it would have to be a much larger fund to enable the poorer Liverpool City children to come to Crosby Hall at half price, the purpose of the fund. The criterion used at Wick was entitlement to free school meals. In the months that followed, Brian would continue to be our most attentive critic and finally our greatest support. Numerous groups of local people were invited to attend a talk on the project at Crosby Hall. They sat around in the magnificent library of the Hall, genuinely interested and many of them ready at once to offer their help.

In our large bedroom at the top of the house there were panelled walls, fine and ancient tapestries and window seats. We looked out on the parkland in front of the house with its individual trees, some of them very old. Beyond the parkland was another wood and, rising above the trees, the spire of Little Crosby church. It had been built in 1847 as soon as the law permitted, but there was always a private chapel in the house, and another one, even more private and secret, in the wood. We could walk across the park to the church and hear Mgr Breen preach perhaps the best sermons we have ever heard. The old traditions lingered on, wonderful hand made decorations for big feasts in the church and Corpus processions in the woods.

Chapter 29
The Blundells of Crosby Hall

The Blundell family arrived in England with William the Conqueror. What became the Crosby branch lived first in Ainsdale, then King John granted them the Manor of Great Crosby in 1189. A Blundell was knighted by Edward 1st; another was killed on Flodden Field. A marriage to Anne Molyneux brought the family the Manor of Little Crosby in 1362, where 23 generations have lived quietly and not so quietly for more than 600 years.

Over the centuries the estate has seen plenty of drama, a Blundell wife with child languishing in Chester jail, a Cavalier crippled by a cannon ball at the siege of Lancaster Castle, a portly Diarist hiding in a priest hole, not to mention the secret burials by night in the wood, or the terrible day the sheriff arrived to dig up the graves. Supporting the King had brought the Blundells honours and land. Opposing the Crown in the 16th and 17th and into the 18th century brought them prison and fines. At one point all their lands were forfeited to the Crown and it was only through the good offices of a Protestant friend that they were able to buy them back and lie low, 'till the persecution passed.' For this reason, until very recent times, the whole village of Little Crosby remained staunchly Catholic. It was remarkable to be breathing this air and sharing this history.

After the Second World War, Liverpool's sprawling mass stretched itself northwards, creating new Crosby housing estates and eating up farmland belonging to the Blundells. No more than a couple of fields now separated the walled estate from this post-war development. Yet it was enough, inside the parkland, ringed by woods, you could forget the city of Liverpool, it might have been a 100 miles away. It was wonderfully quiet except for the squawk of a pheasant or the croak of a frog. Red squirrels played in the branches of the tall trees. Dykes crisscrossed the wood. There was frog spawn in a marl pit and birds nesting. It seemed too good to be true if even part of such a wonderland could be shared with city children.

An architect had already looked at the stables and already made tentative plans. There was much measuring and we had many 'on site' meetings. The biggest challenge, however, was not the detailed plans and necessary planning permission, it was the creation of a charitable Trust and the choice of Trustees who would help to promote the project and raise the substantial funds necessary to get it going. The Trust document was already prepared, the Trustees were still missing.

Much of March was spent preparing propaganda for CHET (Crosby Hall Educational Trust), planning and putting together an initial brochure, long before it would be needed, inviting key people to visit Crosby Hall: the deputy Director of Education in Sefton and the head of adult education in Crosby. Finance loomed large. We sent off 230 CHET letters seeking covenanted 'Chetfriend' support. It was a re-run on a much bigger scale of the struggle to establish Wick Court, raising money for a venture that was still a dream.

Invitations were sent out in March to the head teachers of all Sefton schools, primary and secondary and by 18 April, 90 teachers had accepted, representing 48 schools. On the day itself, Sunday 24 April, about 100 teachers arrived and were all shepherded into the great barn to sit on borrowed stacking chairs.

Five of us sat behind a long trestle table; Mark in the Chair, Bob Miller, head of First Years at Hartcliffe School, Michael Cockett from Manchester, education adviser, and John Malthouse, our Accountant.

There was a daunting sea of faces in front of us and the lighting in the old barn was not brilliant. Bob Miller told them, as was hoped, that Wick Court was an amazing place for city children, Mike Cockett was, enthusiastic about the drama possibilities. It was all upbeat but almost unnecessary for if anybody knew about the Plowden and Newsome Reports and the value of a residential experience for children, it was teachers. But CHET was introducing itself, it would have so many advantages over Wick Court, much greater space, woods and fields that actually belonged to the estate and would always be accessible, buildings that could be designated for art and pottery, the great barn with its walls of enormous stone blocks, its great beams and stage. Sitting there those teachers could not fail to be impressed. There would be a huge dining room next door, a large kitchen and lounge. The plans were clear, the opportunities obvious.

Little Crosby had seen many changes in the past six centuries, but on the whole it had been a conservative place. The proposed Crosby Hall Educational Trust and conversion of the stables into a Centre would be a bold initiative. Each generation of Blundells had carried on and developed traditions received from the past but this venture would be a departure from tradition, a departure, because the traditional way of life that had been carried on for centuries had come to an end and the needs of society had changed.

"The children would be a loss making commodity, numbers of them would have to be subsidised, a large bursary fund would be needed," said John Malthouse dolefully.

The fund had already been started, the target was 250 Chetfriends, expected to covenant £5 per month. This would realise £15,000 p.a. and together with tax relief would ensure an income for the Bursary Fund of £20,000. All school children receiving free school meals would be able to enjoy a week at Crosby Hall at half price.

Tom Massey-Lynch sat at a table, anxious to hand out Covenant forms but was under employed and the slight chill in the air was only dispelled when refreshments arrived, including wine. Gill, in those early years, was often caterer and hostess and on that occasion made 240 sandwiches.

We still had no Trust, no Trustees, and no structure for raising the huge sum of money that would be needed. Something providential had to happen and it turned out to be the unexpected and unannounced arrival of Tony Mould with two friends. They were interested in the pheasant shooting which would be starting again in the autumn and were waiting in the library, the magnificent bay-fronted room with huge windows and doors opening on to the lawn. It was lined almost to the ceiling with ancient tomes and lavishly decorated. When I entered the men were standing by the great French windows, with the light behind them, large intimidating shapes. They had come to talk about pheasants and Mark had been telling them about CHET. Tony's friends were definitely not interested in children, they might get in the way of pheasants, but Tony himself was. He had been listening carefully, a successful business man in Liverpool, President of the Liverpool University Council and a Justice of the Peace, he was widely respected. He came to lunch and accepted the role of a Trustee of a Trust not yet in existence. His acceptance was crucial. He immediately introduced the idea of CHET to the Chancellor of Liverpool University, Lord Leverhulme. They had both been involved in the affairs of the University for some years and knew each other well. It would be a real break through if Leverhulme also agreed to become a Trustee and Mark invited him to the Hall. He was a very wealthy man and supported many charities but was attracted to CHET because of the good use it would make of a country estate for the benefit of the community. He not only became a Trustee but offered financial help as well, and his name was enough to encourage the support of Lady Pilkington, Mary Creagh JP, OBE, Sir Christopher Hewetson and Peter Sutcliffe FRICS, all of whom were creating at last a Trust with a strong board of Trustees.

The fine 18th century stables were listed historic buildings and outline planning permission had to be obtained, which was not easy. The new entrance block we would require and the long corridor connecting the various parts of the Centre had to be in keeping. When permission was finally given, detailed plans were submitted to convert the 5m high stables into accommodation. It took time and endless meetings.

The proposed new Centre would have built-in bunk beds in each room, a wash basin, fitted cupboard, a new window cut in the massive wall, and under it a window seat and radiator. Winstanleys of St Helens were offered the contract at £573,460. We now had a target but would need a year to raise the money.

It was difficult at first to persuade the wealthy in the land that the Blundells were indeed engaged on a worthwhile charitable venture. A fund-raising dinner took place on 25 June for some key business men and their wives. The meal, the wine and the speeches were applauded, but there was no hurry to fill in covenant forms in support of the project. We hoped to find a few major donors prepared to 'prime the pump' with substantial amounts of money and only then, when we had reached half the total needed, or at least £250,000, would we launch a Public Appeal. Mark visited the Duke of Westminster at his Cheshire home and they dined at opposite ends of a long dining table, while the butler brought the Duke a tin of coca-cola on a silver tray. The duke, however, was leaving for his estates in Scotland, so the Duchess came to lunch with us. She was tall and graceful, "Call me Tally," she said, and talked about the work she was doing for young people in the stables of *their* estate. She had an exotic lineage, related to Pushkin and a Prince Michael, but she enjoyed Gill's salmon gateau. It was an interesting occasion but yielded no results.

The strategy, however, eventually succeeded. The Blundell's pledged £40,000, Lord Leverhulme £25,000, Lord Hylton £25,000, but it was only after writing numerous letters to Charitable Trusts and visits from the secretaries of one or two of them that we achieved any further substantial sums. In October Mark was in deepest gloom but by January 1989 larger sums began to arrive. The breakthrough came with £50,000 from the Tudor Trust. By April the building fund had reached £287,500 and Lord Leverhulme launched the planned Public Appeal with a speech in the crowded barn. We had come half way and now hoped for public support, but although CHET certainly had publicity and general goodwill it was probably vain to hope that a public appeal would make much difference to the fund raising.

More Trusts began to respond and in November, Winstanleys began the building work. The stables were quickly gutted and the whole area looked like an immense tithe-barn, with ancient oak rafters in the ceiling and magnificent stone walls all round. The stable nearest to the barn itself would remain untouched with its three huge mangers, original windows, door and high ceiling. This area, about 7m by 9m would be the dining room. The rest of the huge space would be turned into a kitchen and bedrooms on two floors.

The hexagonal threshing floor was gutted and rebuilt using the original brick and timbers. It was to have a new split level floor and large windows on to the cobbled yard with window seats all round. The old paint shop would be rebuilt into an art studio.

By April 1990 the main inside work on the stables had been completed and it was time to build on the long flagstone connecting corridor and the entrance block. On 4 May, Viscount Leverhulme laid the Foundation stone of the Crosby Hall Educational Centre to a fanfare of trumpets and the popping of champagne corks. 140 supporters of CHET were present including the Lord Lieutenant of Merseyside, the deputy Mayor of Crosby, two Bishops, the Moderator of the Methodists, and all the

Trustees. A bevy of helpers, organised by Gill, prepared a mountain of finger food. It was a day of brilliant sunshine and included the public presentation of substantial donations by the Country Landowners Association and the Ford Motor Company. The benefactors of CHET now included 57 trusts, 55 businesses and over 200 individuals and since the launch in April 1989 a further £350,000 had been raised. The fund-raising events put on at the Hall included an Edwardian evening by Chesterfield school, a Carol Concert and the first Art Exhibition in the great barn. Outside in the Crosby Hall gardens, never previously opened to the public, Midsummer Nights Dream was the first of many plays to be performed in successive years, and it did not rain.

All seemed well but, indeed, all was not well. No one could have guessed listening to the speeches, full of high hopes and congratulations, that all was not well in May, that even Lord Leverhulme's magic touch with the trowel was premature, that the bugles could have sounded a false note. Incredibly the quantity surveyors had let us down not by a small margin but substantially. The original figure of £573,460 had been revised upwards to £867,500. There was a gap of £294,000. We had raised £64,000 more than the original target but £230,000 still had to be found.

Unaware of the crisis, the building work continued and would end in November but the payment cheques were due each month. There was no alternative but to return to the big donors and, like Oliver Twist, ask for more. The summer months were extremely anxious. Mark wrote personal letters as Chairman of the Trustees and the break through came when the Tudor Trust gave us another £50,000. By the time the year was out we had reached £900,000, which included a further £120,000 from the Blundell family. The crisis was over.

Chapter 30
Drama at Callow

Meanwhile my mother had reached the point when she wanted nothing more than to return to Callow to die. She had attempted to die several times but had always been thwarted by the doctor and those around her. Maybe, she thought, Wick Court is not the right place for such an important event to happen and she should go back to Callow, her old home. It had been for many years a magical place for all of us, situated on the old Hereford road, about 800ft above Monmouth town, the white house standing out against a background of woods. The move was an imperious and urgent request and Gill drove down from Liverpool to bring her home with as much luggage as could be crammed into the car. Once there, mother decided not to die just yet, but Callow house itself was in disarray, so she was made as comfortable as possible in the 'Shack' - until better provision could be found. She needed to be looked after and Robin offered us the farmhouse, but when she was moved there unexpectedly and hurriedly, there was still nobody to look after her. Desperately Gill drove down again from Liverpool, arrived at midnight and found mother freezing cold and unable to find the bathroom. Gill stayed to care for her for the next seven months. I began to commute between Callow and Liverpool.

Fifteen years had now passed since Callow began to fall apart, both as a home and as a community. I was involved to my cost at the beginning, but afterwards Gill and I became absorbed in our own lives at Shoscombe and Wick and much of the story passed us by. Callow was a place of stark contrasts, extreme beauty, enormous generosity, but later on great pain. The collapse began after the death of my father in 1967. We all became disorientated, our mother, totally devastated. It was as though the ship of state had become rudderless. She left everything intact at the time, dad's clothes still hanging over the bedroom chair, three brothers with wives and children living on the hill, together with various members of a 'second family,' orphans that our parents had cared for. It was a complex situation that needed wise direction. We are all children of our time and the time in which we lived had become materialistic and even hedonistic and Callow had lost its defences. Perhaps, with our wild and wonderful mother, reaching maturity was likely to be painful.

> *'The drive rose steeply from a coniferous valley past a lovely green meadow and through old beech trees. It was early April and the beeches were throwing a veil of green over the potholes to trap an unwary wheel. As I reached the top of the drive the view straight ahead was breathtaking. The ground fell steeply away and you could just see Monmouth in the fertile valley some hundreds of feet below. Beyond, were rolling hills, only their outlines visible in the morning light.'*

Thus wrote Johanna who became Robin's second wife in the summer of 1989 and began to transform once again our beloved Callow. It was such a dramatic year; the Berlin wall came down, tanks crushed the students in Tianamen Square, Nelson Mandela walked free.

"I had known Robin always in spotless white breeches, knee length boots, an elegant long black hunting coat and a top hat."

Johanna's arrival at Callow changed everything. We had glimpsed the possibilities earlier at Wick Court. We had organised a huge 88th birthday party for mother in the gardens there in June 1986. Robin came accompanied by Johanna and a case of champagne. We began drinking it in mother's large book-lined room at 11 am. It was a beautiful summer's day which was fortunate indeed as 173 family members and friends arrived and everybody could be outside. The food and drink was laid out on trestle tables in the shade of enormous, centuries old, yew trees and the Arran Pilots band played brilliantly while mother rocked gently and happily on her swing chair surrounded by bouquets of flowers. There was dancing 'till late on the lawn.

But that was four years earlier. Now she was back on the hill, living in the farmhouse with a big room, her own bathroom, and a wonderful view towards the Brecon Beacons. We occupied the rest of the house and Jessica too had a large bedroom. It was strange returning to the hill but it had become inevitable. By Christmas the new CHET centre was completed and Gill came to Crosby Hall and joined me on 1 January 1991.

'We looked round the Centre, it is really quite magnificent. The children will love it,' she wrote.

On the following day 2 January, Geoff Prest was appointed the first Director. We shared the office in the house until the new CHET office was ready.

Jessica, now living in the farmhouse, was attending the Cathedral School in Hereford for her 6th form 'A' level studies. She was able to ride horses at Callow which she loved and she learnt to play the saxophone. It was good having her with us even though she was breaking free and sparks were already beginning to fly.

I told Jessica I was not prepared to pay for driving lessons if she was not prepared to do her school work. She was 17 and not pleased. I could see what I thought was going to happen, Jessica would have an accident and smash the car up, so I was not surprised when she arrived home one evening with a tarpaulin draped over the back. When I lifted it, the whole of the back of the car was missing, she had been in collision with a bus and of course it was not her fault. Gill, on the other hand, was full of admiration for Jessica because she had driven home on only two wheels, but I was cross that she had been lent the car in the first place. It was a relief to wake up. It was the beginning of a difficult year and a half. Jessica had a high IQ and could have done very well in her 'A' levels but she chose not to. Emotionally it was like winter storms, occasional shafts of sunlight breaking through. One longed for more sunshine.

Education means bringing out and developing the potential of a child and discovering what that unique potential might be. Its task is to open doors for children, to excite their imagination, to inspire them and encourage creative activity. Children cannot develop if they are too submissive and dependent, too bound by rules and regulations, too anxious for rewards or frightened by sanctions. A framework of order is needed but not too much.

Perhaps that was why Jessica had rung up Gill one day from her strict regimented Convent school and said,

"I know I am a rebel and I am ashamed of it," and Gill was wise enough to answer her distress with,

"Don't worry darling, you have to be a rebel if you are going to change the world."

A certain amount of freedom, even freedom to go wrong, is essential to the growth of personality and individuality.

Chapter 31
Princess Margaret

On Wednesday, 8 May, the official ceremonial opening of the Crosby Hall Educational Centre was due to take place. I had been at Callow at the weekend and Gill and I drove up together on the Sunday to spend two days in hectic preparation, Gill taking charge again of the finger food for the 200 guests expected. Caterers were called in to prepare the royal lunch that would be served in the dining room of the Hall. The weather was a worry. For several days there had been no sun and we had been driven back into winter clothes by a cold north easterly. But on the day itself we woke with some astonishment to bright sunshine and a blue, cloudless sky.

For the past week police and security staff had been visiting Crosby Hall and now that the day of the Grand Opening had arrived, they were there in force. Gill wrote: 'We were all still in bed when a posse of the Special Branch began knocking loudly at the back door, sending Bessie, the black Labrador, frantic with excitement. The men moved round to the front of the house where a conference appeared to be taking place. Finally an authoritative voice announced in a slow drawl: "Gentlemen, I would suggest there is no one up yet in this house." Our bedroom windows looked over the front of the house. The policemen moved away, their heavy boots crunching the gravel and we hurriedly dressed. It was only 8 a.m. and the Opening would not happen before noon. At that exact time, 12 o'clock, Princess Margaret arrived in a motorcade of white limousines. With her came her equerry, Lord Napier, her Lady in Waiting, the Honourable Mrs.Whitehead, the Mayor of Sefton, Beryl Lamont, the Lord Lieutenant of Merseyside, Henry Cotton and his wife, and numerous members of the police and security forces. The diminutive princess was dressed in a bright pink fitted coat and blue velvet toque with a diamond brooch. She wore blue sandals with 4 inch heels which brought her up to about 5ft in height.

The cars had stopped in a line outside the entrance block of CHET. Mark was at the door, the rest of us were waiting in the hallway, the trustees, the architect, the surveyor, the builders, Geoffrey Prest, his wife, Sheila, and ourselves. Mark introduced Her Royal Highness to each in turn. There followed a tour of the Centre and then Princess Margaret wanted to see the mini-farm and the adventure playground but she could not manage the cobbles in her high heels. She summoned a car and told me to jump in too and we drove slowly the hundred yards to the farm. Her friend the Countess so-and-so had opened her farm to city children.

"They watched the cows being milked," she said "but when they were asked what they thought about it replied, 'it was disgusting'."

The Princess thought that was very funny. She liked the various animals we had collected, however, sheep, goats, chickens, rabbits. She also thought the Royal Engineers had done a good job building the 'confidence course' as we liked to call the assault course, made up of ropes, ladders, bridges and platforms among the pine trees. It was, in fact, a very superior adventure playground.

The car was waiting and we travelled back in style to where Mark Blundell was waiting. The great moment had come. The Princess was ushered through a crowded barn of chattering people to the stage. Her task was to pull a string and reveal a plaque. Mark was tall and the princess looked smaller than ever. He made a short speech and was clapped, she was clapped too when she pulled the string and signed the Visitors Book, 'Margaret'. The motorcade now collected its various passengers and sped round to the front of the Manor House. All the loyal Chetfriends and other supporters now jostled their way into the dining hall for platters of food and glasses of wine. We almost wished we were there too. We had all walked to the Hall and arrived there before the cars. Now we stood around untidily while the important people were ushered in. Ancestors looked on from large oil paintings. Two groups of halberds or lances stood either side of the inner hall doors adding a baronial touch. Beyond in the main hall, a fine staircase climbed up to a wide landing and all around were the portraits of more ancestors and the massive antlers of a moose.

Everyone moved from the hall into the library. Mark's beautiful wife, Suzanne, and their daughters, Alexandra and Isabel, were introduced to the Princess. Drinks were offered but Her Royal Highness made for the French windows and drew out from her handbag the royal cigarette holder, almost a foot long.

The library had double doors which opened into a panelled dining room. There were twelve chairs round a polished dark wood table and the Blundell crested family silver was making a rare appearance and gleaming at the place settings. There were flowers too, as there had been in profusion in the Centre. The princess sat between Mark and the Lord Lieutenant of Merseyside. I was further down the table but could hear the stilted conversation. Mark tried to educate Her Royal Highness who was not really interested. She ate her quail's eggs in mayonnaise, decorated with tiny red and yellow tomatoes on a couple of watercress leaves, slowly. I was sitting next to the Honourable Mrs Whitehead who told me a sad story about how much money her husband had lost at Lloyds. Then we talked about animals. I suggested that horses were designed to be ridden whereas cows were not. She was ready to agree whereas Mark, who was probably finding conversation difficult with her Royal Highness, interrupted to disagree. The idea of a clear and definite design did not fit in with his convictions concerning evolution. The next course came slowly and Her Royal Highness showed signs of impatience. The menu had been agreed with her in advance and she may have been looking forward to the white fish. It is more likely however, she was looking forward to another cigarette. She pushed the fish almost untouched to one side and out came the long cigarette holder. Would she like coffee? Yes, she would. In no time she was on her feet ready to move. We had all to miss out both on the coffee and the cheese.

"I was particularly looking forward to the cheese," Lord Napier muttered gloomily to Gill.

Princess Margaret was restless. She had to go on to Bootle to open the new Magistrates Courts there, and only after that would be allowed to go home. One did not get the impression that she really enjoyed her official duties.

The Centre was now becoming fully booked and fully staffed. Di Brennan became Geoff's assistant in the office and her expertise and energy did much in the next two years to establish CHET. Brian and Hester in the barn House hardly noticed the crowds of children who came and went and, if they heard them laughing and shouting beyond the high garden walls, enjoyed the realisation that kids from Bootle and other parts of the city were having a good time.

The massive walls round the Barn house gardens had chimneys running through them which could be heated and provide protection to the pear trees against winter frosts. Bob Wright turned the old boiler house on the other side of the wall into a museum. This became quickly overcrowded and had to be transferred to an old farm building in the village where it mushroomed into an extraordinary and unique record of life on the estate in past centuries. From then on learning about the past became part of the experience of staying in the Centre.

On 1 June, a Saturday, there had been a farewell party for us at Crosby Hall. It took place in the Centre and about 60 people came. There were lots of speeches and lots of food and wine. One of the great experiences for us had been the discovery of such warmth and welcome from Lancashire people. We made life-long friends. It was astonishing too what generous support was given to CHET and how many Chetfriends it was possible to enrol, over 200 by the time we left. I became a Trustee then and returned whenever I could.

Chapter 32
Illusion and Loss

Living in the farmhouse at Callow Hill with such magnificent scenery all around us, with a kitchen garden to tend and flowers around the house, with 'grandma' mostly in bed and Jessica late for her bus, with small people in the big house and our five small grandchildren coming and going, with all the friends and well known faces in well-loved Monmouth town, there was plenty to occupy our lives, but storm clouds as well.

Jessica edged her way out of education altogether. She had begun her second year of 6th form studies at the Cathedral School with great reluctance. She was 18 and more interested in raves and all night parties. We tried to restrict her extra-school activities to week-ends only but found ourselves circumvented. "You are more interested in my education than in me," she would say. 'Me' wanted to enjoy the excitements of life, not after 'A' levels, which she did not think she would ever need, but *now,* and because she was Jessica, not only intelligent but forceful, she got her way. She brought home friends who were not stressed out about exams; friends like Steve, Arran, Kimmo, Paul, and spent time with a DJ called Bungy. So Jessica got herself thrown out of the classroom, suspended for 10 days on 7 November and then permanently in January. Twice Gill and I were called up before the headmaster, Mr Tomlinson, warned first and then politely expelled. He made it clear that though he was speaking of Jessica we were the ones misbehaving. Beside Mr Tomlinson stood Mrs Bigley, the tutor, and Mrs Miles the housemistress. They behaved rather like three magistrates.

"She doesn't fit into the school system," they said solemnly.

"But we will correct her essays and write comments if she sends her work in by post." She had signed on for the examinations and was entitled to sit them if she did the required essays and coursework in advance. It was actually what she had asked for in October. "Ask the head," she said, "to let me study in Egypt and return for the exams."

I need not bother you with the story of how, why, or what she was doing in Egypt at Christmas time, although it included galloping past the pyramids on an Arab stallion at midnight, no wonder she found school boring..

In late January 1992, Jessica edged her way out of her home as well. She simply did not come back from Hereford and we did not know where she was. Lucy Eyre, the only school friend she kept in touch with, helped. I rang a number and a voice said, "Try 10 Victoria Street." It was a dingy house in poor repair. Mark let me in and introduced me to Paul, both very friendly, but they kept me in the corridor and would not let me go further. I could hear much laughter and conversation in the back room and could pick out Jessica's voice quite clearly. I told the boys I would like to see Jessica and one of them returned to the back room. There was an immediate silence, the sort of silence that follows the arrival of the police. He came back into the passage and said that Jessica did not want to see me. We talked about her 'A' level studies and both boys agreed that she ought to finish the course and they would encourage her to do her essays. Mark said,

"She fits in very well here." Eventually, he added, "we are hoping to move out of here and rent a farmhouse."

It made up a little for not seeing Jessica that they really tried to be helpful. It was the alternative world that we had first encountered at Wick Court. The next morning Jessica rang up and we talked.

For all the turmoil that Jessica's presence in the house had caused us, interspersed with wonderful days, her absence left a void. She came and went, communicating spasmodically, and we had a party for her 18th birthday, a magnificent cake all ready with 18 candles, a saxophone and a number of presents. Angie and Merilyn came and all the grandchildren but no Jessica. At 5.30 pm she rang up and asked about buses. There were no buses. I went to fetch her. Somehow it seemed to be a turning point. We loved her so much and it was a good party, but after she had blown out her candles and kissed everybody she returned to Hereford. The idea that she might change the world – for the better – might have to be postponed.

Meanwhile I let the past interrupt my life. I slept in the same bed and wrote notes at the same desk, overlooking the same garden. The pictures had not changed either and the little gas fire was still there. Nothing had changed and it was really hard to believe that 28 years had passed. If I had stayed in Holywell I might never have moved.

Bridget suffered from angina now. As you know she had never bothered about her appearance, her hair was wispier and greyer and her face wrinkled but her laugh was exactly the same. No end of priests had come and gone. She served them all faithfully but could not go any longer to the well. The hill was too much.

"Oh," she said, "why can't you come back and stay forever."

It was such a joy being in the old place for a few days, but the parish was sad. Only David Schwarz was bravely optimistic and would achieve a lot eventually to boost morale. It was no pleasure at the time seeing the state of the Well. It was tidier, aesthetically more beautiful, but it was as though someone had spent all their money on cosmetics. Mrs Graham, the old 'battle axe,' heard I was in town and came to see me. She reminded me of the day her eldest son lay in his coffin and she wanted to press £10 into my hands. When I refused her eyes filled with tears and I embraced her. She was unsteady now on her feet. I asked about Hilary and her Inskip children.

"They've all gone, nothing for them here." and I imagined those 11 small boys scattered around Britain producing progeny, more wild redheads.

I had some less emotional meetings with others in the parish but it was the Well that had drawn me back, the Well and Bridget. I wanted to discover again that strange unaccountable relationship with the spiritual world I had discovered in the crypt and in the cold waters of the spring. Perhaps St Winefride could do something about the chaotic state of Yugoslavia for that was very much on my mind. If not, perhaps she could help *me* to do something. I bathed in the well at the height of the pilgrimage season for almost the whole fortnight entirely alone and felt enormously sad.

If the presbytery had not changed, the town had. The large convent next door to the church had disappeared and become a car park. The nuns had evaporated, except for Sister Catherine, the headmistress of the Convent School, and sister Gemma from the Hospice. They were living in a little house called, St. Beuno's, halfway up Whitford Street. It was good to talk to them, both frail but still lively. Living opposite were Francis and Mary Hanson; Francis who had hidden the crutches, and pulled down the last of the bathing cubicles. I was not giving myself an easy time returning to the parish – too much to lament. One should always go on rather than back.

I crossed over to Caldey Island again in November. The sea was rough and it was bitterly cold, so was the monastery. I shivered in the old guest wing until summoned to the evening meal. After the sung Grace everybody carried a steaming bowl of vegetables and a hunk of bread to their place at the refectory table. There was a log fire but it seemed to make little difference to the temperature and the dozen or so monks gave the impression that they were very hungry. Their Spartan life, diet of vegetables, unheated monastery and unsocial hours, bed at 8.30pm on parade at 3.30am, is not a life to choose lightly. It was not surprising there were few monks. Indeed, it was surprising there were any. Such a life of sacrifice, of total giving of oneself, had to be rewarded on a different plane to the life most of us know and delight in. After the meal I walked with them to the Chapel and shared in the final prayer of the day and the very moving chant of the Regina Coeli.

I did not get up when the bell tolled at 3.30 am. In the sub arctic temperature of the place it had been almost impossible to get warm and to get to sleep. After Mass and breakfast Brother Robert called for me and we walked up the hill to the ancient Priory. The castellated mediaeval monastery was built like a fortress with enormous walls which are reflected in the pond in front despite the scaffolding. Inside, the neglect of centuries had taken its toll but it was still possible to identify the refectory, the kitchen, the parlour and the dormitory area. St Illtyd's church next door had a leaning spire (a lookout for pirates), a sanctuary with a pebbled floor and walls that tapered gradually until they met forming a Celtic arch. In a corner was a large memorial stone with an Ogham inscription dating from the 6th century and a Latin inscription, added a century later. It was very likely that Abbot Pyro established a monastic cell on Caldey Island in the 6th century and explained why Ynys Pyr was still the Welsh name for the island.

The monastery had an inner courtyard or garth, a gatehouse with a room over it. It even had a garderobe, or loo. Brother Robert was aware that if the old monastery were restored it could present the religious life of the monks in a dramatic and interesting fashion using videos, models, photographs and history. An example of the history was the record that Abbot Whyting of Glastonbury sent brother 'A' with two sacks of alter plate and diverse other vessels mostly of gold to the island to escape the rapacious hands of Henry VIII but when the brother heard that the king's men were approaching the island, he buried the two sacks deep in a wall. They were never found. Restoring the ancient monastery could have been an exciting project, could have been, but for the tragedy taking place in Europe which pushed the idea sadly out of sight.

Chapter 33
The Bosnia Disaster

A few brave journalists, Ed Vulliamy in particular, had managed to get news and pictures of what was going on in Bosnia published. They were shocking.

It became very clear that once Tito was safely dead, two rapacious leaders in the six autonomous provinces of Yugoslavia had been secretly planning to re-design the Balkan map. They would divide their large mountainous neighbour between them and create a Greater Serbia and a Greater Croatia. Bosnia would cease to exist. The evil of nationalism, nurtured carefully through the media, whipped up by fiery speeches, brought Slobodan Milosevic to power in Serbia and the ferment in Serbia promoted the cause of nationalism in Croatia where the HDZ party and Franjo Tudjman came to power. The two megalomaniacs did not, however, see eye to eye completely.

Milosevic had control of the Yugoslav army and had purged it of dissident generals. In 1991 he decided to forget any vague agreement he had with Tudjman and annex large chunks of Croatia. It was not a sudden inspiration. Milosevic was not capable of honest dealings with anyone. He had been supplying the Serbs of the Krajina, half a million of them in a border country that lay between Bosnia and Croatia, with arms, money and propaganda for months. In the spring of 1991 the insurrection began, supported by the army under the command of the newly appointed General Ratko Mladic. In no time the whole of the Krajina had been 'liberated.' In the autumn of the same year Serbian tanks and artillery pounded the Danubian port of Vukovar. It was a perfectly harmless innocent town but it happened to be the gateway to the rich farming land of Slavonia. Milosevic thought it his duty to 'rescue' the thousands of Serbs stranded in Slavonia. They had been happy for generations, like the Vlach Serbs in the Krajina, and did not need to be rescued, but Milosevic's tanks succeeded and by the end of 1991 one third of Croatia was controlled by the Serbs.

The next stage of the plan was to link up these isolated chunks of Greater Serbia with the mother country. That would mean dismembering Bosnia.

Europe appeared to be bewildered by the destruction of a large part of Croatia and the huge refugee problem that resulted. Lord Carrington chaired an international conference at The Hague and produced a peace plan. It was accepted by all the presidents of all the other regions of Yugoslavia, Slovenia, Montenegro, Croatia, Bosnia, Macedonia, but not by Milosevic. He had his own agenda and it was not complete. The United Nations imposed an arms embargo on the whole of Yugoslavia and sent a peace keeping force to monitor the frozen battle lines.

Three months of partial peace followed while the world learnt more about Milosovic and held its breath. Alija Izetbegovic, president of Bosnia, was more worried than most. For more than a year he had seen troops and armour pass through his country and been powerless to intervene. He was more of an idealist and philosopher than a practical politician. When the blitzkrieg began against his own people, he was aghast. He could not take in the depth of Evil that was suddenly unleashed. The day chosen was 1 April, 1992, not a day for all fools but for all madmen specially selected and trained to murder and terrorise. The disciplined Yugoslav army although purged of dissident officers was not considered up to the job that Milosevic had in mind in Bosnia. He revived the Chetnicks, banned by Tito. They were the ruthless paramilitaries of an earlier age. He encouraged the rabid nationalist, Vojislav Seselj, to conscript and train the White Eagles and put Zeljko Raznatovic (Arkan) a top criminal from Belgrade's underworld in charge of the new, ruthless volunteer force, known as 'The Tigers.' It was these paramilitaries specially trained for months, many offered amnesty from prison, who crossed the Drina River from Serbia on 1 April and devastated the defenceless river towns of Bijelina and Zvornik. They were not fighting a war; they were butchering men, women and children. Those they did not catch and kill, fled. Both towns were 'ethnically cleansed' of Bosnian Moslems in three days. Seselj arrived in Zvornik and said:

"The operation was planned in Belgrade; it had been prepared for a long time. It wasn't carried out in any nervous fashion; everything was well organised and implemented."

Val Newton rang up from Carmarthen. At one time she was the treasurer of the Newcastle Emlyn parish council. Her husband, Bob, had taken early retirement and put his money into a bus. They planned to drive it loaded with food and blankets for the refugees pouring into Rijeka which is a seaside port in Croatia. They planned to go with a Pentecostal bus in January. Would we go too?

"But we have no bus."

"You could hire a van."

In December 1992 we had a meeting in the Lord Mayor's parlour in Monmouth town hall. Seventeen people turned up from the Baptist, Anglican and Catholic churches. It was immediately obvious that a great many people cared deeply about what was happening in Yugoslavia.

"Of course we can hire a van."

"Of course we can collect several tons of food and blankets."

Somebody had an empty shop in town for collecting, packing and weighing the load and it all began to happen. Departure date, 29 January, our load to meet up with the buses at the Severn Bridge service station at midnight. By the third week of January we had almost 3 tons of food but still no van.

"We can't hire you anything. You are going to a war zone."

"Our insurance will only cover you into Austria, after that if anything happens you have to bear the whole cost."

"Sorry, no van."

We put an advert in the Argus. Incredibly, we were offered a vehicle and I went over to Abergavenny to see it. It was an old post office van, equipped with a window from which telegraph poles once protruded.

"It will take three and a half tons," said the owner, hopefully.

It had a notice on the dashboard saying two and a half tons preferred weight.

"That's just a post office precaution," said the owner.

"It's got six wheels and is built like a tank. How about £300? Who knows if you will ever come back?"

It had a powerful diesel engine which made a satisfying roar and I drove it home. £300 would be our contribution to the trip which still seemed unreal but was now unstoppable.

When we came to load the van we could not bear to leave any boxes behind. We ended up carrying closer to 4 tons. Paul Strathern, out of his element and worried lest he couldn't loosen the wheel nuts (if we had a puncture) set about loosening the wheel nuts, 'just a fraction.' I could see catastrophe looming and was inclined to send the van off with my nephew, Saul David and Paul. Gill wouldn't hear of it.

"You can't start something like this and then back out," she said.

Sheepishly I took the wheel and drove the monster down the twisting Wye Valley road to Chepstow, aware of the weight, aware of the steep drop into the river and wondering why it had to start like this in the middle of the night. We arrived on time, no sign of the buses. There was a moon and it was bitterly cold. At 1am the two buses arrived unrepentant and the drivers eyed the post office van suspiciously.

"We want to travel at 60 mph," they said.

"No trouble," I replied, but I wasn't too sure the van would agree.

One of the buses, owned by the Pentecostal church, was carrying hopeful slogans like 'Jesus Saves' and was stuffed with potatoes. The drivers worked for a Swansea bus company. Val and Bill were in the second bus which was loaded like ours with boxes of food and blankets. We headed for Ramsgate and caught the Sally ferry to Dunkirk at 7 am. The buses were charged only £35, return fare, because the company made its money out of the passengers and did not seem to mind that the passengers had turned into potatoes, food and blankets. The Yellow Peril, as we nicknamed the post office van, was charged £107 return. We all enjoyed a free meal with free wine and sat with oily HGV drivers in a special section of the restaurant.

We followed the buses through Belgium and Germany and managed to keep up. Ice formed on the windscreen and we slept the night in sleeping bags, fully clothed. The next night, at Illiria Bistrica in Slovenia, the feared disaster struck. For miles the road had been a succession of hairpin bends and suddenly the van began to shudder violently. We had just reached a small town and could do no more than stagger into a parking lot outside a shop. The buses stopped as well, it was close to another midnight. Both right hand rear wheels were about to fall off.

"They're shot," said the bus drivers gloomily.

We abandoned the van and climbed into one of the buses in total silence. The little town was sound asleep.

Val and Bob had with them a Croat bus driver who had married a Welsh girl and lived in Swansea. He was invaluable. He was also inevitably partisan, all the food and blankets were destined for his own people, the Croat refugees. We had a different agenda with no idea how to carry it out, our load was stuck just over the border, locked up but the flimsy padlocks would present no problem to thieves.

We arrived in Rijeka in the early hours of Sunday morning and slept in the back of the Carmarthen bus until the sun was up and the bells tolled for Mass. The Catholic charity, Caritas, directed us to their depot which was in a seedy area of dockland. The enormous double doors rolled back to reveal six elderly men sitting in the cavernous interior at a large table littered with bottles of plum brandy (Slivovic). They appeared to be very happy and offered us glasses of the fiery liquid and then, with a lot of noise and banter, unloaded the five tons of Pembrokeshire potatoes into the empty warehouse and then attacked the Carmarthen bus with equal gusto.

The Swansea bus drivers now became our stalwart friends and we hurried back to the Slovenian border in their bus, having borrowed the Croat bus driver as interpreter. The border guards waved the empty bus through. Nobody could remember exactly where we had dumped the van but we found it at last, untouched and, in high spirits, we transferred the load to the bus, the drivers complained that we must have had at least four tons on board. It was now Sunday afternoon and it just so happened that the largest lorry repair works in Slovenia was a couple of hundred yards away. If we were destined to break down anywhere it had to be in Illiria Bistrica. The van limped round there shuddering mightily but, of course, the works were locked up, silent, no one around. Then a grey faced elderly watchman peered out of the gatehouse, looked at the post office van and promised to have it fixed by Tuesday. We left him a family box of goodies by way of encouragement. Back at the border the Croat driver took charge of the papers and duly assigned the goods to Caritas. This would fox the customs, two lots of forms for the same vehicle but I had no wish to deliver our load into the Caritas warehouse.

We returned to the huge car park in Rijeka, a river on one side of it, a canal full of small boats on the other, all of it now in bright sunshine, and the Kontinental Hotel well placed for coffee, phone calls and loos. Beyond the canal, tall imperial buildings suggested past splendour. We had time to investigate the city and found it full of Italian and Hapsburg classical houses with large windows, shutters and balconies and delightful piazzas. They were unloading fish in the harbour and the market was busy. Had there been no piles of worthless bank notes floating in the fountains or sunk to the bottom like dead leaves one might have thought all was well. I changed a £1 note for 600 dinars. The next day I could have had 650.

Back in the car park a stocky man was waiting and beside him a tall girl with a shock of black hair, he was Selma's father, Safet, and the girl was Alida, who spoke good English. Selma, herself, was a refugee in England, and had ended up at Callow looking after Robin and Johanna's little daughter, hence the connection. Events now acquired their own logic. Selma's parents knew at least a hundred families in their immediate neighbourhood who had fled from Bosnia. Several hundred more families were stranded in a dilapidated ex-army camp on the hillside miles from anywhere. Ibrahim, director of Merhamet (the Muslim Red Crescent), followed us around like a shadow, repeating a kind of mantra, "the camp does not need help, I need it more. I have seven hundred families to feed tomorrow and have nothing for them except floor" (he meant flour).

What happened that Monday seems like a miracle now. We climbed the mountainside to the decaying huts lined up at the end of a perilous dirt track and were quickly surrounded by a crowd of women and children. Old men watched from a distance. We gave all the children cartons of Ribena and every family a box of food and a blanket, then, wearied already, returned to Safet's house to find a mob of people blocking the road; peasant women with headscarves, numerous children, a few older men. They seemed like a lost people, silent and depressed. Unloading began at once, the men making a chain, then the queue formed, names and numbers in each family were recorded. A dozen helpers broke open boxes, arranged and selected, shared out food and clothes. 96 families took away up to ten kilos each. There was excitement and euphoria. After all that we still had almost two tons for Ibrahim, and that same evening the exhausted bus drivers unloaded it all into his warehouse which was near the end of a cobbled road and close to the river. Just beyond the warehouse was a paper factory. Its effluent often turned the river white. The warehouse belonged to the factory and the next morning the whole road outside it was congested with hundreds of people in drab clothes. We watched them enter the warehouse in single file past hefty doorkeepers, saw them sign at a desk, their names ticked off in a huge register, and move on to collect their rations for the month from another table. No noise, no hassle, each one collected a small bottle of oil, a sachet of sugar, a tin of beef or fish, a bag of beans and a portion of flour. Quantities were strictly rationed and related to the size of the family. Ibrahim had been in the warehouse since 5 am, pouring oil into small bottles and the sugar into paper sachets. It was pitifully little but if we had not arrived they would only have had flour.

We travelled back to Illiria Bistrica in the evangelical bus to find the van repaired as promised and ready to go. It had two shining back wheels but the great workshops were a German subsidiary, the two Swansea bus drivers looked at them doubtfully:

"They are MAN wheels," they said in unison.

"They won't take your spare."

This was ominous but not immediately critical. We drove home fast. The bus drivers had to be back at work.

It was crisis time in the Mayor's parlour. The committee were delighted that all their hard work had been worthwhile but they were hesitant and less than delighted at the suggestion that they continue collecting food,

"Impractical," they said. "How do we get it there?"

I drove the van back to its owner in Abergavenny who was also less than delighted to find it had a new kind of wheel.

"What happens if I get a puncture?" he asked.

"Not very likely," I replied. "It has new tyres."

But I could not ask to hire it again. There now seemed to be an unbridgeable gap between reality, the plight of the refugees, and the possibility of helping them, but unexpectedly the Rotarians of Cardiff were planning a massive convoy to go to Zagreb on March 11. We invited the organizers Mike Rye and Basil Braine, to supper and came to an agreement that, if I went along as a driver I could go to Rijecka instead of Zagreb and Mike would follow with six or seven vehicles, out of the 17 booked on the convoy.

On Friday morning 11 March a Vauxhall saloon car came up our drive, it was owned by a nurse who wore an outsize green t-shirt and had thick glasses and short fuzzy hair, I was to be her co-driver. Gill took one look at her and was no longer worried. We left for Cardiff where the rest of the drivers were collected in the conference room of the Central Police Station. They were all wearing green t-shirts with a Welsh dragon on the front and 'Happiness is Helping Others,' scrawled across the back. Worse still, huge A3 size, bright red hearts were dished out to the drivers to be stuck on the front and back of each vehicle. It was to be a humanitarian effort that everyone should know about so the place was humming with reporters and television cameras and everybody congratulated everybody else, the Mayor, the Police Chief, the Organisers.

Outside, the vehicles were lined up ranging in size from a ten ton lorry to our Vauxhall saloon car with half a ton of medicines. My attention, however, was distracted. The yellow Post Office van was lined up with the rest. I could not believe my eyes and looked at the registration number, OAX 402X, the same van. It was being driven by two impressive Rotarians in green 'T' shirts. One had a pilot's licence and took to the air whenever he had a chance; the other was the manager of a supermarket. They knew about engines.

"It's ticking over like a dream," they said, sitting smugly in the cab ready to go.

I played the innocent.

"You have an odd wheel," I said staring at the back wheel.

"What?" they said, jumping out of the cab.

"It's German, I think, probably MAN."

They made unprintable comments and stomped around. It was the first time they were aware that a puncture in that wheel could be a problem.

"Didn't the owner tell you?" I asked.

"He bloody did not."

They went on stomping and swearing. I had spoilt their day.

"It's very unlikely you will get a puncture," I went on, comfortingly, "But I suggest you stay in sight of the rest of the convoy. You could be stuck for days, even weeks."

They looked at me sourly. Who was I? Then I told them how it got its German wheel and they were good enough to laugh, but they didn't sit in their cab looking quite so smug.

Moving out of Cardiff on to the M4 was stage-managed like a film set. A police car led the way, siren wailing, police motorcycles sped up and down pretending to be sheep dogs, cameras on bridges captured the progress of the raggle-taggle convoy for TV. It was surreal. Out on the M4 we were free, destined for Dover and the P&O ferry. It was hard to analyse motives but they certainly included sharing the distress of people displaced from their homes.

At the Slovenian border it was bitterly cold and the men slept the night on the benches and tables of a service station and Mike, the stressed co-ordinator had a nose bleed. The nurse joined the men. There was no room anyway for the two of us to kip in the car. We reached Rijeka on the evening of the next day and received a great welcome from Safet and Mensura, Selma's parents, but we had no food, only medicines for the children's hospital. Food would come the next day, I promised, but I put too much faith in Mike. On the following morning we were back in the car park waiting as arranged. At last a Renault van appeared bearing a huge red heart on its bonnet. It edged its way through the mass of parked cars slowly.

"Francis is my name," he said, dismounting from the cab.

"And I'm Olivia," his wife added, shaking her red hair and blinking in the sunshine.

"Where are the other vehicles that are supposed to be coming?" I asked.

"The rest of the convoy," Francis replied slowly and pedantically as though it wasn't important, "got lost in a ravine. We were all misdirected."

"We were at the back and saw what was happening," Olivia chipped in, "so we didn't go down - the RAVINE I mean," she added loudly, in case I hadn't understood.

Apparently a 10 ton lorry got stuck and blocked the only way out for everybody else. They were hours late into Zagreb and had to postpone meetings with the Mayor and TV interviews until the next morning. Francis, however, was not a proper Rotarian and opted out. It was hard to be grateful for his arrival and not display huge disappointment at the same time. Ibrahim had been waiting too. He had men in the warehouse ready to unload. His face showed his dismay. I was driven to say "I will come back in April," not knowing how that might be possible. It was clear that the whole of Francis and Olivia's food would be needed for the local distribution. This took place as planned the following afternoon and was as orderly as ever, though the number of families had jumped to 130. At the end of two hours everything had gone. Olivia and the nurse gave away their own coats. Francis looked on askance and when Olivia gave away his sleeping bag as well, showed a touch of irritation.

"We've got another one at home," she said. "Stop fussing."

There was no way I could keep a promise of food for Ibrahim in April without a vehicle. I went back to Abergavenny to see the owner of the post office van. It stood outside his house obscuring the view and had somehow lost its glamour for him. He was not pleased when his Cardiff friends complained that they might have been stranded. He was ready to sell. We agreed a low price.

"After all," I said, kicking the rogue wheel, "it is not worth much. What happens if I get a puncture?"

"You devil," he snorted, but he let me take it away.

We christened the van 'The Yellow Peril' and enjoyed the enormous noise it made when driven through Monmouth, but it was 10 years old. We needed the company and support of another vehicle, ideally the company and support of a mechanic as well.

We began to amass quantities of food. It was stacked up in boxes all over the cottage but we feared to load the van. We feared the long journey to Rijecka alone and wondered what would happen if we did get a puncture – in any of the wheels! The Yellow Peril began to write articles in the local papers and one day there was a phone call.

The Yellow Peril and Drivers

Chapter 34
The Sky grows Darker yet

"My name is Alun. I've been to Bosnia. I'll go with you."

We awaited his arrival with curiosity. His voice had sounded odd and his appearance when he arrived was even odder. He was tall and lanky with a great mane of hair and angular features. He had difficulty edging his way round the boxes in the porch and cracked his head on the lintel of the door. Blood was everywhere.

"Just a scratch," he said.

Alun was strong and quite fearless which had evidently led him into trouble in the past, trouble that he did not mind advertising. GBH (grievous bodily harm) was tattooed prominently on his wrists. He was an HGV driver and a mechanic and had taken his own van into Bosnia alone, crossing from Croatia in December. It was a dangerous if not reckless thing to do but he found a village not reached by anyone else and he said the gratitude of the people was unforgettable.

"I worry about the kids out there," he added. "If I see anyone 'urt a child, that's it."

We didn't enquire what 'it' meant. Alun's van stood outside the farmhouse, a Renault Dodge, we went out to admire it. It had its own kitchen, fridge and sleeping space and could carry two tons. He was ready to collect the food himself and join us on the 14 April. What a relief. The wild pledge to Ibrahim could now be honoured; the families in Safet's neighbourhood supplied again and even UCCA camp re-visited. Hardly had Alun left than Steve Nutt, an undertaker in Newport, rang up.

"I have just read your article in the South Wales Echo and I think I can help."

Business was slack and he thought his funeral parlour would make an excellent collecting point for Humanitarian Aid which proved to be true. A fortnight later he rang up again in panic. He had a body arriving and nowhere to put it. The Yellow Peril hurried down there to relieve the parlour of a mountain of boxes and bags just in time. Steve's bosses, the firm of Tovey and Morris, supported his efforts and one day he turned up at one of our committee meetings in the Town Hall.

"My firm," he said, "is ready to let you have a hearse on permanent loan. It is one they are going to retire from service, a Ford Transit ambulance. The kind we use to collect the body of the deceased at any time of the day or night and put it in a freezer," Steve chuckled.

His droll manner did not quite match the popular image of a worthy undertaker, and discussion of food collection and fund raising came to an abrupt stop. It was obvious that hardly anyone in the room knew that Funeral Director's provided such 'ambulances', and did not much care for the idea that they might in certain circumstances end up in a deep freeze. But the loan of a van that could collect food and take it all the way to Croatia, whatever its previous occupation, sounded too good to be true. The stunned silence was broken by the question,

"How old is this *ambulance*?"

"It is E registration," said Steve, "but the mileage is low. It only runs around Newport when required and that isn't every day." He chuckled again.

The committee did not know quite what to make of him. They presumed he kept his chuckle under control when dealing with his customers.

"The firm will pay the licence and insurance costs," he added.

Two weeks later Steve drove the promised ambulance over to The Callow. It was white and unmarked, but it had clearly been in a scrape with some other vehicle which would account for its early retirement. Its dent did not matter. It was in good order and could carry a ton. Hastily we took the heavy coffin rollers out. No one need know what its occupation had been. We now had two vehicles at our disposal, and the van immediately proved invaluable running round the countryside collecting food. It would stand outside the supermarkets, requesting just one item from a list of 10 handed out to customers. The van could collect a ton in one day, and some people gave not a single item but a whole trolley full. They were clearly responding to the worsening news.

On April 14 we organised our first independent convoy and took several tons of food to Rijeka in 3 vehicles. On May 26 we went again, accompanied by both buses driven once more by Tony and John, Val and Bob. Our destination was still the refugees in Rijeka.

In July and September we had four vehicles because Francis and Olivia came again and so did Alun. Each time it was a different adventure, but declaring our destination in Rijeka as 'Merhamet' instead of 'Caritas' caused us endless difficulties. The Croat customs were not impartial. We were held up for hours and on one occasion all night. The distribution of food to families in Safet and Mensura's neighbourhood was repeated five times. It was immensely rewarding in terms of showing solidarity but by July had become too risky. Numbers had risen from 96 to 190. The road and courtyard of the house was choked with people, a hazard in itself and Croatian flags began to fly in the neighbouring houses, indicating increased tension between Croats and Muslims. The government controlled the media and the anti-Muslim bias continued in the news, preparing the country perhaps to accept the full involvement of the Croatian army in the Bosnian conflict. So persuasive was the propaganda that even the Croatian bishops were reported to have sought an interview with Tudjman and requested more robust intervention to save Catholic communities inside Bosnia. We were not on the right side and were penalised accordingly.

Likewise the news from Sarajevo was increasingly tragic. We tried in July to join a convoy going there, listened to a British officer in Split pointing out on a huge map the hazards on the way, and the recent fate of a Muslim convoy. Other drivers were listening but did not say anything. They just did not turn up the next morning. We drove off alone into Bosnia on a spectacular mountainous route to Duvno, renamed Tomislavgrad, and found the fortified British compound there. The CO was very kind. He explained that vans like ours were routinely high jacked and emptied of their contents if they were not protected by his armoured cars. One would go ahead and one would follow behind the convoy but he could not provide that support for only two vans. We sat in our vans considering the matter. Alun was ready to go on, the others were less enthusiastic and we decided to make for Mostar instead.

Medugorje, on the way and 18 miles from Mostar, is a shrine and a place of pilgrimage, but its failure to become involved, its apparent capacity to ignore what was happening all around, was almost sadder than the Serb sniper fire and shells falling on Sarajevo and the long battle over Mostar. Sadder, because that revered place had become a prey to the propaganda machine, the Franciscan friars saying they did not approve of the ethnic cleansing in Capljina and all around but they understood it. How can you 'understand' turning your neighbour out of his home and imprisoning the menfolk? It seemed incongruous that American pilgrims were there in Medugorje and telling us they had an interview with 'Our Lady' at 10pm at the Blue Cross. Ivan, one of the five visionaries, would fall into a trance and have a message for them. Would the messages waken the world to what was happening? Not at all. They all began with 'My little children' and were mostly about personal piety and salvation, no mention of saving the Muslims. It was an unreal world. The real world in Medjugorje was occupied by the HOS, the Croatian Defence Organisation. They were militantly nationalist, wore black clothes and dark glasses. We did not see any display of the swastika itself, but you could find that grim reminder of the nationalist hysteria among the pious objects sold in the streets. The drip feed of Propaganda was the problem. Many people believed the Muslims were evil invaders who had stolen their property and they were justified in stealing it back.

The battle news was bad. There was no way we could reach beleaguered East Mostar. What on earth should we do with all our food? We had stopped in the main street opposite the huge pilgrimage church and, while Gill made tea, I went in seeking help. When I came out a man was standing by the vans who spoke good English. No, this is not a fairy tale it is what actually happened, he asked what we were doing.

"We have humanitarian aid."

I was afraid to say it was for the Muslims; the real victims in this made up war, and expected him to direct us to some Croat controlled warehouse. Instead he said:

"Go to Bruno Maillard."

The man described how to get there and we drove down a steep unmade road on the edge of the small town to find Bruno loading up his van with bread and pizzas. He was risking his life supplying food to isolated Muslim villagers who had had their cars destroyed and electricity cut off. The HOS had threatened death to anyone harbouring or assisting the Muslims and Bruno knew he was a marked man. Eventually, members of the HOS stole his four wheel drive vehicle. They put on a different number plate but Bruno could still recognise it and the Authorities could not or would not help him. He carried on his secret mission until the day his house mysteriously burnt down. The Franciscans, in charge of the enormous pilgrimage Church, preached charity but left it to Bruno to carry it out.

After leaving all we had with Bruno, we were on our way home with our empty vans when we stopped unwisely to photograph a destroyed Muslim village full of devastated villas and gardens. Three of us were arrested, Saul, who had driven the post office van on its first trip, Alun, driving his own van and myself. We could not argue with a Kalashnikov and we all had to drive obediently into Caplijna. In no time we were standing before the 'Kapetan' in the Caplijna Police Station. Our cameras were displayed on a long table at which sat a plump uniformed officer. He had short cropped hair and a round face, his eyes showed no sign of animation. The soldier who had arrested us described our crime and a junior officer opened both cameras. The chief's cold eyes looked at the camcorder and the officer took out the video cassette. A soldier came in and left his automatic weapon on the table.

Then my nephew, Saul, the camcorder and the video cassette were all taken to another room. The chief sat in his big chair ignoring us. Time became intense. Saul, however, had not used the camcorder to film the village, that would have been the offence, not because the filming could be considered criminal but because it would have recorded a crime. The inscrutable chief seemed to have lost interest in us, provided we just stood there.

At last Saul returned clearly shaken. Going through the video had taken a long time. He didn't think there was anything incriminating in the pictures but was not so sure about his comments. More soldiers came in leaving their weapons on the table which now looked like an armoury. Finally an interpreter arrived, she was a Croat who had lived in America and France and returned to answer the Croat leader, Mate Boban's call, to all ex-patriots to come home and support the cause.

"We was taking photographs to show how the Serbs destroyed Croat villages," Alun began.

The woman laughed, "Don't be silly, you know perfectly well we did that."

But she was not unfriendly and seemed to relay to the chief a positive picture of who we were and what we were doing in Bosnia. Even so we were not given our cameras back and had to leave clutching a piece of paper typed and signed by the chief, which the woman declined to interpret.

"Take it to the Mayor of Grude," she said. "You cannot have your cameras back without his permission.

"You will have to go on Tuesday," she added. "He will be away on Monday."

Grude was the temporary capital of Croat controlled Hercegovina. The real capital, of course, was going to be Mostar when it had been fully 'liberated'. Gill, who had escaped arrest, was sitting in our van outside. When she heard shots fired she busied herself writing little notes and hiding them, expecting an independent investigator to find them one day and solve the mystery of our disappearance.

For the sake of the camcorder which we had only borrowed and the cameras, Alun and I drove to Grude and parked outside a massive church. We sent Saul and Gill back to Rijeka. It was Sunday night. The bells were ringing for an evening Mass and a Franciscan preached with fervour on the merits of the Rosary. Early the next morning we were waiting in a dilapidated municipal building outside the Mayor's office. By 8.30 am the building was alive with people. At nine o'clock a dapper, smartly dressed man arrived followed by several others, he took the Caplijna police chiefs note and disappeared into his office. Nothing happened for half an hour, then a police woman arrived and went into the office. The Mayor came out, handed the policewoman the note, she was ice cold and simply told us to follow her. A police car was waiting outside.

"You will do," she said to me and let Alun go.

He stayed in his van while I was driven to the police station and put into a room with one window high up, out of reach, walls floor and ceiling entirely bare, the only furniture a table and chair. Outside a soldier stood on guard with a Kalashnikov. All this petty punishment for the sake of a few photographs and we had not even taken pictures of 'USTASHA' scrawled on the ruins of one of the wrecked villas which would indeed have indicated who the culprits were. The Ustasha came into existence under Ante Pavelic in 1941 when Hitler recognised Croatia as an independent country and included the whole of Bosnia in its boundaries. Pavelic had imbibed fascism during 12 years of self-imposed exile in Italy. He became a fervent Nazi, not only eliminating the Jews in the new greater Croatia, but killing or driving out thousands of Serbs as well. A memorial to those who died in the Jasenova concentration camp used to be visible from the motorway built to link Zagreb with Belgrade, but under Tudjman and the HDZ party first the museum was vandalised and then the memorial itself, a huge black memorial chalice rising above the trees completely disappeared. The black uniformed H.O.S now strutting around in Medugorie revived the Ustasha. They were under the command of the H.V.O. (Herzegovina Croat army), but were effectively paramilitaries and a law unto themselves.

The punishment for not respecting Croat susceptibilities may well have been set out in the Mayor's instruction. We will never know what it contained. 'Lock him up,' seemed quite on the cards. After half an hour I tried the handle of the cell door, it opened and I pointed to my watch in an agitated manner, indicating that I would be late for my next appointment. The soldier waved his Kalashnikov and shut the door. I wondered if the translator in Caplijna was responsible. She could have listened to the video and not enjoyed certain remarks. Saul had been uncomplimentary about the Croat boss of Gasinci camp which we had visited on the way. The real reason, however, was different. Caplijna was peculiarly sensitive to prying eyes. It had recently rounded up its Muslim inhabitants. All the men were herded into underground hangers at Dretelj on the hillside. All the women and children were driven to the battlefield area around Mostar and Blagai and told to walk across to the Bosnian army side. We did not discover the enormity of this crime until later.

At last the door opened and the soldier invited me out with the help of his Kalashnikov. The ice cold policewoman had another piece of paper in her hand.

"Take this to the Mayor," she said "when he has signed it take it to the Mayor in Caplijna."

She forgot to say she was sorry for keeping me waiting. The soldier gestured me into the waiting police car and I was driven back to the municipal buildings to find the Mayor just about to get into his own chauffeur driven black limousine. He was off to see the Serb mayor of Banja Luka. It appeared the Croats and Serbs were able to divide Bosnia between them quite happily, without the help of Stoltenberg, David Owen or anyone else. The mayor paused, stiffly, unsmilingly, to sign the incomprehensible bit of typescript and was off.

I returned to Alun's van, expecting him to be worried sick. He was asleep.

"Wake up. You should have been in that police station. I couldn't cope.

"Just as well I wasn't. I'd 'ave thumped them."

"And you've had breakfast and it's now midday and I'm starving."

"Not my fault, you was late."

We sped out of Grude across a plateau of open country with small trees and outcrops of rock, a land of magic. Twice we passed strange standing stones.

"They could be ancient Bogomil burial stones," I said, pointing them out to Alun.   "I'm not stopping," he replied.

"But its history, before the Turks conquered Bosnia there was a heretical Christian sect living here called the Bogomils.

"Bugger them, I'm not stopping."

It was just as well. A wild mob of uncouth soldiers with guns sticking out of their unmarked cars passed us, not the sort of people anyone would wish to talk to on a deserted road.

"We are supposed to go to the mayor of Caplijna with this silly bit of paper but I want to give him a miss. His name is Pero Markevic and he is not likely to be friendly."

Alun thought for a moment and said:

"If 'e's responsible for that wrecked village and thinks we've been gathering evidence that could put him in jail, 'e might decide to put us there instead. It all depends what's on that bit of paper."

"Right, we leave him out and go straight to the police station."

It was not a bad road, Klobuk, Vitina, Ljubuski and down the valley to Caplijna. We parked once more outside the grim police station and the bear like guard waved us up the stairs when he saw our bit of paper.

The office was full of soldiers and Kalashnikovs but the chief was not there. A young officer read the note and actually smiled. He handed back the cameras, the camcorder and, after some haggling, even the video cassette. We were back on the road and this time did stop briefly on the open plateau in the evening sun to touch those extraordinary standing stones. They are unique. Only an expert could decipher the hieroglyphics but touching the stone was like touching the history of a thousand years. There was no border but we crossed into Croatia itself at Runovic and over a wonderful range of mountains in the last of the sunlight. There were distant rumbles and flashing lights in the sky.

"Gunfire," said Alun.

The Serbs were disappointed by the opening of the Maslenica Bridge which enabled traffic to avoid having to queue for the ferry to Pag Island and were lobbing shells into Sibenic. They were also lobbing shells onto the bridge but by the time we arrived all was quiet. We reached the ghost like country around Zadar with its grim burnt-out ruins and approached the Maslenica pontoon bridge. The soldiers ordered us to switch off all the lights, it was quite dark but mercifully the moon rose. We crossed, clankety-clank, from one pontoon to the next, wondering whether the chance of a Serb shell was not preferable to falling into the sea. Alun had his face glued to the windscreen and was staring like a maniac. The moon had gone behind a cloud. The Serbs were only 800 metres away and could probably see us and even hear us. Over the other side we were safe and arrived in Rijeka at last in the early hours of the next day, shattered, but nobody had gone to bed.

Chapter 35
The Loss that Overshadows All

In July 1993 mother had died. We had postponed the event long enough with the help of Complan and the doctor. At the beginning of the year she had refused her daily diet of digitalis, the little blue heart pills, and refused as well the antibiotics prescribed for a bladder infection. The result was inevitable. Her heart beats became irregular and before long her feet were swollen and then her legs. She was still just able to get in and out of bed but her fantasies increased. Unable to see, she still managed to scrawl a few lines to her beloved husband, 'Aubs', telling him of her love and ending, 'Come quickly.' The 26 years since his death had become just an uncomprehending absence. 'I need you,' she wrote. It was fantasy and yet had meaning because they loved each other deeply, and because there is Reality beyond the grave. I felt sure he would come quickly. The last kiss we shared, as she lost consciousness, remains with me still. We are all part of each other. As John Donne wrote, 'any man's death diminishes me because I am involved in Mankind.' I felt hugely diminished.

We ignored the usual funeral protocol, laid her in a simple coffin, dressed in her favourite Palestinian gown, a shroud they say has no pockets, and she had emptied hers long since. No obituary could mention what she was worth. There was no will to read out. She had given everything away and now, believing she was a burden, had given her life deliberately away, back to God. She knew the verse: 'thou shalt not kill but need not strive officiously to stay alive.'

The tump on the edge of the Callow lawn where Dad was buried was solid rock beneath a foot of soil. The struggle to break through it was an exhausting, lengthy process. A drill was not allowed. It was a kind of collective therapy to wield the pickaxe in turn and shovel out the broken stone. Fr. John Kelly, a friend, and Fr. David Smith, the parish priest, officiated together. There was Mass in the crowded drawing room and then the coffin was carried the 150 yards to the open rock-lined grave. Charlotte and Frank, great grandchildren, carried the big candles.

"I am so glad," said Charlotte, "Grandma is going to be with her husband. She has not seen him for such a long time."

An effort was made to lower the coffin down but it got stuck halfway and had to be brought up again. Even that was somehow fitting. There was hilarity as the volunteers descended once more into the bowels of the hillside to perfect their work. A wildly generous life was over. She lay next to her beloved Aubrey.

The Bosnian trips had been a distraction from watching mother's painful decline. They continued in that role, an antidote to her loss, but there was an inevitable void in our lives. No one is replaceable, least of all parents. After the funeral our little convoy drove again to Croatia carrying 8 tons of food and nearly £5,000 worth of medicines. The food was destined for the Muslim refugees in Rijeka, the medicines for Muslims stranded in Banja Luka, too old or too poor to join the exodus in the previous year, but the city had become the administrative capital of Serb controlled 'Spska,' and we handed our drugs over to drivers who knew the back roads, except for 7 boxes. These, Gill and I, planned to take to Merhamet in Zagreb concealed under duvets and sleeping bags. The van was otherwise empty. The other drivers went home

We had an address in Zagreb where we could stay the night but our secret load made us feel uneasy and we missed Alun in particular. We could not this time enjoy the spectacular scenery. The road runs close to the Serb lines and was alive with military police. At the first check point they were busy examining a lorry and let us pass. At the next one we were lucky again. A line of vehicles were awaiting attention and they waved us on but at the third check point close to Karlovac we were stopped. One officer looked at our green card and passports. Another demanded that the back door be opened. I had a sickening image of a very long detention somewhere and hoped I might share a cell with Gill. Was I worried about her? Indeed I was. We had no papers to say we had come through customs and no way of explaining why we were in the country at all. The officer only examined the bedding with his eyes and did not notice how unnecessarily bulky it was. I am sure there are angels whose job it is to protect you, at least if you are trying to be on their side.

We were allowed to drive on, reached Zagreb safely and stayed with a family who had made a hair-raising escape from Sarajevo. The UN connived in making that city a prison but there was a tunnel that the Serbs could not control. The next morning we drove to the Velesajem industrial complex, straight through the gates past the customs office as though we had nothing to declare. The Merhamet warehouse seemed to be full of Zimmer frames but there were offices at the back and two doctors were there. It was such a relief to arrive safely that it was hard to take in that we were not exactly welcome. The doctors were cautious, tired and obviously under strain.

"You have no customs papers, we can't take them."

The younger of the two spoke good English and explained that Croatian customs were demanding a share of all medicines and drugs destined for Merhamet and we had not declared the drugs. We had lined up the seven boxes inside the warehouse only too grateful to get them out of the van, and had no wish to take them back again. The doctors were afraid, they had never seen us before and we could be those dreadful people called undercover agents. The anti-Muslim propaganda machine was now producing horrendous TV news. Only the night before we had had to watch sickening pictures, worse than a horror film, of machine-gunned bodies in a village. Five villagers gunned down somewhere by Muslim terrorists and the camera did not spare you. It was no doubt a genuine atrocity but Croatian 'ethnic cleansing' and concentration camps were never made public news. They had been taking place in an organised fashion since the beginning of July. At the same time the fight to subdue the Muslims in East Mostar and create a capital for the Croat majority in Hercegovina was being stepped up, supported by the Croatian army with tanks and artillery. The oldest part of the historic city with a population swollen with refugees was being constantly shelled. There was good reason for the doctors to be fearful. Later on we got to know the Zagreb Merhamet well, took them an electric typewriter, lots of food and more smuggled medicines, but that night they really wanted us to go away. Eventually, they opened one of the boxes and immediately changed their minds.

"They will go to Brcko," the young doctor said. "They are badly needed there."

Our involvement in the Bosnian tragedy became ever more intense.

It was a little war on its own waged on several fronts. Fund raising for drugs had become a priority, the habit of standing outside supermarkets with the van suitably placarded was the main source of food but it was being collected too in Newport and Hereford. The Monmouthshire Beacon carried regular articles written, of course, by the Yellow Peril. Our meetings continued in the Mayor's parlour and the mayor herself was usually there.

I was doing something mother would have done and felt I was doing it for her. Our warehouse now was a redundant school in Monmouth town. The main hall cum dining room, still decorated with children's drawings, became choked with boxes, clothes, mattresses. We could not move it all fast enough until we had bought another larger van, the Currant Bun. It was full of order books for Mother's Pride and had spent its time running round Hereford for ten years. Gill was General Manager of our warehouse and worked indefatigably with a team of helpers, packing, labelling in both English and Serbo-Croat and weighing. The vans could load up in the school yard but each journey became progressively more difficult and expensive. The Slovenians imposed a tax and demanded extra insurance. They became paranoid if they discovered tinned meat. The Croats were difficult if you wanted to go anywhere except a specific Croat controlled Caritas, this despite the fact that Merhamet was an internationally registered charity. In December Alun collected hundreds of toys for the children in Gasinci camp and we crossed the Channel with five vehicles and ten tons of food. In one van we carried 2.000 pairs of knickers for the vast underground Merhamet warehouse in Zagreb.

"They bring everything else," a doctor's wife wailed, "but no knickers."

We were able to respond to particular requests, a load of dates for the end of Ramadan, saucepans, sewing machines and wool for UCCA camp, bicycles and tricycles and especially particular medicines and antibiotics. It was a very small contribution but a large number of individuals and organisations throughout Europe were doing the same.

In Gasinci camp near Osiek, we met thousands of displaced peasants, some of them quite wealthy farmers who had fled across the border with their tractors, trailers, lorries and carts, carrying everything they could with them. There the Norwegians provided a large number of little huts but not enough. Tents were everywhere in the woods. That December it was all under snow. Warm clothes and Wellington boots were needed.

The ten of us will not forget that December trip. It was bitterly cold and the fog was so dense we got lost. We pulled of the road just inside East Croatia on the road to Varazdin. Ice formed inside the cab but the next morning the fog lifted and we found ourselves with a petrol station on one side and a café opposite. We needed both. It didn't matter that two vans were frozen up and wouldn't start; the Yellow Peril pulled them into life. As well as Alun's toys and warm clothes we carried food parcels for Spansko Muslim camp and the neighbouring Croat camp for Vukovar refugees. Their loss of home and men folk was equally grievous, their stories equally heartrending. By now we were filling in forms at the border but delivering our aid where we chose, though usually some of it went to the destination named. We were never sure if they might not check up, but we were not just carrying aid but compassion, not just delivering parcels but meeting and embracing a stricken people. Our Christmas card carried this verse:

There were ten of us. We set out in a raging storm to follow a
star
It led us over the sea, across plains and mountains.
We went in search of the Child in hundreds of refugee
children
We went in search of the old folk, driven from their homes into
the snow
In search of young men, wounded and missing
In search of the orphans and women bereaved.
We carried presents, given by the children of Hereford and
Monmouth
Like Gold for the children of Bosnia
We carried medicines, analgesics, antibiotics, insulin, precious
as Myrrh
Food for the hungry, jerseys, coats and boots against the cold

We carried the love of hundreds of people, and prayer was our
Frankincense
It was a long journey and hard on the way. But to laugh with
the children
At play on homemade sledges, to weep with the women
bereaved
To take with a grimace the hugs of unshaven men. All this was
our task
It was a long journey. But the Star rested over many places
And we would do it again.

PART 5
Different Levels of Tragedy and Need

Chapter 36
East Mostar

Gill's diaries are remarkable for 1994. We shared so much together and worked so hard. When I put my back out lifting boxes she took charge of the January convoy and fortunately Alun joined her and proved indispensable. The preparations for each journey, the gathering, sorting, packing of goods, the raising of money, the visits to schools, the talks, all of that was exhausting enough. The Currant Bun doubled our capacity but meant extra drivers, extra maintenance, extra paper work. At this time we were still only reaching refugees from Bosnia and seldom going into Bosnia itself. Rijecka however was no longer the only destination but one of many, except in March when we managed to divert a whole Rotarian convoy there. In May our destination changed, in May for the first time we reached East Mostar. Getting there was hair raising and pretty miraculous. It is a story on its own but our arrival with the Yellow Peril and the Currant Bun with some eight tons of food was unimaginable and unforgettable. Shell holes in the road were a warning but nothing could have prepared us for the devastation that met us in the town itself. There was no electricity and no traffic; it was eerily quiet. We had no idea where to go and stopped alongside a small terraced park that was attached to a mosque, or what remained of a mosque. The park was filled with graves. We had hardly stopped when out of the ruined streets and houses came a crowd of people. The whole road was choked with chattering people, and then, because our two vans were clearly objects of extreme interest, excited children suddenly appeared everywhere and were clambering over the vehicles as monkeys do in a Safari park. Worse still they managed to get the back of the Currant Bun open and their little hands were pulling out boxes and running off with them. The drivers had sweets to give out but wisely refrained from doing so. Then a woman's booming voice in the crowd shouted, 'stop,' or words to that effect, as one of the drivers ran after a youth who was carrying off a box while the others secured the back of the van again.

After that mayhem I went off to find the mayor, led by the woman with the booming voice who clearly exercised some authority and was probably a teacher. In her hand she carried the envelope we had brought with us, it contained a message in Croatian for the mayor. We negotiated the rubble, the tangle of cables and wires that seemed to festoon the streets and houses, and climbed a cobbled alleyway to an old house with walls a meter thick. Our guide knocked on the solid oak door with its oriental knocker and it was opened at once. A whole group of men and women were sitting round a table in the front room discussing something, but when one of them read the note they all became animated. One of the men was given instructions and returned with us to the vans. He didn't try to speak, he used signs and grunted. He squeezed between Bruce who was driving the Yellow Peril and myself, and grunted loudly when he saw how the van had to be started with a screwdriver. A broken ignition key was one of the hazards we had faced on the way, a broken exhaust pipe another.

We drove further into the old town past fine buildings; some of them shelled or gutted by fire and then had to stop as the Currant Bun was being plundered again. A mass of young people were chasing us and some had to be ejected from the van itself. It was a great game for them, survivors of pretty continuous bombardment for almost a year. The shelling had stopped in March and there was now a truce, if not peace. It was resented by the Croats who were sullen and hostile at the Buna border crossing, but welcome to the Moslems who were close to starvation and despair. They had survived horrific experiences and the people themselves expressed this sense of achievement and elation in graffiti on the ruined walls. Victory was written in large letters, victory at a huge cost. Later we would come to know more about the cost, the cellars where many of them still had to live, the rape victims banded together, shamed and self-exiled from society. There was no greater crime committed by the terror gangs in Milosevic's war. We proceeded slowly, turned left and left again, room for single traffic only, half the road and much of the sidewalks littered with rubble, a whole family seemed to be sitting in the ruins of a house with blankets and a small fire burning. At another spot there were standpipes and queues of people with plastic containers, collecting water. Our guide pointed this way and that between grunts and we found ourselves making our way out of town and following an old railway line to what had once been marshalling yards. It was evening now and the light was fading but the yellow vans could still be seen clearly from the houses in Lijeva Obaca on the outskirts of town. They must have looked unusual, for a woman appeared at her door and waved. A driver in the Currant Bun waved back and she seemed to take that as a kind of invitation for, almost at once, two women were running behind us. Our grunting guide took us to a large warehouse, mysteriously already manned and ready for our arrival. The two women arrived breathless at the same moment. There was just time in the failing light to unload both vans, detach the boxes of medicines which we wanted to deliver personally to the hospital next day, and rescue one or two boxes from the hands of the men to give to the two women. Their eyes filled with tears.

The men locked up the warehouse which until that night was quite empty except for some sacks of UN flour and crates of bottled water. The tap water in the town was contaminated. Our guide then motioned us to return with him to the town but Hajra with the dark eyes and her sister-in-law, Seka, invited us to stay with them. It made sense; Hajra spoke some English.

A quarter of an hour later we were sitting on the balcony of a house on the eastern edge of the city, immediately under the mountain still held by the Serbs. It was a warm, dark night. There was no breeze and the only noise came from cicadas and someone sawing wood, a strange sound since there was now no longer any need to work in the dark. Hajra put two candles on the table. She had dark burning eyes and was struggling with her school English. Her husband stood beside her, tall, moustachioed, handsome. Supper was white bread made from U.N. flour and jam from berries gathered on the hillside. It was the same fare at breakfast, they had nothing else.

The warm evening and the candlelight seemed magical, too rare an experience in Britain, but we were quickly reminded that for too long the valley had been a crucible of pain. The big gun on the hill suddenly fired and a tongue of flame came from the muzzle, and the roar reverberated down the valley. None of the company at the table moved. It was Serb artillery on the mountain behind us saying, 'We are still here.' Next to Salko sat his brother-in-law, Halko, and his sister, Seka. Hovering in the background, in and out of the house, giggling and curious, were the four children, a boy and a girl in each family.

Salko produced an enormous bullet which he said was from an anti-aircraft gun. They had been fired on from the hills on the Croatian side, and in the morning we saw the damaged walls and windows of the house.

"This is not our house," said Hajra. "The Moslem family who lived here went to Germany when the war started. We lived in Stolac. I come from Sarajevo and met Salko in the university there. We married and I came to live in Stolac, my husband's town. I was working in the hospital as a dental technician and my husband was a teacher in the secondary school. Stolac is small and beautiful; it has a little river, museum, swimming pool, library and an orthodox and Catholic Church, four mosques, an orthopaedic hospital and many fine old houses in the Turkish style of architecture.

We lived in a village 2 km outside Stolac and built our own house. About 7,000 people lived in the town and 18,000 in the villages around. In Stolac 51% of the population were Moslem, 37% were Catholic Croatian, and 11% were Orthodox Serbs. But it did not matter then, we were all Bosnians, all Yugoslavs."

Hajra and Our Two Vans

Chapter 37
Hajra's Story

"On 3 July last year at 6 am there was a lot of noise outside the house. I went out to see what was happening. In the street were a big lorry and an armoured personnel carrier. Everywhere there were soldiers, they surrounded our house and fired their guns in the air, as though playing a game, but it was no game. I recognised some of our neighbours from Stolac but with them were some from the Croatian army, you could tell that from their speech and their accents. The soldiers were carrying pistols as well as guns, and some wore black uniforms and had swastikas on their sleeves. I said, 'What do you want?' Then I saw a good friend from Stolac. 'Nicolo, what's happening? What do they want?' But he turned away and went into the street. He had not expected to see me. 'Where's your husband?' one of the soldiers asked. 'Why is he not outside?' Our rotweiler leapt up to give him his answer and he shouted, 'Hold your dog or I will kill him.' He repeated, 'Where is your husband?' Salko appeared in shorts and T-shirt, it was hot weather. The soldier said, 'Good morning, you will go with us.' He was not an officer, the commandant was in the street, but he took Salko to the lorry.

By now Ismir and Emina had come to the door and the three of us were crying. 'Where are you taking him?' I asked. The soldier then said to Emina 'Don't cry, your Daddy will come home again.' Then he said to me, 'We are only taking your husband for interrogation. We will bring him back.' I think our wailing had unnerved him. But they did not bring him back. He was pushed into the lorry with all the other men who came from everywhere around. Other lorries stood in other streets, we were frantic. The cries of women and the wailing of children grew louder, but we could do nothing. They just fired more shots in the air and drove off. They took Salko's brother, Enes. He had a two year old son and his wife, Aida, was about to have another baby.

We were told not to lock up our houses as our husbands might come back at any time, but the real reason was they wanted to be free to walk in at any time. After a few days 3 soldiers in khaki, heavily armed, came into the house at 5 am without knocking. They went round every room. I jumped up and told them, 'Hush, my children are sleeping.' They found my son, and when he stood up he was as tall as the soldiers. They wanted to take him away but I said, 'You cannot take him he is only 14.' One of the soldiers had worked with Salko and we knew him as a friend. He said, 'We won't take him, but if other soldiers come, they may.' "

"Then," said Hajra wearily, "I was ill for a month, I was running a temperature. We had no water, it had been cut off and I had to go with all the other women to a well. We would stand there silently weeping, waiting for each other to fill a jug or a pail, no longer believing our men would ever come back.

A Croatian soldier from Neum who knew me gave me some tablets, and another soldier gave me a packet of cigarettes. They did not like what was happening. But when a soldier asked me one day to give him a cup of coffee, I could not. I said to him, 'When you bring my husband back, then I will give you coffee.'

Three other groups of soldiers came for our son Ismir, but I had his Yugoslav passport and his date of birth, yet every time they came I shook with fear.

At 6am on 4 August the soldiers and the lorries came back. They knocked at the door this time. 'This is an evacuation,' they said. 'You may take one bag with you.' We hastily packed three bags, one for each of us. Then they bundled us into the waiting lorries, not just women and children but babies and the very old. We were crushed together, the babies crying, all of us frightened. They took us to a factory outside Stolac and left us there. We did not know what would happen next. We looked a wretched crowd sitting on our bundles in the factory yard, watched by soldiers, some of whom we knew.

They opened the factory and took people in 5 or 6 at a time. When the first group came out they told us they had been searched and all their money and valuables stolen, including their wedding rings. I felt desperate, I had little money but some people had a lot. I put 5 rings and a gold necklace into the top pocket of our daughter Emina's T-shirt.

Many women were coming out of the factory crying, they had lost everything. At last it was our turn to go in, I was shaking. It was a small room. An officer sat at a large table and around him were 5 or 6 soldiers. In the middle of the table was a big box. A farmer's wife stood beside me, a big woman with rough hands. A soldier had just rifled through her bag and stolen her money and she was very angry. Then he pointed to her bust. 'What are you hiding there?' he said. She retorted, 'Nothing, nothing,' and threw up her blouse, she was wearing no bra.

The officer turned to me. 'What do you have in the bag?' he asked. 'Photographs,' I replied. He opened all our bags and said, 'Where is your money? Where is your gold?' He uttered threats about what he would do if he found money, and started to search Ismir. I gave him what money we had, he would have found it anyway. Another soldier searched me and Emina but did not find the rings and necklace. It was a crazy risk for the sake of a wedding ring and a few heirlooms, but we were lucky. The box on the table was already full of gold and bank notes. Most of the women were too terrified to hide their wealth and many had been rich. They had also been carrying too much baggage, and a large pile of clothes had been confiscated.

When they had stolen everything we had, or they could find, they put us into long container trucks and locked us in. One woman tried to save a bag she had, and was hit in the face by a soldier who fancied it. It was a nightmare. They locked 30 or 40 of us in each truck, it was completely dark and the only sound was of people sobbing.

They took us up the Neretva valley to Buna, which is about 8 or 9 miles from Mostar. There, they unlocked the lorries and we all got out and lay on the grass, there were many hundreds of us. I thought, 'Thank God we are free.' But then they began to round up the boys. I said to Ismir, 'Make yourself small.' Somehow they did not take him, but they filled a bus with boys they snatched from the crowd, and their mothers, distraught already, were screaming. It was no good. They formed us up in a long column, several hundred people, and told us to walk. Soldiers with guns walked beside us. It was very hot. Many old people collapsed and died. They were left by the roadside. Aida had given birth to a little girl in July, and now she was carrying her baby, only twenty days old. On that terrible day the baby died, someone else carried her little boy.

I was so exhausted myself I could not carry my bag any more. I just dropped it.

I don't remember how many kilometres it was, but when we reached the front line the soldiers left us. 'Go to Blagai,' they said. We staggered on. Government soldiers came to meet us. Just to be among friends and not enemies was a relief and at last we reached Blagai. It is little more than a village but now it was crowded, they said there were 11,000 people there. They came not only from Stolac but from Caplijna, Pocitelj, Ljubuski and many other places. Every house in Blagai was packed with people. In our house there were 52 women and children.

We stayed in Blagai three days. How we lived I don't know. There was hardly any food. You can imagine what it was like. On top of everything we were shelled every day and many people were killed."

Hajra's face looked whiter than ever and she began to shake.

"You must tell the world," she added.

For the first time I felt I might have to try, it was as though we had come on our journey just to hear her story. She went on:

"After three days the Bosnian army brought trucks for the old people, the rest of us had to walk. We walked and walked, Seka, my sister-in-law, and her children joined us, and the army gave us food and water. It was about 10 kilometres, and on the way we were shelled again. Seeing the craters and burnt out buildings on the edge of Mostar, we seemed to be going towards hell. Merhamet, the Red Crescent, commandeered all the empty houses and gave us this one, and that is how we came from Stolac and are living here. We had been taken from our homes and put in the front line. For eight months we had to live underground like rabbits. We had no electricity or gas, no water, no wood to light the fire with, and no food. But we had a cellar. I will show you the cellar tomorrow." Hajra managed a smile and we sat there in silence.

"You see," she said sadly. "It wasn't a war against soldiers; it was a war against us. It didn't matter if it was a woman fetching water or a child playing, we were targets. They must have thought if they could kill enough of us we would surrender but we would never surrender."

There was anger in her voice and fire in her eyes.

Chapter 38
The Disgrace of Gabela

Seka took a candle from the house and led me round the back to a home-made loo. It was a trench in the garden. Then she discreetly left me. The stars were bright, the air very warm, and the cicadas seemed to have multiplied and were noisier.

"But we had a problem," said Hajra. "We were literally starving; Merhamet had no food at all. Then we thought of the army, they had to have food otherwise they could not fight." Then she added bitterly, eyes flashing, "We had one battalion, 1,800 men, defending East Mostar. The Croats had five battalions and all the guns and ammunition they needed.

We did not want to take food from the army but we thought we could ask if there was anything left over. The cookhouse was the other side of the railway lines, beyond the warehouse where you went with your vans. One day, Seka and I left the children in the cellar and ran across the railway lines, it was embarrassing but what could we do? The soldier on guard took us in, and one of the cooks gave us two loaves, our first food for many days. It was like gold.

On 25 August the first UNHCR convoy reached East Mostar, 19 trucks carrying 200 tons of flour. Gerry Hulme organised it, he is a hero for us now. It was accompanied by Spanish troops and you can imagine how the people went wild. There was a ceasefire to allow the convoy in but everyone knew that as soon as it left, the shelling would start again, so we stopped the convoy going out. It did not help much. The next day about sixty shells hit the hospital. They were careful not to aim at the UN trucks themselves. On the third day we let them go. Now Merhamet could set up field kitchens, 15 of them, one of them close to us. You could have a bowl of watery soup and a piece of bread each night, it kept people alive.

Merhamet was giving everybody some flour and we had a stove in the cellar, so Seka and I went off very early at 5 am to find some wood. A neighbour lent us a trolley and we found a bit of tree. We had nearly got our load back to the house when a shell fell. You could hear it coming, and we both fell to the ground, but Seka was not quick enough and a piece of shrapnel went through her hair. We abandoned the wood and the trolley and just ran. It was miserable for the children to be stuck in the cellar all day but on the other hand it was safe. On one occasion when Nedim went outside he was nearly killed."

Nedim was Seka's eight year old son. She brought out his T-shirt, it had a hole right through the back, it had billowed out a bit and a bullet went straight through.

"What happened to the men when the soldiers took them away?"

"They were taken to Gabela," said Hajra. "It is a little place near the border at Metkovic but on the other side of the river; you would think it was a nice place. They were taken there on 3 July 1993, to an army warehouse with small high windows and double doors at the entrance. It was 40 metres long by 12 metres wide."

"We were taken there," said Salko, (Hajra translating), "in the summer clothes we were wearing. We could take nothing with us. When they opened the double doors it was almost dark inside. In fact, once inside it was difficult to tell night from day. They crowded us in, using their rifle butts, lorry load after lorry load, until there was no space left. Sometimes you could not find enough space even to lie down. The wall and floor were concrete and dirty. There was nothing to lie on. There was nothing in that warehouse except a bucket in a corner, meant to serve the needs of 700 men, packed into that stinking place."

The candle flickered in a slight draught of air; it was not difficult to imagine the atmosphere in that warehouse.

"One man was asthmatic. He begged them to allow him some air. He only lived a few days. They tried to destroy us without actually killing us. Every night they took a few of us out of the warehouse, made us stand against a wall with our hands behind our heads while they beat us, or they would make us crawl on concrete, all the time kicking and beating us. Each night you heard screams and the men come back bent and broken, and you knew that you would be next."

"We became very weak," Salko continued quietly, "and I think none of us knew if we would live or not. Our food was about 5 spoonfuls of poor quality soup and a small piece of bread a day. The bread was a 600 gram loaf between 18 men. The soup was ladled out of a cauldron into 20 bowls and the first 20 men were given spoons. 'Start,' they shouted and then, 'stop.' We handed our dirty bowls and dirty spoons to the next 20."

Salko got up, went out and brought back a metal bowl. He had smuggled it out when they were finally released.

"You see why you have to tell the world," Hajra said.

Salko continued. "Apart from the beatings, the worst suffering was thirst. We were given 10 litres a day to be shared out between 700. Just imagine the heat of the place and no water. We did not even have a spoonful of water each. Many of us went without any all day. We took it in turns to be first to have a mouthful the next day but that was even more painful. We were parched all the time." We sat there in stunned silence. The candle was flickering low and casting queer shadows, it was getting cold. We slept uneasily on mattresses and sofas that night, and tried to spare the precious bucket of water in the bathroom. By the door were a candle and a box of matches. The weather was good enough for breakfast outside. It was a re-run of supper, bread, jam, coffee and juice. We could now see the railway lines and marshalling yards, the tangled mass of overhead power lines, the burnt out sheds and factories. In one corner were a line of buses listing at curious angles."

"They are all wrecked," said Hajra. "Not one of them will ever go again."

Salko went on with his story.

"For the next two months we were like dead people, lost to the world. No Red Cross or UN representative came to see us. For 45 days the double doors were never opened except briefly once a day, or when they wanted to take men out for a beating. As I told you we had hardly any water to drink and none to wash with. When the Bosnian army began to have some success against the Croats we suffered even more. For three days, between 13 and 17 July, we were given no food or water at all, only the beatings continued. Several men died.

We were covered in lice and many had scabies. This gave them the pleasure of shaving our hair so that we really looked like convicts. Then one day all the teenage boys and men over 65 were taken out and we knew something was going to happen. Suddenly we were allowed water for a wash. They even opened the doors and let some fresh air in. We did not know until later that the final indignity the old men and boys suffered was to be stripped naked at the Croatian front line, and sent running down the hill to the Bosnian troops defending Jablanica. We all looked like skeletons and could not believe that if anyone came to see us they would not notice what we had suffered. At last Red Cross officials did come. The Croats said we were prisoners of war captured with our weapons, but the Red Cross realised that even if we were, we were being kept in inhuman conditions. From the date of the Red Cross visit, life became slightly better. We had water to drink and to wash with, a blanket each, and a little more food. They had to give us more food. They took us out part of the day to work, but we were dizzy with weakness and blinded by the light, so the work teams were given more bread.

We were always searched when we returned and one boy, he was 18, concealed a piece of bread under his shirt. The officer shot him in front of us all. We think at least 13 men were shot at Gabela, apart from those who died. Then, quite suddenly, a soldier came up to me and said, "Friend, today you go to Mostar, be happy." He did not seem to know or understand what his people had done to us. They brought trucks round. We had no baggage so they could crush us in. It was 15 December 1993 and we had been prisoners in Gabela for six months."

"A neighbour came to our house," said Hajra. "She was excited and said, 'I hear on the radio that a lot of your men will be free today.' I ran and called Seka and fearing it wasn't true said, 'It cannot be true.' But Seka immediately put water on the fire, 'So that they can wash,' and both of us forgot the danger and went to Merhamet to try to find trousers and shirts. We were lucky."

"When we got home," said Hajra, "I was depressed, it just could not be true. Then suddenly at 3 pm lorries full of men with shaven heads began to pass our house. Our road is a dust track but the main road into Mostar is too dangerous and has not been used for months, so these lorries passed our gate. I counted 10 or 12 of them and was so excited and frightened I could hardly breathe. There was no sign of Salko or Halko on those first lorries. We watched them go back to Buna empty.

238

Then at 6 pm, they all came past again, crowded with more men. Seka said 'I will just go to the gate and wait.' She took Ismir and Nedim with her but instead of waiting at the gate, they walked into Mostar."

"In the tunnel under the railway line men were passing us," said Seka. "Then one of them stopped and asked me where Hajra Mulac lived and it was Salko."

"Ismir did not recognise his Dad," said Hajra, "and nor did I. He was terribly thin. He looked as though he could have come out of Belsen with his head shaven, sunken eyes and protruding bones. His clothes were stiff and stinking. We had a ceremonial burning. 'It's over,' I said to him, 'over forever' but he would not let me say that."

It seemed like a great burden to carry, this knowledge that the Croats had been led to behave so brutally. Was this too to be kept a dark secret, the re-awakening of fascism in a country 90% Catholic? Could Cardinal Kuharic of Zagreb know what had been going on? How the basic badge of a Christian, love for your neighbour, had been discarded so disgracefully? We returned to the ruins of the town in sombre mood, looked into the dark fast flowing Neretva River where the broken pieces of the Stari Most bridge lay buried, climbed the stairs of the secondary school that had lost one wall, climbed down into the basement of the hospital, the only part of it still in use. There was still no water in the hospital. The loo was a dank decayed wooden cubicle with a bucket and though the doctor welcomed us, he was dispirited, shattered by his experiences, and missing his wife and three daughters whom he had sent to England.

"Medicines? Wonderful," he said. "Take them to the dispensary."

The dispensary up the road had power but no refrigerator.

"We are desperate for a refrigerator. It gets very hot in July and August."

We returned to Mostar in July, brought both big vans and the hearse, and included in the load an enormous refrigerator. We made several more journeys in 1993, only made possible with the help of a German team who led us into East Mostar by a secret route.

Yellow Peril' in East Mostar)

Chapter 39
A Different Journey

At the end of December 1994 we bought a Renault Traffic van and began a journey to Lanzarote in the Canary Islands. The cruise ship left Portsmouth with 2,000 happy passengers on board. It was a special Christmas offer, a delightful cruise to Bilbao, a shopping spree and a pleasant journey home. The storm began before we were out of the harbour, the Pride of Bilbao, a sizeable craft, began rising and dipping alarmingly and, as soon as it had turned south into the bay of Biscay, it began rolling from side to side. Nobody dared climb the stairs to watch the special film, 'Four Weddings and a Funeral,' you could not even enjoy a meal. Indeed most people never seemed to leave their cabins. We did struggle up to the restaurant for breakfast and one other couple made it there too, parents of Paul Harris, who had worked in Yugoslavia in '91 and '92 and written, 'Somebody Else's War.' We talked, holding on to tables and chairs well bolted to the floor, and watched our breakfast jump off and slither across the deck. Conversation was necessarily brief.

For those taking a short holiday it was a disaster, arriving at Bilbao the ship could not dock and went on rolling from side to side. You could imagine the wailings and recriminations going on in the various cabins and when eventually we did dock, we were among the few allowed off. Too much time had been lost; there was no time for shopping. We watched a group of pale seasick passengers besieging the Purser to find them some other way of getting home. There wasn't any other way. Only those fortunate enough, *not* to be going home, could have a reprieve and our van chained to the floor, the contents tightly packed, was unharmed.

We had over-filled the van; we were rather used to doing that, but now we had no Alun with us and were on our own. The hazards became alarmingly clear when we could not stop going down a steep hill into Bilbao. We were not supposed to be going into Bilbao; we were on our way to Cadiz. We were becoming refugees ourselves; leaving the tragedy of human greed and pride behind, leaving the suffering it can cause innocent people, and hoping to find our own peace. It was a difficult decision to make but we left behind an organisation and hoped it would go on, which it did for a while and then was taken over, or over taken, by Hereford Humanitarian Aid.

We drove out of Bilbao and eventually, after going round Madrid, arrived at a hostelry for the night and found the Harrises already there!

This time we could enjoy a conversation and share a table. Bosnia, Bosnia, it would haunt us all the way.

We had made 13 journeys to Croatia and Bosnia, more than half to East Mostar, overcoming the border problems by donating our vans and their contents to the Bosnian government at the beginning of each trip. You can imagine how pleased the Croat Customs were to see us. They still made difficulties, holding us up overnight on one occasion, but legally after that they could not stop us. There was a cease fire in Mostar but no real sense of peace. We could crunch our way over thousands of spent cartridges and watch the sullen backs of Croat soldiers peering across the river at their Muslim enemies who were far more relaxed and, as we discovered earlier, believed they had won the war. The Spanbats (the Spanish battalion, part of UNPROFOR) were a jumpy lot, turning our drivers away from sensitive spots. In West Mostar the HOS were still in evidence, vigilantes in dark glasses who would confiscate your camera if you were pointing it in the wrong direction. One of our drivers, Ian Brice, had been photographing the stadium, when suddenly, asking no questions, two hefty men stood beside him and took his camera away. He did not know the stadium held a secret, a place where the Muslims of the west bank had been rounded up. The beautiful ancient damaged city, especially devastated on the east side, was a long way from recovering 'brotherly love.' A flimsy swaying footbridge had replaced the famous 'Stari Most' built by Suleiman the Magnificent, but no one was crossing over. The great building blocks of the famous bridge, like the love of Christians for Muslims, lay buried deep in the fast flowing waters of the river.

On the deck of the ferry heading for Tenerife, Gill wrote a four page letter to Tomislav and Tatjana Coric in West Mostar. They had become part of our lives. There were many good Croats in the city but most were cowed by the xenophobic frenzy. Tomislav Coric was not one of them. His wife, Tatjana, from Montenegro, was not one of them either. They both lived in the house of a Muslim family that had fled to Germany. Tomislav's parents lived in the same street and had access to a stream that was flowing into the Neretva. They annexed a bit of it and kept ducks. Like most people they hid away in their houses when the Croat militia were around, but Tomislav went out into the street and saved a Muslim woman by claiming she was his mother.

The way we met Tomislav was another of those extraordinary chances, another moment when you felt someone else was directing operations. Our two vans, the Yellow Peril and Currant Bun, had been held up at the Metkovic border Customs. There was no way they would let us through with goods destined for Merhamet in East Mostar. We had to have special permission from Siroki Brigge, a small town some miles from Mostar itself, and there was no way we could get that permission without a recommendation from the Croat municipal offices in West Mostar. The obstacles were precise and purposeful. We emptied the Yellow Peril in the UN car park and left one driver to look after the contents, then drove the empty van back to the border and satisfied the suspicious Customs men we had nothing on board. Driving down the twisting treacherous road into the city of Mostar would have been a waste of time if it had not been for Tomislav. He seemed to be waiting for us and spoke English. He stayed with us all day, acted as our interpreter in office after office, all of them seemed to be involved in obstructing the process, but finally after a nail biting wait for the Fax machine in a warehouse that we could never have found for ourselves, permission came through. We hurried back to the border, reloaded the van and got both vans through to East Mostar. After that we always stayed on the West side with the Coric family and on the East side with Hajra and Salko.

But now, on our way to the Canary Islands, there was a chess game being played on board. The champion chess player beating everybody was a Muslim professor from Mostar University, but he had been fortunate to move to Geneva long before the so-called 'civil war.' One of the vanquished competitors lived in Santa Cruz, Tenerife, and when we docked there, he hurried to his offices and gave us two Spanbat medals. His company minted them; on one side is a picture of the 'Stari Most' and on the other a soldier holding out his hand to help. The words around the edge were: 'Cascos Azules Españoles, Acción Humanitaria.'

We changed ferries in Santa Cruz and eventually reached Lanzarote, via Gran Canaria and Fuerteventura, early on 3 January, 1995, ignoring the Customs, which proved a mistake. When we swapped our van for a car the new owners tried to go back to England in the van, but the Customs people said no such van existed on the island and made a great fuss.

In our first year on the island we made many friends but Desmond and Dorothea Goode became more than friends, they changed the direction of our lives. They had been farmers in England, mainland Spain and Tenerife. He was a yachtsman, happier on the sea than on land, but Dorothea suffered from sickness if anything moved under her at all. When he went to sea, she stayed at home and prayed, and when he came back with wonderful stories of South America, she would invite us to supper. For years Desmond worked for GORTA which was a wonderful excuse for his frequent sailing trips across the Atlantic. GORTA was a Charity 'against hunger' set up by the Council of Ireland and based in Dublin. Its principle was; 'do not give a man a fish which will last him a day, teach him how to fish.' Desmond's task was to teach people how to farm, or rather improve their farming methods. He was responsible for setting up numerous agricultural cooperatives and institutes on the long Pacific coast of Chile, had a hand in the introduction of a monetary system in Tongo, helped tribes in the Amazon and thought he was establishing an agricultural school in Ecuador. This last project turned into something rather different. He might have guessed it would, since it was prompted by the secretary of the Bishop of Riobamba. The secretary was Thomas Walsh who knew Desmond Goode rather well. They had met 20 years earlier when Thomas was riding round the world on a bicycle and had ended up one afternoon on Playa Blanca beach, on the southern coast of Lanzarote. Desmond was trying to push his Landrover which had become stuck in the sand, so he hailed Thomas. Thomas not only gave him a hand but later sailed across the Atlantic with him and that changed the direction of *his* life. The problem with Desmond was his overwhelming commitment in the last ten years of his life to improve the lot of the poor, and Thomas caught this infectious disease.

The Goodes retired to Playa Blanca and bought a house overlooking the small bay, as it then was. From the house Desmond could see his yacht and when the sun went down over the yardarm could drink his Jamaican rum, and dream about his voyages. They celebrated their Golden wedding in a nearby Chinese Restaurant and invited us. Would we make the next journey to South America and check out the latest project? We were not sure. Bosnia was still on our minds and we returned to the shattered beauty of that country three times in our first two years on Lanzarote.

In September I went alone with money raised in Lanzarote, for a rehabilitation music centre in East Mostar, a project sponsored by Pavarotti. That was positive, but I travelled from the airport in Split to Medjugorje with a bus load of American pilgrims, misled, I believe, in their quest, which seemed negative, yet who is to know in the mystery of things. From there I took a taxi into Mostar and found Tomislav, Tatjana and their children, made homeless when the Muslim owners of their house returned from Germany. The stress of the war had already caused Tatjana to become an alcoholic and her marriage was on the edge of collapse. The same terrible stress, that is hard to imagine, caused Hajra in East Mostar to have a breakdown, she had had to give up her job in a nursery school and looked white and distressed, such a terrible war should never have begun and should long ago have been stopped at the gates of Vukovar.

We were at supper again in the Goode's house. Desmond had reached the age of 78 and given up crossing the Atlantic. He had twice been mugged but reasonably gently, even so it unnerved him. Having been thus warned, we began our next adventure at his behest. It was May 1997, a dramatic experience from the moment we landed in Quito, capital of Ecuador. You land in the bowl of an enormous crater, which is almost entirely surrounded by city. Thomas Walsh was waiting for us, saving us from a swarm of small Ecuadorians anxious to carry our bags, helping us into his ancient truck. He drove up and down the rolling beautiful countryside, most of it around 10.000 ft above sea level, the air thin, the sun burning hot. Thomas, as secretary to the Bishop, was in charge of the project we had come to see, and was one of those rare people who put you at ease at once and whose friendship is forever. He talked about the bishop's dream which Desmond had not mentioned, indeed may not have known about, and after four hours driving we arrived at an old dilapidated Rectory on the edge of a little town called Chambo. Four young men were waiting for us, also eager and anxious to carry our bags. They constituted the bishop's wild dream. Thomas introduced us briefly and took us through the old building to our bedroom, a high-ceilinged room with no furniture except for a large bed. "You have a bathroom," he said proudly, "with hot water, operated like this." It was electric, looked dangerous and exploded as soon as we switched it on. So, in fact, we never had hot water.

The once fine Spanish colonial L-shaped building, with two acres of land around it, high walls and gates, an avenue of ancient yew, was built on the edge of the sleepy town, 10km from the provincial capital, Riobamba. Funding for such a place came in the past from estates belonging to the Church; yes, the Church too, the Dominicans and the Franciscans as well, owned and profited from big estates until the previous Bishop, Leonidas Proaño, whose life is legendary, insisted that church estates be returned to the people. That was in the 1970s.

On the way to Chambo we had passed women coming up the road carrying so much on their backs they looked like walking haystacks. We would later see them, minding or milking a cow, sowing, reaping, harvesting, often with a child on their back and barefoot. Then it would be time for them to carry what they could to the market and we would find ourselves sharing bus rides with live chickens, guinea-pigs, rabbits, and pretend we did not mind the animal smells and unwashed bodies. They were always crowding into the buses, off to one of the markets in Riobamba, in colourful ponchos and strange hats, once with a goat standing upright on the roof amid sacks of potatoes.

Around the old neglected square in the town they set up braziers each day, cooked a whole pig and sold it in slices, and you could buy strong drink for nearly nothing, and two paracetamols at the Chemist to calm the consequent headache. Nobody expected you to buy a whole packet of cigarettes in the shop or a whole box of pills. We happened to be there for the great event of the year, the bullfight, but the bulls, though quite skittish and dangerous are too precious to kill. They are teased to exhaustion and then let go, presumably returned to their owners until the next bull fight.

The single naked 40w bulb high up in the ceiling of our bedroom, mocked us that first night. The bed was so hard, the heater on the shower out of action, and we did not know how long we could take the young men's cooking. We noted with alarm that there was no hot water for washing up in the kitchen and, of course, no hot water for washing clothes in a big tank outside.

Early next morning we woke to the sound of activity in the rest of the house, cleaning going on, then a pause, then out of tune singing in the narrow chapel next door. Supper had meant that we did not really look forward to breakfast, and now we could not even shower. It was cold, high up, close to a line of volcanoes in the Cordillera of the Andes and not far from the great snow covered Chimborazo mountain, all on the wrong side of the equator. Breakfast was pappy bread, soggy cooked bananas, hot milk with just a pinch of Nescafè, and sometimes a hard boiled egg, or an apple. We had to brave the buses and go into Riobamba to supplement our diet.

The young men were cheerful, especially the smallest, a true blooded Quichua peasant from the hills around Alaussi, who found everything amusing and made everyone laugh, but all four of them were really very serious. They had taken over the derelict property in January 1994 with the task of growing enough food for themselves and enough left over to sell. It was quite a sacrifice to leave their own families to survive without them, but at Chambo they would not only work the land but study as well for a secondary education certificate, and after that they expected to begin Philosophy and Theology. That was the plan Desmond did not know about. Our job was simply to inform the parish of Shepton Mallet in Somerset that their money had been well spent and was creating a thriving Agricultural School with four students.

Bishop Victor Corral was a cautious man. He knew what he wanted but he did not mention it for a year. He worked with the 'boys' in the garden, said Mass in the home-made chapel once a week and began calling the old rectory a Seminary under his breath in January 1996, but did not dare put up a notice to that effect. The papal Nuncio and the Cardinal Archbishop in Quito had no idea what he was up to.

In May 1997 the four 'boys', most of them over 30, completed their Secondary education successfully and we arrived in time to celebrate with them. Thomas organised a picnic and drove from Riobamba with his pick up van, destination a secret. Gill and I sat in front, the four students bounced about in the back in great good humour - until it began to rain. We climbed forever to a mountain lake shrouded in mist and learnt that it rained or snowed up there almost all the year round. The picnic was not in my memory a huge success but it was rewarding in another way. We learnt more about the 'boys:' Serafino was the youngest, 24, Manuel the joker, 31, Luis, 33 and Isaias, 34. They had all been studying at the Centre for the Formation of Campesinos in Guano, one of four Centres set up by Bishop Proaño, who made it his priority to educate the peasant farmers and, indeed, gave up his Episcopal palace in Riobamba to go and live close to them in the Santa Cruz Centre. These formation centres produced Catechists, Animators, Musicians and Organisers for the numerous remote and scattered parishes of the diocese, all of which had communities living in the hills who could often only expect to see a priest once or twice a year. Their task was to help the priests in those parishes by going out to the surrounding remote villages, prepare children for Communion, baptise and bury if necessary, organise bible groups and singing, and generally animate the communities for the priest's visit and Mass on feast days. They were Bishop Proaño's secret army, designed to evangelise and save the 'Roman' faith from the growing threat of American Evangelicals who had more money, nice wives, and taught a fundamentalist form of Christianity. The advantage enjoyed by the bishop's missionary army was that, unlike priests, they could have nice wives too. The bishop suspected that the Evangelical missionaries were having an easy ride convincing gullible natives, happy to have somebody looking after them, while Rome was a long way away and did not care. His successor, Bishop Victor, wanted to go further and give the campesinos a chance of becoming priests as well, but this time nice wives were out and only young men prepared to be celibate required. The need for more priests was and remains urgent, every year more so with the gradual demise and disappearance of many missionaries from Europe and North America

Unexpectedly, we became involved. We liked Bishop Victor, a courageous man, responsible for the poorest diocese in one of the poorest countries in the world. The mountainous province of Chimborazo was 67% indigenous or native Puruha, 91% lived at subsistence level, 60% in extreme poverty. No health care or pensions of any kind. For example Manuel came from a family of 7, struggling to survive on a small mountain farm with no water, electricity, or drainage. He said his family was often hungry and because of the work, the children, like their parents, had almost no education. He was one of the Puruha, quichua speaking 'Indians' as they were called incorrectly, a gentle, dark haired, bright eyed people, with shining white teeth. They were small but able to carry heavy loads on their heads and backs. They were often barefoot but all wore hats and brightly coloured ponchos or shawls and smiled readily. You met them on every dusty mountain track, the children struggling with pigs, sheep, or heavily laden donkeys, all trekking to a huge open air market in the hills every Friday. It is their own market, not simply a place of endless barter and gossip but a reunion of the tribe, a much more interesting market than those in Riobamba. Who would take us there first but Eulogio? We were to meet him for the first time in Pulingui.

The bishop had his plans but his secretary, Thomas, had other wild ideas. He was planning a community centre at Pulingui San Pablo, 12.000ft above sea level. He took us there in his pick up van which was true to its name; it acted as an unofficial taxi. Anyone was free to climb aboard and they would tap on the window when they wanted to get off. On that and other trips we were safely in the front seat, watching through the mirror poncho-ed figures, wearing Wellington boots and curious hats, clambering on and glad of the ride, bumpy though it was. We would discover where many of them lived, not anywhere that a western person would want to live.

When we had climbed to Pulingui, which is at the foot of the great Chimborazo volcano, 26.000 ft high, its head in the clouds, snow covered, treacherous, it was to find homes looking like bee hives, men and animals, cows, chickens, sheep, the hillside well cultivated, a rushing stream twisting its way down the valley. An important event was about to take place. Padre Eulogio, the first native priest for the diocese, was about to bless the foundation stones of a community centre. He had been ordained in the Cathedral in Riobamba only a year before, the Cathedral packed and overflowing with the excitement of the native

Puruha, all gaily dressed, so proud to have a priest of their own. Now Eulogio was the parish priest of San Juan, which included many hill settlements in the foothills of the volcano, including Pulingui. He had come to bless three big stones (standing for the Christian three-in-one God). These would be the foundation stones for Thomas's village centre, a school, workshops, clinic, meeting room, showers, loos, all built in the layout of an enormous Condor. It was a dream of such grandeur it was hard for the people to take it in. Care International were properly distressed to find the people had no loos and built little sentry boxes painted white all over the place with doors and septic tanks. The people, however, had a perfectly good mountainside and were not going to share such places so they turned them into tool sheds. The Condor idea was different.

A Chozo in Pulingui

A young wife outside her home, her mother lived with the cow

Chapter 40
A Mission in the Mountains

All the villagers were now crowding round the makeshift altar where lay the three big stones and a sheaf of wheat and the elected representatives began making interminable speeches, and they all took their hats off and bowed their heads until it began to rain when they all put them on again hastily. Padre Eulogio, robed, waited patiently while musicians played and it rained again. At last he blessed the three stones and we retired for 'refreshments,' roast guinea pig and potatoes in a nearby shack.

The wind got up and it was obviously going to rain once more. A young woman in a blue wrap-over skirt and shawl and the inevitable pudding bowl hat, was cutting grass for her cow with a sharp, curved knife. I asked if she would show me her house and she smiled shyly and without saying anything took me to her 'chozo.' The door was small and low and inside it was at first completely dark. It smelt of smoke and small chickens ran away under the bed which occupied more than half the room. It was a huge double-decker bed, parents slept on the lower deck, the girl and two other siblings above.

I could see where the cooking was done in a circle of stones with a huge black cooking pot beside it. No chimney, the smoke just went through the thatched roof. There were strange shapes hanging from a line among the eucalyptus branches which made up the framework of the 'home', chunks of meat were hanging there, probably guinea-pig, or rabbit, obviously getting smoked and preserved. There was no furniture so the family had to squat on the mud floor for their two meals a day. There must have been somewhere in the darkness for spare clothes to hang. Apparently they would take off their outer garments at night and lay them on top of a thick blanket on the bed, but otherwise they did not undress and wore the same clothes night and day. It was hard to believe that a whole family could live like that, no light and nothing but the freezing stream to wash in. I saw the precious cow in its special hovel next door and learnt that the Grandmother slept there too. She spoke no Spanish, was small and wizened, bright eyed, no teeth. She might have been any age but was probably only 60 or so. She seemed fearful of a white face and turned away.

This glimpse of the way life was still being lived in the mountains, made it easier to understand why Mariano Toazo Toazo stank to high heaven. In the open air the smell was scarcely noticeable, in a small room excruciating for any sensitive nose. I pretended it was important to record his answers to questions from further away and sat at the far end of the table. It was an interview set up by Thomas who thought I should know more about the background to Pulingui and the Condor Centre, so he booked a room in the Curia offices in Riobamba. Mariano was the elected and much respected president of the Pulingui San Pablo community.

"I used to work with my parents as a slave for the masters of the Hacienda," he told me. "They forced us to work from early morning until dusk, making ditches, carrying firewood, rounding up horses, cattle, sheep and moving them from one place to another to fertilize their land. They did not pay us a cent. Often we would be out all night following the sheep from one planted field to another. We were often far from our own hut and would fall asleep on the ground and sometimes wake in a downpour. Then we would spend the day soaked to the skin and hungry."

He did not speak clearly and Thomas later transcribed the tape. It was a tale of great suffering. They were not properly clad and always barefoot in a climate that was often awful.

"We did not have enough to eat, just gruel for breakfast which had to last us the day, then more gruel at night and a little potato. The masters beat us with whips or clubs and we were held in a stranglehold by them. The overseer, the farm manager and even the cowman beat us and there was nothing we could do. Our huts became neglected and the grass roofs let in the rain. We had no time to repair them."

Mariano went on to describe how they had no education and grew up unable to read or write.

"We lived without knowing where we were going, with no future for our children." Then he described the change that took place in 1974 when bishop Proaño arrived in Riobamba and, at the same time, there was a change of government. The big landowners came under pressure to part with their land and the Church, more powerful in those days, backed the Land Reform, so the mountain communities first formed themselves into Associations and then into a Federation. Mariano spoke of the privations from which they still suffered and how grateful they were to Thomas and his Condor plan.

"There is hope now for the communities," he said, and I hoped he might have a bath one day as well.

We were woken in the old Rectory by mopping and brushing and clatter as usual but there was an added noise, the sound of flapping wings and squawking. Clearly chicken might be on the menu and indeed it was. The first indication was chicken feet or talons appearing at the bottom of the soup, a delicacy we were told. You were expected to chew the scales off them. Luis, sitting next to me, suddenly asked:

"Why do you think we have to be celibate in order to become priests?"

I was not prepared for such a question but, since there is as yet no alternative, there was no point in doing anything other than encourage him, which could, I said, be for the best. He was the one who would go off on his bike every day to collect the milk and the farmer's daughter was a beautiful girl and a catechist in the parish. Eventually Luis married her, created a chapel on the roof of his house, and together with his wife prepares children for their First Communion. Yet he was an excellent leader and could have made an excellent parish priest. They now have two fine sons Luis Carlos and young Christopher Francisco.

That dramatic fortnight, a glimpse of a vibrant but very different world, came to an end too quickly. Three more young men joined the original four and the bishop became animated. He appointed Fr Frank Hegel to be the first Rector of his proposed seminary and when we were back in England sent us a request: 'Would we please come back?'

At the end of February in the following year 1998, Gill and I sat round the bishop's table in a large house next to the Cathedral, with the Rector of the Seminary, Frank Hegel, the bishop's mother and sister, a nun, and the bishop himself in expansive mood, pouring glass after glass of wine. It was a good meal, the conversation desultory. We had no idea what was going to happen. After coffee he took us into a smaller room and showed us his plans for the new Seminary. It was certainly ambitious, on two floors round a quadrangle, bedrooms for 12 students, two bathroom blocks, two rooms with en suite bathrooms for staff, chapel, library, lecture rooms, kitchen, dining room, IT room, office, not to mention entrance lobby and gallery, all separated from but linked to the old building. The bishop had gone slightly mad. I looked at Frank Hegel who was seeing the plans for the first time too. He looked suitably shocked. I had guessed the bishop had an extension planned but it was a far bolder project than we could have imagined, and the estimated cost was $80.000, much lower than almost anywhere else in the world but still a substantial sum. He hoped with extraordinary optimism we might raise the money for him.

I went to stay with Fr. Frank for the next few days in his 5th floor apartment, while Gill went off to the Galapagos Islands which she found a lot more interesting. Eulogio called the very next day and we went off to see his family home.

"Time to discuss important things tomorrow," I said to Frank, making for the door rather too eagerly.

A forest of eucalyptus trees rose up behind Eulogio's house and we climbed together through the trees to the top and surveyed the beautiful valley on the other side, then down to a meal prepared by his mother and aunt. Yes, it was a real house, still a hovel but a house, no sitting room, kitchen or bathroom and only a mud floor but a house all the same. Cooking was done outside in a separate shed, behind it there was a tethered black pig and a number of chickens. Eulogio had two sisters, the elder one married, the younger one still at Secondary school which meant a two hour walk each morning and a two hour walk back in the evening and homework after that.

Back in Frank's apartment we discussed tactics. Frank took on writing to his Canadian friends and I agreed to harass the parishes and communities of Britain and Ireland, supported by a letter from the bishop carrying his seal. The clouds lifted. We had a magnificent view of snow covered Chimborazo and the bishop laid the foundation stones of his new Seminary on the feast of The Good Shepherd in April, with no idea whether we could raise the money or not. Frank was jumpy, but the building started as soon as the first cheque arrived and was completed in exactly one year, including the extra needed for furniture, just before an economic downturn and the collapse of an Ecuadorian bank.

The celebrations took place on the same feast day, Good Shepherd Sunday, in April 1999, and were organised by Thomas. A street theatre group called YAWAR came by bus from Lima and arrived in colourful costumes, played their flutes, danced and sang in a long 'pasacalle' around the town, followed by a bemused white haired bishop and his cohort of priests and acolytes and led by two seminarians carrying a cauldron of fire. Eulogio stood out as the only truly indigenous priest, and you could feel yourself back in Inca times.

A canopied altar had been prepared in the grounds of the new Seminary. Luis was the spokes person for the 7 seminarians. Frank was overwhelmed and almost in tears. The bishop spoke at length while we all melted quietly in our plastic seats under a burning sun. A blind and barefoot woman, muttering prayers, was close to us and Gill and I took her grubby hands at the kiss of peace without enthusiasm, but when she tottered up to receive Communion she seemed to be in a heaven of her own and greeted everyone with her toothless smile. They had gathered everybody from the highways and byways to share the good meal afterwards, and the blind old lady was not quite so blind and had no need of a knife and fork.

Chambo Seminary

The gardens, old rectory and the new Seminary beyond

Chapter 41
YAWAR in Lima

The street theatre group, Yawar, had intrigued me and after the fanfare and feasting that followed the solemn opening of the Chambo diocesan Seminary, one of the actors, Juan Carlos Cesped, invited me to stay with him for a week in Lima. He said I would see their acting workshop and go to one of their performances, so I flew to Lima in May 2000. It was another cultural shock. The airport was chaotic but at least Juan Carlos was there. What was not there was his car. First shock, no car, we scrambled into a minibus with a hundred other people, second shock, no seat. We joined the amazing traffic pouring into the suburbs of Lima until a few passengers left and we could grab a seat. At one stop we got out and joined a hubbub of people waiting for a variety of other minibuses. They came in packs, elbowing each other out of the way, almost all bearing battle scars, young conductors shouting destinations. Eventually we climbed into one which seemed to know where it was going and had an elderly driver, calmer than the others, but not so calm when we became inextricably stuck in a traffic jam, vehicles hooting and shouting from all sides. Some minibus had not just bumped another but more or less laid it out. Apart from arresting the bus driver, who would have no insurance and probably only get out of prison if his family paid, the police seemed powerless.

"It's not far from here. Shall we walk?"

I was travelling light so we got out, weaved our way through the lines of frustrated, stationary traffic to the pavement, and began to walk. It was a really seedy part of the city and we had only gone a few hundred yards when I realised we were being followed by 5 men and we were about to walk through a tunnel. It was one of those dreams you wake up from in a sweat. Juan Carlos turned pale. "We have to get back on the bus," he said, and slid into and among a large group of people waiting at a stop just before the mouth of the tunnel. I was not really enjoying Lima at this point. Eventually, the same bus we were on before turned up and I hoped it might be taking us to a more civilised part of the city. It was not. We walked in a limbo land of half finished houses, rubbish-strewn streets, few people about now.

"This is it."

It was a ramshackle building, never completed like so many others. We were in a kind of lobby with stairs going up on one side to a door and presumably another apartment but our door was unpretentious and immediately in front of us. I expected Juan Carlos to take out his key, instead he rang. Not only did he have no car, he seemed to have nowhere to live. I might have learnt more about Juan Carlos if my Spanish had been better than it was. No one came to the door.

"I have a friend down the road," he said, "We will have to come back later."

It was Saturday evening, various shops had already shut, but one had a light in an upper room. Juan Carlos shouted, he had a good theatrical voice, a head appeared at the window, and in a couple of minutes we were in the shop and climbing a ladder to the upstairs workshop. Yes, it was a ladder, and a nice voluble Peruvian was at work making trainers. He was not just making any kind of trainers; he was sewing in ADIDAS, the brand name, and making professional household name trainers. I thought I could be in Alice's Wonderland. He went on working and talking at the same time and I looked round his collection of pirated shoes. He *needed* to live at the top of a ladder.

We returned to the apartment Juan Carlos did not own, and he explained that when he asked me to stay with him he *did* have an apartment, but just now he did not have one. He had had to go back to live with his parents. 'But it is OK,' he insisted, 'you will be staying with a friend.' I thought he might have let me know earlier this change of plan. The woman I would stay with was a teacher working in the same College as himself. He rang the bell again. This time the door was opened and we walked in to find not just one woman but three. They sat on plastic chairs, chatting happily. There was a slip of a kitchen to one side and a 'bathroom' which did not deserve the name on the other. It had a window on to an enclosed space open to the sky, but the window itself was missing. Opposite there was another window, the kitchen window. There seemed to be no curtain which would make the bathroom even slightly private. On the other side of the 'sitting room,' correctly named, people *did* sit there, was a big curtain. This concealed the bedroom. The women were not unfriendly but they did seem surprised, not, of course, as surprised as I was. Juan Carlos was oblivious to the delicate situation and left me with,

"I will come back tomorrow and we will go to YAWAR."

That evening is blurred in my memory. I ate what they gave me, ventured into their dreadful bathroom, and asked if I could go to bed early. The weather was cold and the bedroom very cold. It had a large double bed and bunk beds. I soon realised that the light covering on the main bed would never keep me warm and asked for a blanket. The good lady, whose name I have forgotten, did not give me a blanket from one of the bunk beds as I had expected, but opened a chest full of thin counterpanes. I am sometimes slow to recognise the signs but that seemed significant. There were three ladies in the house. Where would they sleep? I was too tired to worry. I slept soundly which was just as well, and lay on the right side of the bed, facing the bunk beds. Would they be empty when I woke up? They were not empty. There were large lumps in those beds and quantities of black tousled hair protruded. I wondered if they had bothered to take off their clothes since there did not seem to be any on the only chair. But then I became a little more concerned, what about the third lady? Could she be behind me? It was not a situation which made me feel comfortable and relaxed. It would probably be the owner of the bed which was reasonable enough. She had to sleep somewhere and could hardly sit up all night on a plastic chair. I lay perfectly still, listening. *I* had undressed and was wearing pyjamas. What on earth might she be wearing or not wearing. There was no sound, it was a Sunday after all and people sleep in on a Sunday. I slipped out of bed, out of the room and into the bathroom which at least I had to myself.

Thousands of people must live like this, hugger mugger, and not mind the lack of privacy, or perhaps they mind and there is just no alternative. In the past 50 years the population of Lima had grown from about a million to more than seven million. The beautiful city was surrounded by new suburbs in a reasonable state and others that were huge shanty areas that stretched into the hills. For millions of people today it is a real struggle to survive, and round other great cities like Jakarta, Mumbai, Calcutta, Sao Paulo, Rio de Janeiro, conditions of life are worse. Tomás Temoche was an angry Socialist, railing against injustice. He wrote plays which portrayed the struggle of the poor against the rich and founded the street theatre group, YAWAR, thirty years ago. He could have been a successful businessman like his brother but chose to live with and work for the Quechua people, many thousands of whom flooded into the city, fleeing the 'Shining Path' guerrillas, government troops, civil war and economic collapse. His purpose had always been not just to entertain but to educate, inspire and animate.

He lived in a narrow street in a two storey house with a bay window and a large attic. The attic was the YAWAR workshop. All the walls were plastered with YAWAR posters and photographs, and children from the streets came in to play recorders and drums and the classes were free. Young men and women took part, some working on a play, some practicing music. I sat with a group of children being taught simple tunes on the recorder by Tomás, and became aware that the little boy next to me had wet his trousers, too excited to contain himself. At the same time, in the other half of the room, young people, including Juan Carlos, were practicing a play and on the next day, masked and splendidly dressed, he played the Jester before a large and noisy crowd in the vast and ugly square of some suburb. Tomás was acting too, but his acting was rather eclipsed by the outstanding performance of a horse which won the most laughter and applause. Afterwards the municipality produced refreshments, but YAWAR was not offered any money. It is a voluntary organisation and depends on voluntary support. It was clearly difficult for all the actors with their gear and instruments to meet together for performances so later we bought YAWAR a bus and Tomas knocked out his bay window and turned his front room into a garage. It was not safe to leave it in the street. After the meal and a speech by somebody important, Juan Carlos changed and we made our way back to the wonderful apartment he had organised for me. I had the intention of returning only to pick up my clothes.

"I can't stay here any longer. The apartment has only one bedroom – and it has only one bed." Juan Carlos muttered something.

He seemed to think I was making too much fuss.

"I don't think she will be disappointed if I am not here tonight."

"But where will you go?"

"Tell me how to get to Carabayllo."

I was carrying an emergency alternative address. This was an emergency. Thomas had given me Gricel's address in Carabayllo, one of the most remote and dilapidated suburbs in Lima, 20km from the city centre. It was a nightmare getting there in the awful minibuses and I was not encouraged by the run down appearance of the properties on the way, but I made it and Gricel gave me a great welcome and a very good meal. Her husband was more aloof and important, but then he had once been the Mayor and seemed to think he still was. It was a pleasure to have a whole room and a bed to myself next to a bathroom, one with a real window and plumbing that actually worked. The front room even contained antique furniture. Their son had a room in the attic and was studying at the University, and there was a very nice garden outside. Gricel was one of the founders of C.A.N. (Centro de Apoyo a la Niñez). It was started in 1985 with the aim of feeding and educating the children of immigrant families. It went on to include the education of parents and by 2000 was running 10 one room schools with 20 teachers and over 350 small children.

Gricel, and several other CAN teachers, took me to a barren desert high up in the hills. I was sure they were doing it on purpose to show me one of the most wretched and impoverished places on earth, but they had a school there. Well, it was a hut and it did have a door and inside a real plastic window, but a mud floor. All around were the weirdest homes you could imagine, constructed from anything that could be salvaged from rubbish dumps, only the pigs nearby lived in breeze block pigsties with good roofs. There was no electricity, water or amenities of any kind, but there seemed to be crowds of children. A water lorry arrived periodically and a nurse set up home within reach and showed us a book of all the children and people she had treated and all the promised payments she had never received. We left the dust and the wind and the frequently sick children to climb down the hillside. They showed me the cemetery with earth mounds over recently buried children, unmarked graves, a huge rubbish dump with scavenging kids nearby. Nothing grows in the hard rock as it hardly ever rains and people cough the dust from their lungs. It was not somewhere where anyone would want to live, and yet for the children's sake the women were right to build a school.

"It just needs a basin and a lavatory," they said.

Later, we were able to provide that and rebuild the hut as well.

Suburb of Lima City

From the hill we could see the smog hanging over the city, where 80% of the cars and vans choking the roads are over 20 years old and the street cleaners wear masks. Strange things were happening in Peru. The whole country was holding its breath, wondering if things could ever get better or become even worse. Alberto Fujimori seemed to bring hope when elected President in 1990, but he had an 'evil genius' advising him and nobody seemed to know how that happened. Under the pretext of controlling drug trafficking and fighting the Maoist group 'Sendero Luminoso,' this shadowy figure behind the throne, gained more and more power. Fujimori celebrated his birthday while I was there. He had just persuaded a docile parliament to allow him to run for a third term and the city was humming with nervous expectation. Few wanted him to have a third term but everyone was afraid. There was a permanent presence of disgruntled peasants camping in the gardens outside his palace, so he chose another square for his birthday speech and bussed in hundreds of supporters with offers of food and drink. Meanwhile the papers headlined the crisis, 50% unemployed, 15.000 prostitutes many with AIDs, prisons overcrowded, street children scavenging and living like rats on the banks of the river. I saw some of them. Yet the polls gave him 36% of the vote and his nearest rival 30%. Elections were due on April 9.

The government controlled the armed forces, the national police, the judiciary and the public ministries. Those who opposed Fujimori in the judiciary and ministries had already been removed form office. Those who opposed him publicly had already been slandered in public. Fujimori's strongest critic was the newspaper, La República, but a new satirical newspaper had appeared on the streets called La Repúdica. Its purpose to calumniate the opposition and though its writers were anonymous, it was said to be funded and directed by the national Intelligence Agency, controlled by 'this shadowy figure, Vladimiro Montesinos, another Rasputin.' It was a dangerous allegation. Vladimiro took the newspaper, El Comercio, to court and won.

On April 9 Fujimori failed by only 0.13% to win a third term in office but he finally won in a second ballot against Alejandro Toledo on May 29. It was not a free and fair election, a third of the votes were declared invalid, but it made Montesinos safe. No one discovered until later that the ship load of armaments, he bought legally from Jordan, would be sold to the FARC rebels in Colombia. No one publicly denounced him for the bribes he received from drug traffickers but what brought him down was a secret video, released on September 14 which showed him attempting to bribe a Congressman, Alberto Kouri, with $15.000. Alberto Fujimori took fright, announced on TV that he would call fresh elections in 2001 and, more importantly, that he would not be a candidate. Montesinos fled and the Ministry of the Interior offered five million dollars for his capture. For his extraordinary story read 'El Espia Imperfecto' by Sally Bowen and Jane Holligan.

Chapter 42
Haidee Zauny and the Water Project

Gill and I returned to Lima in the following May. Alejandro Toledo was the new president, Montesinos was in hiding and Fujimori had wisely retired to Japan. We stayed with Haidee Zauny, the new president of C.A.N. and visited the schools we had begun to support.

We arrived at a school that was just about to begin the days work. It was in two downstairs rooms of a small house and was full of young children. A large woman was at the door with her little daughter aged 5. The teacher took one look at the child, felt the swollen glands in her neck and said:

"You must take her straight home and put her to bed."

"Where does she live?" we asked.

"Up the mountain."

A few minutes later we were following Beatriz and her little daughter up a mountain path of shifting stones, steep enough without that extra hazard. Two or three hundred feet up, we came to a ledge just wide enough to get past a series of home-made shacks. Beatriz's home was made of bits of wood and plastic sheets. It had a tin roof, a door but no window. You would think it would be stuffy inside with the door shut but in fact the shed, for it was little more than that, did not fit well together. It let in plenty of air and quite a bit of light. Outside the view was panoramic, inside mostly darkness but there was a light bulb, even a fridge near the entrance, and the woman sold fizzy drinks and various other items to her neighbours. A young girl arrived wanting to buy some 'special' and the woman fumbled on a shelf for some dark looking stuff, tobacco perhaps, and put it in an envelope. The entrance-cum-lobby-cum-shop, ended in a curtain. Behind the curtain a little boy was playing on the mud floor beside a big bed. There was no man around. He had gone off in search of work, even though he had made a kind of workshop beyond another curtain. He professed to be a car upholsterer and, apart from the bed, an old car seat was the only furniture in the room. Clearly they all had to sleep in the one big bed.

The woman put her daughter to bed and grabbed the little boy who was watching us. He was obviously used to being shut up in the house when his mother was out. There was a sink in the tiny lobby and a gas cooker but nothing else. They had to go out to a loo which was just a hole in the ground and it was now obvious why the good woman smelled strongly of disinfectant. There was no water. She had to carry every drop in plastic containers up from the valley and never had enough to keep herself and her family clean.

"But if there is water in the valley, why can't it be pumped up here?"

"They can't get it up here." We did not know what she meant at the time.

"We will try to get water to you," I said, hopefully.

Beatriz was 37. She had left her home in the province of Huarochirre when Fujimori came to power. Her father had been killed, either by the 'Sendero Luminoso' revolutionaries or by government forces, she never knew which. Her mother struggled on but died of cancer aged 54, and Beatriz joined the thousands of displaced peasants who poured into the suburbs of Lima in those turbulent years. She met Auber, the upholsterer, and they planned a temporary home on the hillside but became trapped in their poverty.

Her little girl had gone to sleep, and her small son was still playing on the mud floor with little stones when we began the laborious climb down, more perilous than the climb up.

"Beatriz and her neighbours have to carry all the water they need in plastic containers up that treacherous path. That is why the child is ill. They cannot wash properly, the lavatory is unsanitary, the water unsafe to drink. It's a major health hazard, worse than no education." Haidee had to agree.

The water board was in fact willing to provide clean water and mains drainage if the steep hillside was made safe. It could only be made safe by pretty massive 'containment walls.' We might have given up at that point but Haidee had a younger brother who had just qualified as an architect. His struggle to achieve that was extraordinary, as the family had no money for his education, and without the kindness of a friendly neighbour who fed him when he did not have enough money to eat (let alone buy both books), he might never have succeeded. He chose not to work for a big firm in the city; he wanted to help the poor, among whom he had grown up. Juan knew what could be done and had already drafted plans for containment walls. The problem was funding. The 'shanty town' around the mountain had formed themselves into 27 self-governing communities with 60 to 100 families in each. They could get electricity but none had water.

The local Authority was bankrupt, unable to keep the streets clear of garbage, pay the police or provide public transport. Most businesses, such as they were, did not pay their taxes. Haidee's husband, Paul, an engineer, with a garage in his mother's sitting room, did not pay taxes. The barricaded shop keepers behind their metal grills did not pay taxes – for good reason they were not safe. They could not expect the police to come to their aid if they were robbed. When a fight took place outside Haidee's house between two gangs of youths, the police only came in the end on the promise of having their petrol paid. No wonder Paul built the house like a small fortress.

There are many different levels of privation. Paul had had to work in Panama for 3 years to earn the money to build his house. They gave us their double bed in the front room with a covering that felt like a carpet, no furniture except a rickety cupboard and a vast television, single strip-light in the ceiling, and a cement floor. Converting his mother's front room, and making it an open workshop on to the Tupac Amaru highway, kept Paul busy but poorly paid. He kept cars on the road which should have been on the scrap heap.

"They are mostly unofficial taxis and if I don't keep them on the road their owners won't be able to feed their families."

He lived on promises of payment. I watched a barefoot old woman wearing little better than rags crossing a square to give money to a cripple.

We woke the next morning to what we thought was another riot outside the house, an enormous and frightening racket. Gill hid under the heavy blanket but it was only the television news, timed to come on at 6.30am. It was a real riot but in Arequipa, a city in the south of Peru, rejecting violently the government's plans to privatise the water supply.

The family was getting up by now and the next step was to find the right moment to occupy the bathroom, careful listening required, careful treatment of the loo which easily got blocked. Outside a succession of street vendors were shouting their wares or honking their horns, bread, milk, fruit. Breakfast was ready.

We climbed the hill again outside the Zauny house. The enormous barren hills were empty of all life when the family first proudly settled in that corner of the valley and children arrived; first Susana, then Paul junior, and finally Gabriel. Now shacks climbed the mountain in all directions. They disappeared into the haze that seemed a permanent feature of the place, a haze that was partly dust in the very dry climate and partly pollution. It hung yellow over the city and made you cough. It was not just Beatriz, not just her community that needed water and drainage. The pathetic canvas cubicles over disgusting holes that would not drain away, accompanied hundreds of shacks all over the grey, stony mountainside. It was a strange coincidence that a possible access for water to reach all of them could only happen by way of 'Comitè 60,' the community to which Beatriz belonged. We stayed a week in 2001 and left with the plans for a water project well advanced, that is to say two containment walls were to be built by the people themselves. The two communities involved would work one day a week preparing the ground, pickaxe foundations, carry sand in sacks, cement, water, reinforcement iron bars. They would be working in 'faenas' as they had done hundreds of years ago in the Inca empire. Haidee would organise the purchase and distribution of the materials. Juan would make the plans, liaise with the Water Board and supervise, we would send out money to pay for the plans and materials.

On our next visit in 2002, all 11 communities around that mountainside had joined in the work, all 1,260 families, over 6,000 people and they were building 19 walls, 3 and 4 metres high and up to 200 metres long. You can imagine the rather frantic efforts to finance such a programme. We plagued our friends and maybe lost some, and in Lanzarote Kevin and Claudine Roper's Dinner Dances and Auctions became critically important fund raisers.

Meanwhile, Vladimiro Montesinos had been captured in Venezuela and brought back to Lima. His false identity papers and plastic surgery did not save him; the price on his head was too high. But he now found himself in a prison that he himself had designed to solve a serious problem, how to safeguard a prison from underground escape tunnels. Simple, he thought, build the prison itself underground. Never again would terrorists be able to mount a rescue mission by digging a 330 metre long tunnel under the then maximum security prison of Canto Grande, turn up in the exercise yard, and rescue 47 condemned terrorists. They even saved their leader, Commandante Roland, who had been kept in solitary confinement in a different part of the prison. Montesinos was determined such a disaster would not happen again. No one would rescue anybody from the new prison at Callao, but he had not expected to be put there himself.

Chapter 43
Living in the Chambo Seminary

Numerous young men now joined the Seminary but few stayed; an average of 15 slept in the new and old building. The reason for the chaos was the large, comfortable, happy Rector, Fr Gerardo Nieves, who was also the parish priest of Chambo and preferred to stay in his presbytery and operate from there. There was thus nobody in charge of the Seminary itself for most of the time and, however well intentioned the young men may have been, they took advantage of the vacuum and all sorts of odd things began to happen there. TV sets were appearing in individual rooms, two of the boys had charge of the Seminary vehicle, two others got up at half past four and turned the kitchen into a bake house and were selling freshly made bread as a commercial enterprise. Wires trailed across the back yard to a hut turned into a workshop making picture frames, and a large hutch appeared in another place with privately owned rabbits. It was all enterprising but causing conflict, about which Padre Gerardo was blissfully unaware. He was very busy in the parish and thought his duties were fulfilled if he got the 'boys' to join him for festive Masses. "What?" he said, when told things were not right, but then he called an emergency meeting of all the students at which it became slowly, painfully, evident to him that all indeed was not well, but still he did not leave his comfortable room and live in the Seminary.

The bishop was waiting for his new Rector to arrive from Madrid but Fr. Frank Cepedes had to complete his studies first. In the meantime Gill and I offered to stay in the old building next to the Seminary. The bishop was delighted. It was October 2003. To begin with Gerardo invited us to stay with him, while a proper bathroom was made in the Seminary, and that first 3 months were not easy. It was not just 'third world' disorder and discomfort, the kitchen was also a disaster and the presbytery was like a station waiting room, likely to be invaded by anyone at any time. That autumn, Thomas was our lifeline and it was a joy to see the Condor Centre up and running in Pulingui, full of school children in one wing and women weaving in another. They even had an outlet for selling their goods, a habitable hut on the roadside to ensnare the tourists on their way to climb Chimborazo. The children were being taught in two languages, their own Quichua and Spanish. Some of the Pulingui girls were training in Riobamba to be nurses, a doctor was coming to Pulingui once a month, and the 'campesinos' were getting agricultural advice as well. Then at Christmas we joined Thomas's wife, Julia and family for 10 days holiday and spent much of that time on the Pacific coast in a small resort, hardly any people there and such a joy to walk and swim, bird watch, relax and picnic. It was called Los Piqueros, a bit run down like the rest of Ecuador, with a museum, a little lake, a bridge about to collapse and enormous orange crabs. We stayed in comfortable wooden huts with excellent shower rooms and spent our days relaxing in the warmth of the coastal climate.

Back in Chambo I organised restoration work. Both the old and new buildings of the Seminary had been neglected for almost five years. The roof needed repairs, the windows painting. More funds from England made it possible to transform one wing of the old building into a workshop, store room, and four more bedrooms, two with en suite bathrooms. The work was done by two small Ecuadorians and Clive Muskus from Lanzarote who did the plumbing and electrics, and cost us almost nothing as he did not seem to need any food. Gill and I moved into our original bedroom in early February, hot water at last. We furnished it with a splendid chest of drawers, a small table and two comfortable chairs. We had a sink and two burners to cook on in another room and Gill divided her time between cataloguing 600 books in the library, painting on pieces of slate and working in the garden. Peace at last. Benjamin lived opposite, completing his secondary education. Fidel and Fausto had taken over two of the new bedrooms. Padre Carlos kept some sort of order in the new building and we all waited for Frank Cepeda to arrive from Madrid.

That Easter Eulogio invited us to his parish for the Easter ceremonies. He had moved to Sibambe. He did not tell us what Sibambe was like as a place or what kind of weather to expect. We arrived on the evening of Maundy Thursday. The town was wrapped in a dense wet fog. This seemed at the time just a little bit of bad luck. No one was about, yet when the great bell of the Santiago church in the square began to toll figures appeared from nowhere, whole families shuffled into the huge church. Outside, in the wet, a double line of men collected, wearing white albs and carrying staves. They called themselves 'Slaves of Jesus,' an ancient and privileged order of laymen. They processed into the church barefoot, mounted the sanctuary steps and sat like a choir of monks around the altar. The church was packed, every bench filled, the overflow stood around the walls, yet it was not a night to encourage anyone to step out of doors. Traditions remain strong in the hills of Ecuador. There was much pealing of bells and the 'slaves,' standing in for the Apostles had their muddy feet washed while the congregation raised the roof with their hymns which they all knew by heart. At the end of the Mass the 'slaves' led the way to the flower decked altar of Repose and then returned to strip the high altar bare, unhesitatingly, knowing the ritual well. We went out into the fog and were instructed to follow the shadowy figure of a nun to a cold supper and a cold bed, sharing the room with sacks of flour given by the diocese for the poor. On the next morning, Good Friday, the weather was as bad. We took against Sibambe.

Huigra, further down the valley had much better weather and Eulogio, thoughtfully, took us there. It had another big church and another falling down presbytery. Eulogio was busy collecting funds to build a new presbytery in both parishes. They were both his responsibility. He showed us the plans. He seemed to have found friends and funds in Italy, probably because Huigra was looked after for years by an Italian missionary. Back in Sibambe we met the wet fog again and the bell was already tolling for the evening service, the 'slaves' lined up as before waiting to process in. Branches of pine had converted the Sanctuary into a forest and in the middle was one tree on which hung a man, on one side of him stood the figure of Mary and on the other St John. Again the church was packed to the doors. Between hymns and the rest of the liturgy the 'slaves' read out the seven last words of Christ spoken from the cross, and then took the body down with elaborate ritual, venerating each nail, folding the arms and placing the body in a tomb. Much of the play-acting liturgy of Spain can be found in South America. The people did not have books and could not read anyway.

On the Saturday the sun shone mercifully and we went for a beautiful walk in the hills but by midday the fog had come down again. In the evening, despite the fog, two teams of youths played a game with a ball in the huge square. They threw it at each other and tried to catch it but it was hardly possible to see them clearly, let alone the ball. That night fires were lit and masses of candles and the liturgy continued with baptisms, singing and bells. On Easter morning the 'slaves' were in action again. The risen Jesus was carried on a dais by one group of men while Mary was carried by another group. The two processions went in opposite directions round the enormous square but when they met the men carrying Jesus knelt three times before Mary, his mother. Then the men carrying Mary knelt three times before Jesus. It was another bit of drama. A crowd of people followed each procession, then joined together to follow both figures back into the church. Meanwhile the nuns smoked out a little room in their efforts to make a fire between stones on the floor. They roasted a pig and made a great feast and we promised to do something about the deplorable school yard and the absence of a proper kitchen for school meals.

The six or seven thousand inhabitants of Sibambe suffer an atrocious climate, damp fog for most of six months of the year, strong winds in the summer. The 3 nuns at least had their own company; the priest was on his own. The people liked him and he worked hard but he already carried a secret legacy from a previous parish. I met her later, a fine motherly Quichua lady, from the parish of St Juan. They had had a little girl together, a beautiful child, which prompted the bishop to transfer Eulogio to Sibambe. He really wanted to be a priest, believed that was his vocation, but mourned his wife and little girl. He could not refuse to see her sometimes and so it happened that a second child was born, another little girl. The bishop could forgive one but not two. After that Eulogio was forced to give up working as a priest in the diocese. He faced a crisis that was insoluble and is now working with an Anglican community, but he is not really happy. Anglicans are scattered and poorly organised in Ecuador. The good nuns who loved him found it hard to forgive him, but later on when I met his wife and beautiful children, a strange providence and God's love was there too. For the native Quichua celibacy seems almost impossible.

On Easter Monday Eulogio took us by car to Alaussi to catch a bus back to Riobamba. We left, aware that the extremely poor are inevitably less attached to the things of this world. They have so little to be attached to. The church provides them with some comfort and hope, but the people of Sibambe were about to lose their priest, one who spoke their native language and shared their culture, one they loved.

Chapter 44
Crisis and Celebration

In January 2004, I returned to Lima city while Gill took a break visiting the family in England. It was indeed crisis time. The water board had become impatient. They had promised their water pipes and drainage to all 11 communities on condition that the containment walls were built. Progress was too slow. SEDAPAL, (the state water company) sent an official letter from their city offices terminating the agreement. The reaction in the communities was not just consternation but anger. I arrived in the middle of it, a noisy meeting was taking place in the Zauny house, all the 'dirigentes' (Community leaders) were talking at once and accusing each other. The simple fact was that not all the 19 walls that had to be built, half a kilometre in length, could be continued simultaneously. We were not sending Haidee enough money. They agreed on one thing, a delegation had to go to the SEDAPAL offices and argue their case. I had to go too. A decrepit vehicle turned up the next morning to take us into town, 5 dirigentes, four men, a woman, and myself. We all climbed aboard or got into the boot. Yes, two men got into the boot and a third slammed the lid down, and we were not just going round the corner. It took an hour in the awful traffic to get into the city and I really wondered if the two crushed into the boot would survive it.

We were not welcomed in the offices of the water board with joy. We were putting pressure on them they did not need and we were herded into a room with not enough chairs. Eventually the boss man deigned to see us but not everyone, only two of us. I thought the men who had emerged from the boot shaken but cheerful should be chosen, but they all insisted that I had to go in and they chose the woman to go with me. It was a wise decision, she was young and attractive, a community leader with plenty of passion, and she was able to communicate this passion to

274

the unhappy man sitting behind his immense desk. Finally he agreed to reinstate the water project and I committed myself to giving it full support. The waiting men were so relieved

they were ready to cheer but the hero of the hour was the girl, and now the awful cramped discomfort of travelling in a car boot for two of them did not matter anymore, they even tried to sing.

It turned out to be a stimulus for the whole venture. The elected leader of the project, chosen to liaise with and support the architect, Juan Zauny, was Rodriguez. Together they now had fewer problems getting people out of bed on a Sunday morning. There was more urgency and we made more money available. The headache of handing out 'multas,' fines, for not turning up (commuted usually to commitments to do better next time) was over. During the two and a half years it took to complete the work, Rodriguez was often close to despair and it took Juan's diplomacy and skill to smooth things over. Everyone was to benefit, so every adult was expected to take part but the show of hands at meetings did not always translate into action.

By the end of 2004 the walls were completed and the Water Board machinery moved along the new paths which turned out to serve a double purpose. Hundreds of flimsily built homes with slippery access now had protective walls and respectable paths to their front doors, underneath the paths ran the new water pipes and drains. Only the inspection chambers betrayed the secret, clean water, and a tap outside every shack. Bathrooms had to wait a bit longer.

The celebrations were planned for February 2005. Seven of us went out from Lanzarote and met in a hotel in Miraflor in Lima which had every modern convenience including a casino in the basement. It was a different world from Carabayllo. It was a modern world with big shops and well dressed people. We had a meal in an expensive restaurant overlooking the sea. The seafront, the trees, the gardens, everything in fact, made you feel at home. There were no beggars, nothing shabby like that; we could have stayed on happily. The next day we piled into two taxis and braved the dreaded journey through the traffic-choked city. The scenery became less and less entrancing, more and more wretched. Only Gill and I knew where we were heading and even we had forebodings. Why would you bring elegantly dressed people with

275

manicured finger nails and high heeled shoes to Carabayllo, much of it a virtual slum?

But they had left all their elegance behind and were ready to brave the edge of the civilised world where it never rains and one-room shack after shack disappear up the hillsides, the furthest ones hardly visible in the polluted air. We tumbled out of the ancient taxis at about 11am at Haidee's house. She was there at the door with Rodriguez, signs of impending festivity already evident, a marquee occupied the whole road alongside the house, but she was impatient to start the guided tour. The seven of us began the climb, at times a scramble, up dusty crumbling paths, shepherded by Haidee, Rodriguez, Juan the architect, and someone with a video camera. It was very hot and very dusty. You did not have to think too much about the quality of life. Nothing grows on the mountainside, the dust gets into your lungs, and the people suffer infections that lack of water and sanitation inevitably bring. But it was celebration time, each little community had prepared a welcome with banners and flags, a tape to cut, cheap champagne bottles to smash, speeches to make, knots of people clapping, clapping for themselves too for they had done all the work. It was so hot, one or two in the party put their heads under new cold water taps. Mains drainage was in too, manholes all over the place, and a sad little loo already connected stood ready for the basic needs of a family, but the walls still had to be built around it.

Back down in the valley an Inca meal had been prepared with quantities of meat and sweet potatoes cooked on an open fire, and after that came dancing and endless speeches, 'till a troop of musicians, gaily dressed marched in with panpipes and drums, YAWAR! So the day ended with a play performed in the open air and a homemade air balloon, fitted with its own small flame took off into the sky trailing a banner which just said 'Gracias.'

This was supposed to be the end of the affair but in fact we continued supporting further extensions of the water system while Gill began a much bigger project, a new school in Huanca Pallaguchi for 240 children and accommodation for 12 teachers, who have to stay in the mountains with the children from Monday to Friday. It was an enterprise too big for us but Gill and Sue, who accompanied her, managed to enthuse a group of Canadians on holiday. They went home and raised the major part of the money. All the building work was done by volunteers from four communities, but they had an architect and the invaluable supervision of Hector Garcia, just released from prison. Hector was a Union leader, condemned by hooded judges to life imprisonment for belonging to the Tupac Amaru revolutionary movement. The man who put him in prison is now there himself. Alberto Fujimori, President of Peru from 1990 until 2000, extradited from Chile on December 10 2007, and tried for crimes against humanity. On 3 April 2009 he was sentenced to six years in prison and could be keeping Vladimiro Montesinos company.

Gill & The Girls

Angela, Jessica and Merilyn
The Author and his wife, Gill

More than 36 years have now passed since Gill and I married and it is not possible to express adequately what those years have meant for us in joy and fulfilment. We have seen the girls grow up and get married, worried over them and over grandchildren, the eldest grandchild is now married herself. We travel to Milwaukee to find Jessica, and she travels to Britain and Lanzarote to find us, bringing her remarkable seven year old son. It has been a brilliant partnership, and we have been able to achieve things together which neither of us could have managed on our own.

Epilogue

We get many things wrong in life and perhaps it does not matter in the end, particularly if we become aware of values greater than ourselves and a destiny beyond this world. That changes the focus of everything we do.

The Churches, I believe, have much to offer mankind, essentially a message of joy and hope, but the message is entrusted to human beings and becomes obscured if it is not humbly lived.

The instruction that Jesus gave to the Apostles is clear (Matthew 23.10); 'You must not allow yourselves to be called Rabbi, since you have only one Master and you are all brothers. You must call no one on earth your father since you have only one Father and he is in heaven. Nor must you allow yourselves to be called teachers for you have only one Teacher, the Christ.' Jesus was marking out the distance he wanted his followers to make between themselves and the pride of the priests and Pharisees, and the passage ends with, 'anyone who exalts himself will be humbled.' Human nature does not change, and pride is the greatest threat we all face as followers of Christ. It obscures our witness to Christ in the world. Jesus did not wish his followers to claim status or privileges. He rebuked his disciples when they argued among themselves as to who was the greatest.

Probably out of the pain of poverty better things have happened in Ecuador. Leonidas Proaño, bishop of Riobamba, gave his life in service to the poor, leaving his Episcopal palace in the city to live with them. He founded Catechetical Centres and a radio station and was interrogated by the police for his socialist views. He died in 1988. His successor, Victor Corral is equally simple, no mitre, ring or crozier, not even a wide cummerbund or purple stock. Out there Christian names are used and here in the Canary Islands it is the same. It is rare to see a priest wearing a soutane or a clerical collar. Gradually it is becoming evident that the dress has nothing to do with the mission. Rather it sets men apart, gives them position and authority and can be a temptation to self importance. It is hard to reconcile elaborate dress and titles like, 'your Lordship, your Grace, your Eminence,' or any pomp and ceremony with the simplicity of Christ's life or with his instructions to his first followers.

The Gospel 'Good News,' can set men free, give them hope and joy, help them to be aware of their spiritual nature and destiny. But the Church has to live like the Saviour himself for the message to carry conviction.

The second cause of concern is a failure to recognise the unique condition the world finds itself in today. 'Increase and multiply and fill the earth and make it yours,' was the command given to the human race and recorded in the Bible. Mankind has achieved exactly that today. We can truly say, we have filled the earth and made it ours, discovered many of its secrets, explored the oceans and the skies. No mountain has been left unclimbed, no river not followed to its source, no desert not crossed, no forest unexplored. In addition, discoveries in technology, medicine, travel, have transformed the world we live in. We live longer. We know what goes on everywhere.

'Increase and multiply' was dramatically fulfilled when the UN recorded the arrival in Sarajevo of a baby who brought the population of the world to 6 billion. The world population had doubled, from 3 to 6 billion, between 1960 and 2000. Many countries by then had a surplus population in the countryside, and they flooded into shanty towns around the big cities. At the same time, to meet increased demand, the resources of the world were exploited as never before, whole forests cut down, fish stocks threatened, the very earth forced to produce more with chemicals and pesticides, and it has all happened so fast and so recently in the long history of the world. The situation is urgent. The world population is still increasing by about 750 million a year and is set to reach 9.2 billion by 2050. This inevitably means more millions will starve and conflicts over diminished resources can only increase, yet people in the poorest countries continue to multiply while Authority in the Church is silent, recommending only abstinence, because it cannot accept that the 'means' now available for controlling population come from God. It still considers 'nature' to be a statement of God's will and everything that is contrary to nature to be wrong.

It was John 23rd again who had the courage to establish a commission to study the matter. His successor Pope Paul, clearly anxious, enlarged the commission, but when after two years it came to the wrong conclusion in his eyes, he issued the encyclical 'Humanae Vitae' which condemned all artificial forms of birth control. There was never in the recent history of the Church a sadder day and Cardinal John Heenan, co-chairman of the Papal Commission on Birth Control, wrote in his memoir: 'A Crown of Thorns,' 'it was the greatest shock the Church has suffered since the Reformation.'

Thus the vital message of the Church, that has nothing to do with this kind of ruling, suffers again.

Thirdly, enough has been written about the rule of celibacy for priests by eminent scholars, but the debate is still closed as far as the Pope and the Vatican are concerned. There are said to be a 100,000 who have opted out of the priesthood, most of them in order to be free to marry. The cost is high for the individual priest and for the Church. My own distress surfaced in a recurrent dream. I would be saying Mass in a packed church and all would be going well until the end. When I came to give everyone the blessing with the words; 'go in peace to love and serve the Lord,' I would find no one left in the church. I would wake up with two emotions, sadness and relief, sadness because it spoke of my failure, relief because I was married and should not be saying Mass anyway. I accept the ruling of the Church but believe it should be changed and in this respect there is one further point to make.

It may be crisis time financially, everyone scared about material prosperity, but it is also crisis time spiritually. Christian communities everywhere but particularly in the Roman Catholic Church are suffering from an increasing shortage of priests which has meant empty churches and amalgamating parishes. Karl Rahner SJ, a great and much respected theologian, was quoted in a Tablet article in May 2002, as having written an 'Open Letter to a Brother Priest' in which he called celibacy 'a crucial factor of life, as vast and enigmatic as life itself.' He was scornful of a certain naïve expectation of marriage on the part of celibates but concluded; 'if the Church everywhere, or in certain areas, is unable to find enough clergy unless she abandons celibacy, then she must abandon it; for the obligation to provide enough pastors for the Christian people takes precedence.'

Inside the Catholic Church, Newcastle Emlyn, the people wait, but not for their own priest.
When Fr. Higham died in 2005 no parish priest was appointed

Acknowledgments

We are all of us dependent on each other, and can scarcely live a day without support. So it is that hundreds of people play a part, of greater and lesser significance, in everyone's life, too many to acknowledge and thank. Just a few should be mentioned by name: Angela Charles, David Halpin, and Gill for editing; Ned Benjamin, Ron Ballantine, and Juliet David, for technical help and photographs; Mark Blundel, Julian David and Guy Neely for comments.

Lightning Source UK Ltd.
Milton Keynes UK
UKOW04f0220280315

248685UK00003B/71/P